Derrick Greaves

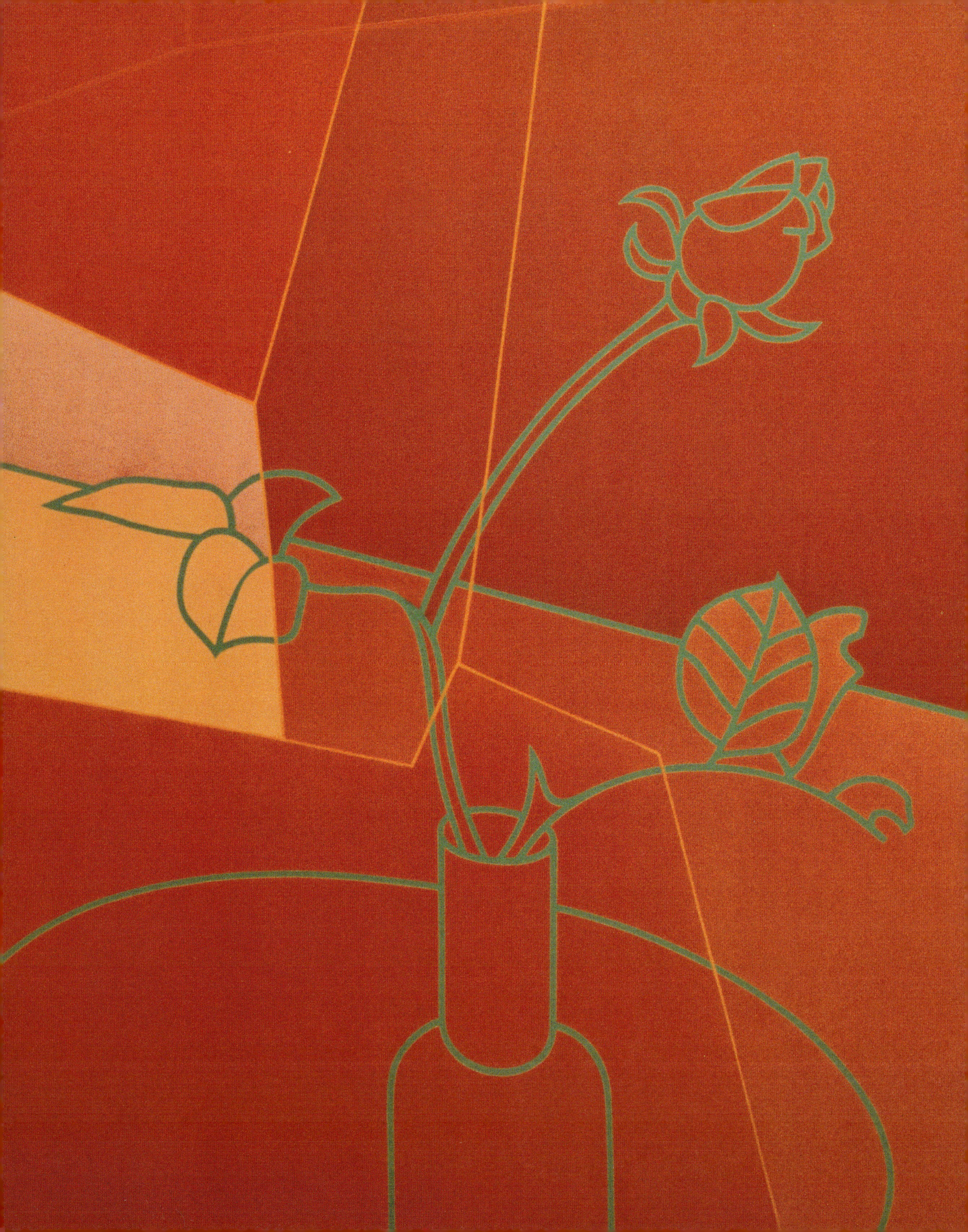

Derrick Greaves

From Kitchen-Sink to Shangri-La

James Hyman

Lund Humphries

First published in 2007 by

Lund Humphries
Gower House
Croft Road
Aldershot
Hampshire GU11 3HR

and

Lund Humphries
Suite 420
101 Cherry Street
Burlington
VT 05401-4405
USA

www.lundhumphries.com

Lund Humphries is part of
Ashgate Publishing

British Library Cataloguing in
  Publication Data

Hyman, James
    Derrick Greaves: from kitchen
      sink to Shangri-La
    1. Greaves, Derrick - Criticism
      and Interpretation
    I. Title
    759.2

    ISBN-13: 978-0-85331-957-3

Library of Congress Control
Number: 2007924095

Edited by Howard Watson
Designed by Peter Willberg
Printed in Hong Kong

Frontispiece: Detail from *Entering
a Room with Difficulty*, 1979

Contents

For Eden Rose

Acknowledgements

Above all, I am indebted to Derrick Greaves. Our friendship has made working on this book a pleasure. I know that for him it is the next picture that matters, and that he would rather look forwards than backwards, but he has been unfailingly generous with his time and patient in his responses to my questions. I am also extremely grateful to his wife, Sally, not only for her hospitality but for her assistance, not least in the laborious task of tracking down reproductions of the illustrated works. I also appreciate the help of numerous public and private collections in granting access to pictures and supplying reproductions. Many others have also helped, among them the artist's family and friends. I am also grateful to Caroline Cook and Christabel Armsden, without whom this book would not have been completed; to Peter Willberg for his exceptional design; to Howard Watson for the clarity of his editing; and to all those at Lund Humphries, especially Nigel Farrow, Lucy Myers and Miranda Harrison. Last but not least, I would like to thank my parents, Robin and Inge Hyman, for their ongoing support, and my wife, Claire, for her continuing patience during the lengthy period that it has taken to complete this book.

James Hyman

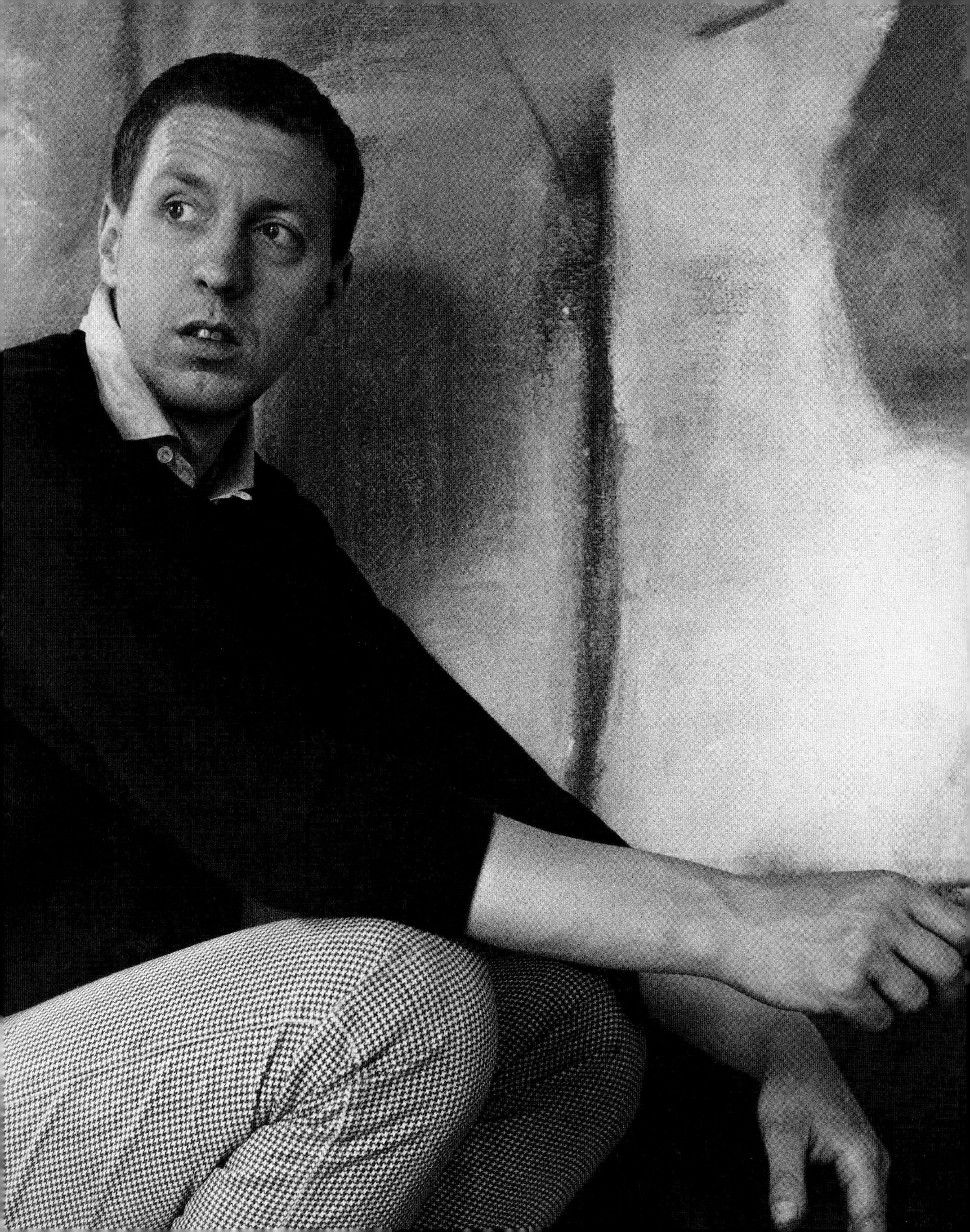

Introduction

I don't think one paints for any other reason than to produce something new. My painting now has little resemblance to that of the 1950s – as though one has any choice about one's own development! All one can do is forge one's own path, respond to the last painting and hope that the present painting leaves a clue for the next one.

Derrick Greaves, interview, 1999[1]

Derrick Greaves was an instant success. He was still a student when he had his first solo show at Helen Lessore's famous Beaux Arts Gallery, London, in 1953. Then the leading gallery for young figurative painters, the Beaux Arts was responsible for seminal exhibitions of, among others, Craigie Aitchison, Michael Andrews, Frank Auerbach, Francis Bacon, John Bratby, Jeffrey Camp, Edward Middleditch, Jack Smith and Euan Uglow. Held at the same time as a selection of recent paintings by Francis Bacon (Greaves showed upstairs and Bacon downstairs), Greaves's first exhibition gained enthusiastic coverage from the leading critics of the day including Stephen Bone in the *Manchester Guardian*, John Russell in the *Sunday Times*, Nevile Wallis in the *Observer* and John Berger in the *New Statesman*. So commercially successful was it that, having graduated, Greaves was able to live on the proceeds for a year without needing to take on teaching. Swiftly, the work was bought by major museums and taken up by the British Council, who presented it at the Venice Biennale in 1956 alongside the artists with whom Greaves soon became grouped, the 'Beaux Arts Quartet' or 'Kitchen-Sink painters': John Bratby, Edward Middleditch and Jack Smith.

The result of such meteoric success was to brand Greaves, seemingly forever, as a Kitchen-Sink painter. The effect of this was to bestow historical significance on the work of an artist barely formed. Forty years later, in an article for *Art Review*, Derrick Greaves would write eloquently about the fate of the artist whose early work gains such rapid acclaim, eclipsing everything that follows, and

Facing page:
1 Derrick Greaves, 1957

ensuring the artist a category and place in the history books at the beginning, and
not at the end, of his career.[2] In the case of Derrick Greaves, atypical works from
just a handful of years, many done while he was still a student, have dominated
perceptions of a career that spans over half a century. It is hoped that the present
monograph – the first overview of the artist's work – will remedy this bias.

Paradoxically, had Greaves's star not shone so brightly his mature work might
have received more immediate acclaim, but the branding of 'Kitchen-Sink painter'
was strong and as the artist, with characteristic wit, has observed: 'There is an
idea that the painter has an egg he lays of identical shape from birth to death like
a battery hen.'[3]

From Greaves's five-and-a-half years as an apprentice sign writer (1943–8)
to his celebrated social realist paintings of the 1950s, through to his later heraldic
works, there has been a desire not only to forge a personal language but also
to communicate with an audience in as direct a means as possible. These two
aspects – the personal and the public – are united by a desire for clarity:

*My desire is to be clear in what I am doing and through that clarity to be clear as
well for any spectator looking at the work. I never had in my mind an hypothetical
audience in any form or any shape, I just wanted people to feel clear in their mind
like I felt clear in my mind. The difficulties came later when unlike the earlier
works my work started to include other aspects of the creative mind such as the
subconscious or dreams, although even then I was concerned to have as much
clarity as possible.[4]*

Surveying half a century of achievement, one might even argue that
Greaves established his reputation with the least typical paintings of his career.
His 'Kitchen-Sink' period works of the mid 1950s have little in common with
either the sign writing that preceded them or the radical reformulation of his
visual language that followed. Without these works of the 1950s Greaves would
not have received acclaim so early, yet with them his wider achievements have
been obscured, as have the essential continuities of his work.

Indeed, although chronology is important, it is also apposite to consider
Greaves's mature work as a series of returns to themes and ideas that transcend
the passing of years, and as a series of interlinked bodies of work. Themes recur,
as do the clarity of line and an emphasis on flatness. A graphic, notational
boldness bestows an iconic quality on mundane items and an enlarged scale
gives grandeur even to the most banal of objects.

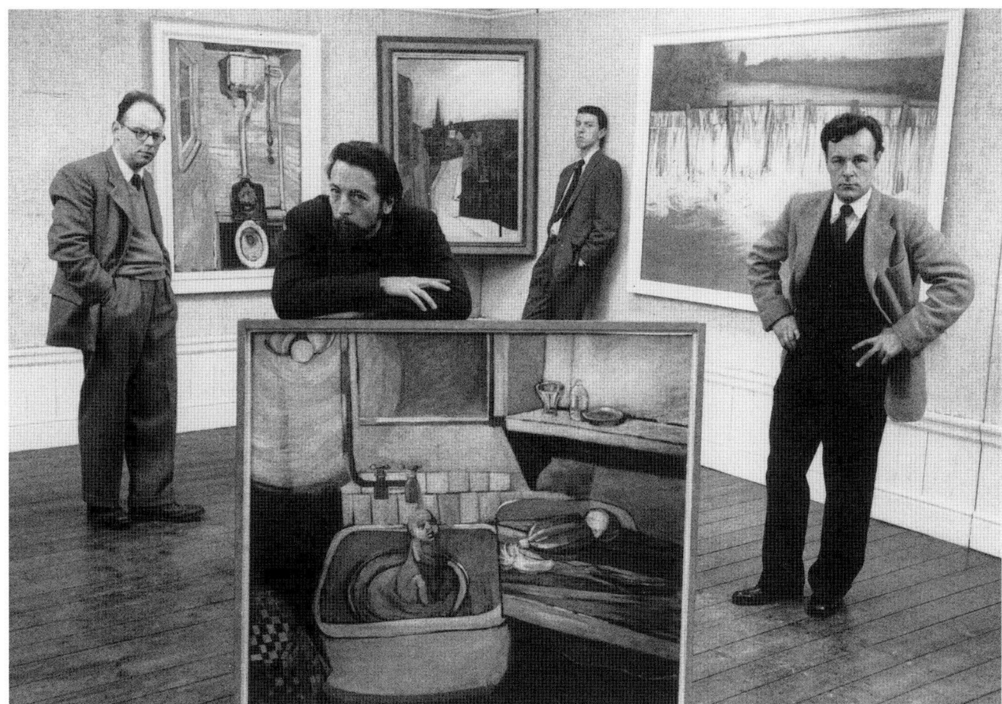

2 John Bratby, Jack Smith, Derrick Greaves and Edward Middleditch at the Beaux Arts Gallery, 1956

The task of the art historian is to present, discuss, analyse and explain, to try and understand a rich, complex, still changing body of work and address its significance. For the artist, however, the task is rather different: it is an ongoing urge to translate his obsessions into paint, to remain open to chance and to be receptive to change. It is the nature of any such study to imply seamless production and to suggest a reasoned development. It is hoped, however, that the present book also preserves something of the risk-taking and something, too, of the spirit of enquiry and discovery that lie at the heart of the work and life of Derrick Greaves. Although this is not a biography, it is intended that this monograph will also convey something of the man: his love of good food, wine and music; his gift for friendship and love of storytelling; his conviviality and humour, sociability and sensitivity. Above all, though, it should be the pictures that speak most loudly, illustrating an extraordinary journey of discovery.

Notes

1. Derrick Greaves, interview with Cathy Courtney, 1999, tape 1, side 2. In this book quotations from the artist come from two main sources. Firstly, tape recordings made by Cathy Courtney for the British Library Living History Sound Archive that were recorded over 1999–2000. These amount to almost 13 hours of reminiscence and are especially full on Greaves's childhood and youth. Secondly, letters, conversations and interviews with James Hyman from 1994–2006 in connection with previous essays by the author and for the present publication.

2. Derrick Greaves, 'Studios I Have Known', *Art Review*, 1995.

3. Courtney, tape 2, side 1.

4. Derrick Greaves, unpublished text, June 2006.

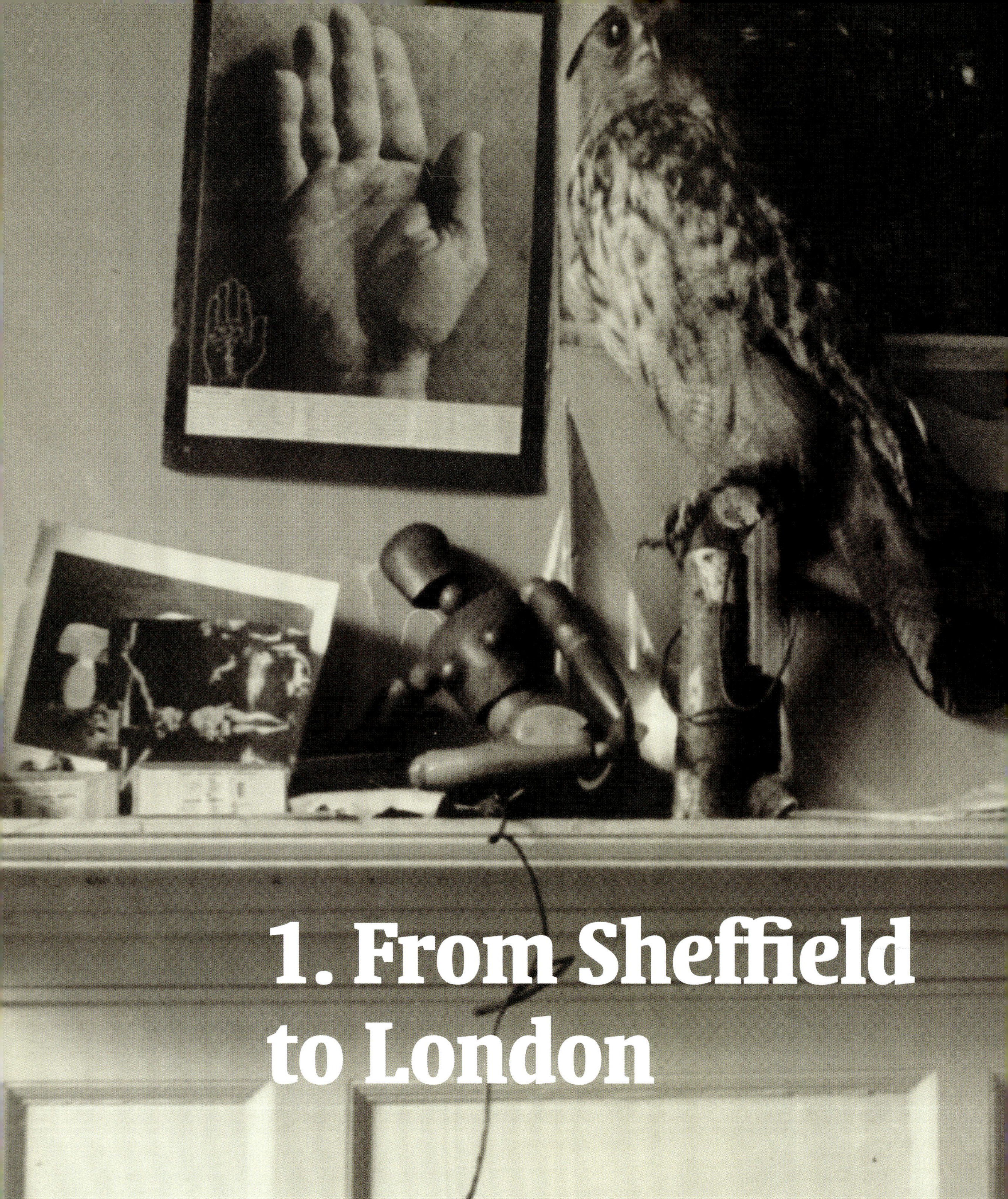

1. From Sheffield to London

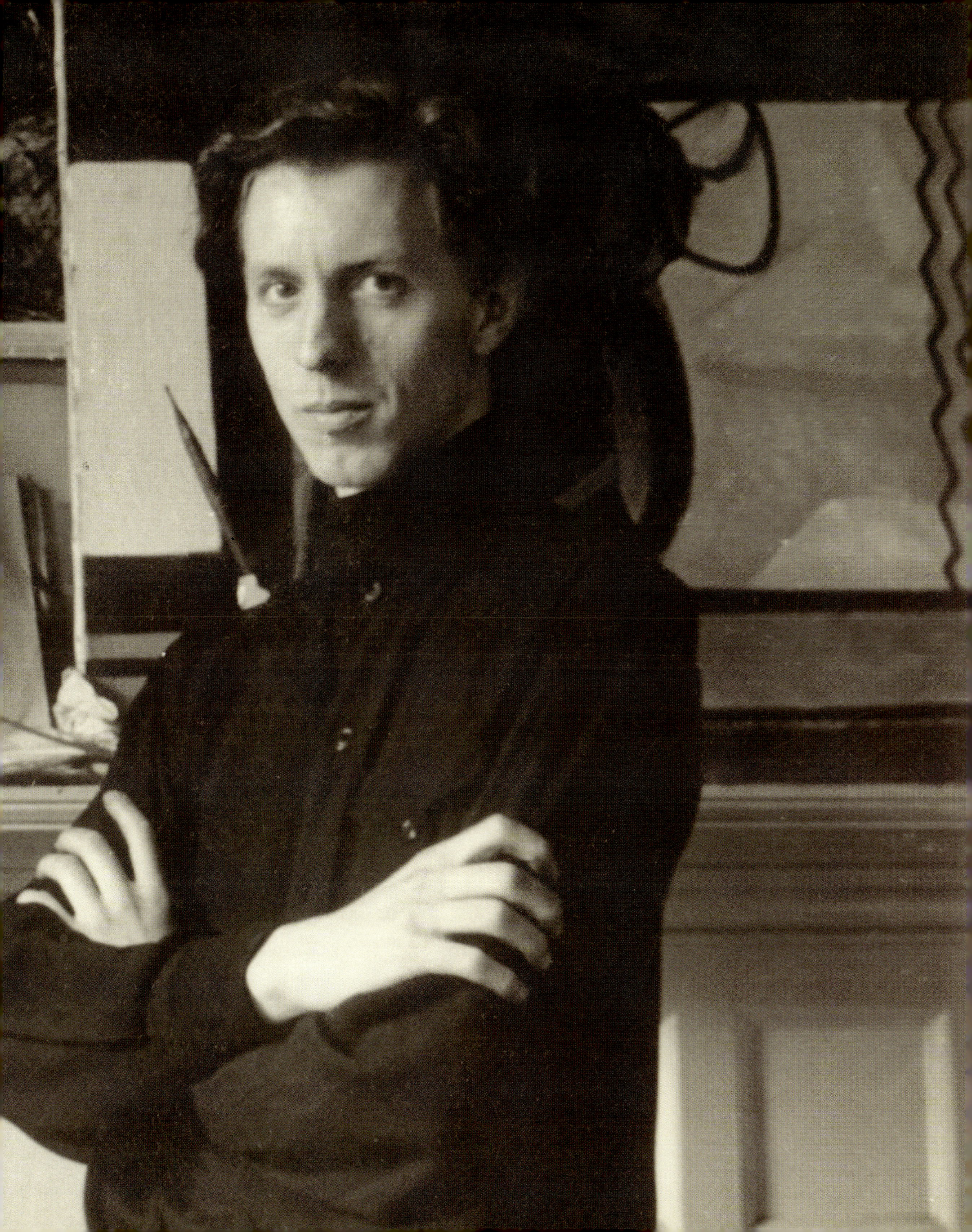

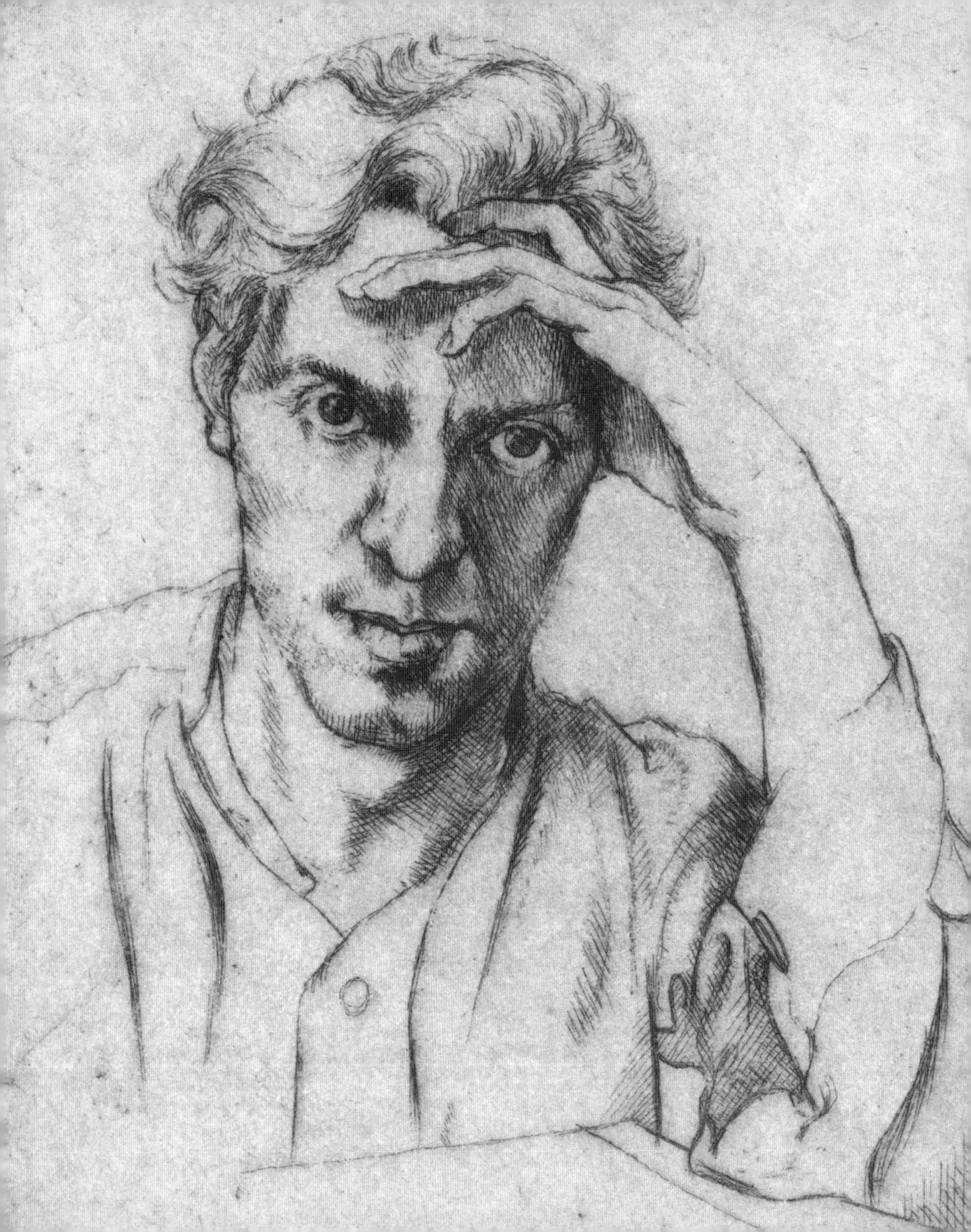

1. From Sheffield to London: The Artist's Formative Years

> *To begin drawing is like putting the first spade in the earth of previously uncultivated or ignored terrain in the blithe hope that this time there'll be a garden at the end of it! One begins with high hopes and diligence that some kind of garden (or previously unknown coherence) will ultimately declare itself. I've done this since I was a child. The results of hundreds and hundreds of drawings over the years have been unpredictable to say the least but whether mad or bad the necessity to persist remains. Garden indeed!*
>
> Derrick Greaves, undated[1]

The earliest surviving drawings by Derrick Greaves date from his childhood in Sheffield and show an astonishing facility. Presciently, given his early fame as a Kitchen-Sink painter, this precocious talent is nowhere more evident than in *The Kitchen* (plate 5). Drawn at the family home in Mitchell Road, Sheffield, this drawing in green ink may owe much to Camden Town School picture-making and especially the marks of Harold Gilman, but it is still an extraordinary achievement for an artist who was barely 15. A self portrait (plate 6) from this time, one of only a few such pictures the artist has ever made, also shows this legacy and shares a similar confidence. The rakishness of the artist, in a specially borrowed fedora, belies the provincialism that he felt. A related etching of the artist (plate 4) is no less proficient and demonstrates how early he was introduced to a life-long love: printmaking.

An only child, Derrick Harry Greaves was born in 1927 but nearly did not survive the birth. He was given up for dead and cast at the end of the bed whilst attempts were made to save his mother's life. Fortunately, at his mother's insistence a clout brought him crying into the world, and his mother's life was also saved. The family into which he was born was poor and working class. Life was tough, although Greaves recalls that his childhood was happy. His father, although under age, had served in the First World War and suffered severe trauma that affected him for the rest of his life and Greaves recalls him as a distantly affectionate father, but not one with whom he was ever really intimate.

Previous page:
3 Derrick Greaves,
Pembroke Road Studio, *c.*1950

Facing page:
4 *Self Portrait*, 1943
Etching
15 × 10.6cm (5.9 × 4.2in)
University of Wales, Aberystwyth

His father worked as a skilled cabinet-case maker producing presentation cutlery cases and his mother was also highly skilled, having fulfilled her apprenticeship to costumier and dressmaking workshops in Sheffield. In the Depression years of the 1930s both of them kept the family going, taking other jobs to make ends meet. During these times his mother made clothes from second-hand garments for the young boy. Both parents shared the maxim, as a result of their own apprenticeships, that a job undertaken should be 'properly done' or 'left well-alone'. This attitude made a deep impression on Greaves even as a child.

Home was a small two-up, two-down terraced industrial cottage with no bathroom and a tin bath to drag upstairs on bath night. The heart of the house was the kitchen and the front room was never used, even at Christmas. As a child, Greaves realised that he was lower class, that there were 'posh' people who lived across town. At infant school, he went to his first party and realised that other children were more expensively dressed and brought more lavish presents, and for many years he felt considerable shame because he didn't have a bathroom.

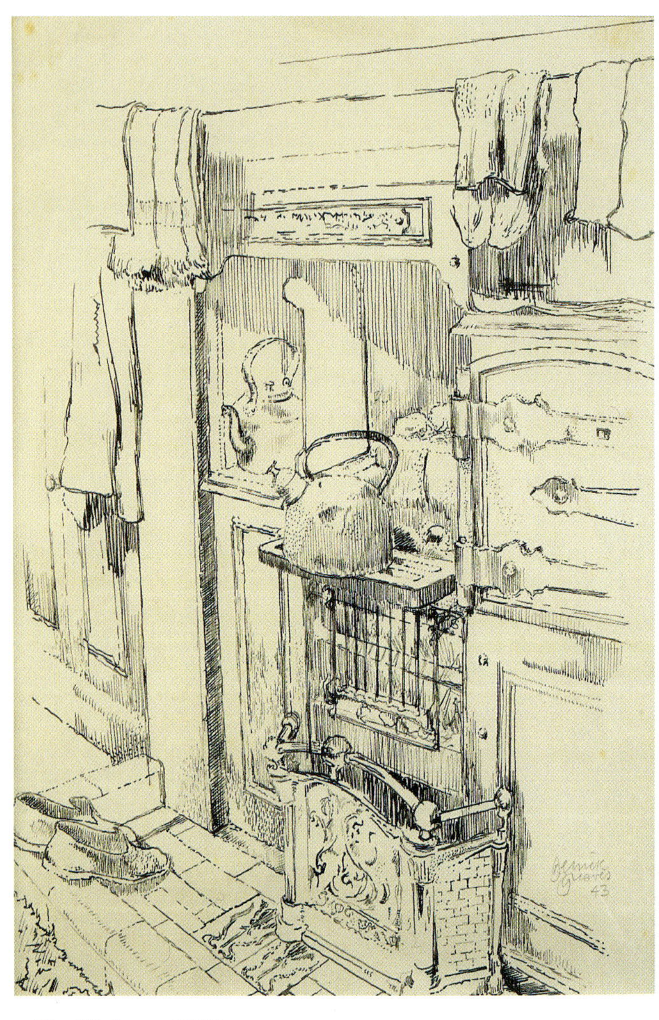

5 *The Kitchen*, c.1943
Ink on paper
37.5 × 27cm (14.8 × 10.6in)

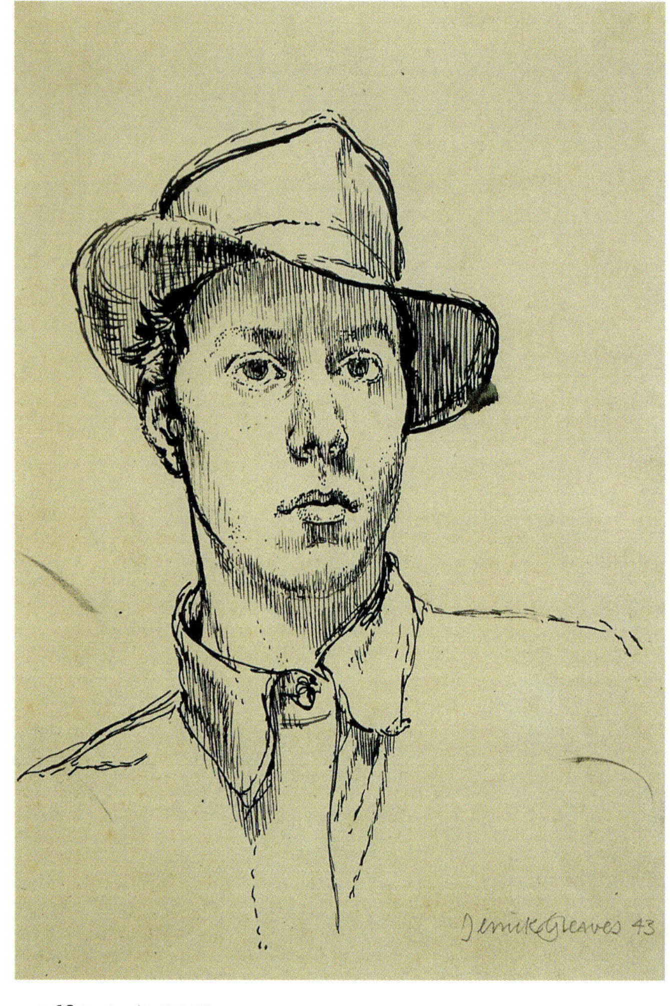

6 *Self Portrait*, 1943
Ink on paper
26 × 17cm (10.2 × 6.7in)

Drawing was important from childhood, and has been at the centre of
Greaves's life ever since. This is a person who drew since he was five years old,
habitually, almost every day. Drawing was almost more natural to him than
writing and it was often easier to communicate through drawing. As a small
child he found the illustrations in children's books to be more vivid and original
than the words around them. If one was to have a *grand projet*, as Sigmund
Freud advocated, then his was always drawing.

As early as his time at infant school, at the Abbey Lane Council School,
Greaves had been singled out and allowed to go into a room to draw, and at eight
or nine he was given larger and larger pieces of paper, coloured crayons, pencils
and poster paints, using them for pictures of galleons. Even at this stage, the
desire to create was married to the desire to communicate: at the Junior Art
Department of Sheffield College of Art Greaves tried to start a student newspaper
using a home-made printing kit. The Junior Art Department, which he selected to
go to in favour of other grammar schools, turned out to be an important school
for Greaves in the sense that it gave him his first sense of structural anarchy.

Most memorably, Greaves recalls that the principal, 'Pop Glover', decided
that the whole of the school, involving pupils from ages 11–14, would combine
in the creation of an exhibition which could be toured around other schools. Its
subject was the historic development of England, starting in Stone Age times
and concluding with the nineteenth and twentieth centuries. It involved making
charts, measurements, working models and painting murals in full colour to
represent the period. For a considerable time, normal lessons were completely
suspended as the pupils spent each day constructing, modelling, and talking
about agrarian subjects and industrialisation. Greaves and a friend, Ken Wootten,
worked on a large mural on thick paper, which measured approximately 6×15ft
(1.8 × 4.6m), involving the transition from the nineteenth to the twentieth
century. For the first time, he was able to go out into the streets of Sheffield
and make on-the-spot drawings which were later used for painting the mural:
'this was a great realisation for me – the making of a drawing to be immediately
used in a developed painting form – and also a very valuable lesson in a rather
exciting yet anarchic approach to educational understanding'.[2]

However, what Greaves knew of art was limited, gleaned from local libraries,
from the Graves Art Gallery, which was not far from the Junior Art Department,
and later from occasional visits to London: 'When I realised you could paint
pictures and some people did it all the time, I used Sheffield City Library and very

quickly exhausted all their books on art. Fuddy duddy books on amateur painters, specialists in Scottish heather lands; how to draw trees by Adrian Hill; Ruskin's *Stones of Venice*.'[3]

It is difficult to imagine how little information there was in the provinces at that time about painting and, as for modern art, there was almost nothing to be found. The Graves Art Gallery, Sheffield, was a local pick-up place for teenagers who would check their appearance in the reflective glass on the darker pictures. In contrast, Greaves recalls solemnly trying to draw from a William Blake engraving before being unceremoniously moved on by an attendant. He would later recall that it was in the reference library that he first saw a book on Pablo Picasso and that until then he had been principally aware of British art through such sources as Herbert Read's *Art Now* and library books on John and Paul Nash, Eric Ravilious and Blake. To gain a glimpse of contemporary art he was dependent on the 'little magazines', such as Cyril Connolly's *Horizon* and John Lehmann's *Penguin New Writing*. Reproduced in their pages he saw illustrations of works by Francis Bacon, Graham Sutherland, Prunella Clough, John Minton, Keith Vaughan, Robert Colquhoun and Robert MacBryde. About Paris he knew almost nothing, which made the celebrated Henri Matisse and Pablo Picasso exhibition at the Victoria and Albert Museum of 1945–6 a revelation. To Greaves at that time, Matisse seemed rather decorative, but the scale of the Picassos was stunning, providing evidence of a painter working at full stretch with no holds barred.

Greaves left school at 14 to work in a progress office at a foundry with the aim of becoming a draughtsman but, seeing the depressing working conditions, he quickly changed his mind. He would go onto the shop floor to get components progressed, monitoring their casting, milling, polishing and wrapping. It was wartime and this was a protected trade, so the office was filled by older men who provided the teenager with a wealth of life-changing experiences. His boss, John Watson, was a concert pianist who sparked Greaves's life-long love of music, playing him records that he had been sent from a music club and introducing him to symphonies by Mozart and Beethoven. Another colleague was the sports writer of the *Sheffield Telegraph*, Frank Stainton, who would come dressed in a long fur coat and open sandals, and another was a car salesman. It was Stainton who first encouraged Greaves to find a job that would allow him to pursue his interest in art. Seeing that Greaves was always drawing, he suggested that he get a job as an illustrator and even advised him how to go about it. Greaves never followed his advice, but it provided a lesson to him: rather than accept his lot, as his parents' generation had done, Greaves realised that if you took the initiative there were opportunities.

Whilst working in the progress office, Greaves also met one of the biggest influences on his early life, Sybil Barker, a woman twice his age whose husband was fighting in Burma. She was the first person Greaves had met who had been to art school and she became a mentor to the 15-year-old. On Saturdays, work finished at lunchtime and they would go into Sheffield to bookshops, filling her basket with Graham Greene, Aldous Huxley and other new novels. They would go to a restaurant for lunch and, since it was expected that the man should pay, she would pass him the money under the table. Then they would go to the cinema – anything from *Fantasia* to Orson Welles films – and she would talk about film-making techniques and camera angles: 'I was like blotting paper, soaking all this up'. The day would end in the upstairs room of her parents' pub where they would read books and have drinks sent up from the bar, and Greaves would entertain her by playing boogie-woogie on the piano. It was an innocent but revelatory friendship.

Following the foundry, Greaves took up an apprenticeship as a sign writer. He also attended three evening classes a week at Sheffield College of Art where a teacher, Eric Jones, taught drawing. Greaves later recalled that Jones was a draughtsman *par excellence* in a manner that was not entirely his own. Greaves would take what he soon regarded as a rather mannered, even effete, style of drawing with him to the Royal College of Art in London, although once there he soon expunged it completely in favour of a more flexible and direct way of drawing, an approach that was less bothered by the elegance or finish of the final picture.

It was Jones who suggested that Greaves apply to the Royal College of Art. The prospect was daunting. Greaves hardly knew London and what he did know was from visiting the capital on his fortnight's holiday a year, when he had gone to exhibitions such as the Leicester Galleries showcase, *Artists of Fame and Promise*, or 'Artists of Shame and Compromise' as he came to call it. Nonetheless, Greaves took a day off work and, in his best green Harris Tweed suit, travelled by train to Manchester where the Principal of the Royal College of Art, Robin Darwin, was holding interviews. Getting into the Royal College seemed beyond Greaves and his nerves were not helped by going out the evening before the interview and having beer knocked over his suit. As Greaves later recalled, he was eventually shown into an enormous room where Robin Darwin was flanked by people behind a large table. The room was over-heated and, crossing the huge red Axminster carpet, Greaves was aware of nothing so much as the smell of the stale beer so that when he finally sat down he was in a state of mind that was half-larky and half-despairing. Fortunately, the interview went well, with Greaves talking at length about Sutherland's wartime paintings of bomb sites and the way that he could identify with them, as he had known bombing in Sheffield and the aftermath of ruin and desolation in the city.

Greaves was amazed to be accepted and to be awarded the Royal Scholarship of about £600, a sizeable sum, although half what he might have earned as a sign writer. His peers at the college, such as Frank Auerbach, regarded him as one of the star students and when he graduated his tutors awarded Greaves a First.

Greaves's most celebrated paintings of the 1950s and their idiom owe much to his years of studying painting at the Royal College from 1948–52. In London, Greaves felt at first 'naively provincial compared to more urbane students'. He recalls, for example, that on his second day at the college a fellow student, Carl Cheek, praised a still-life he was painting for its tonal qualities. For Greaves it had been entirely intuitive, but the comment led him to think more consciously about tone and colour.

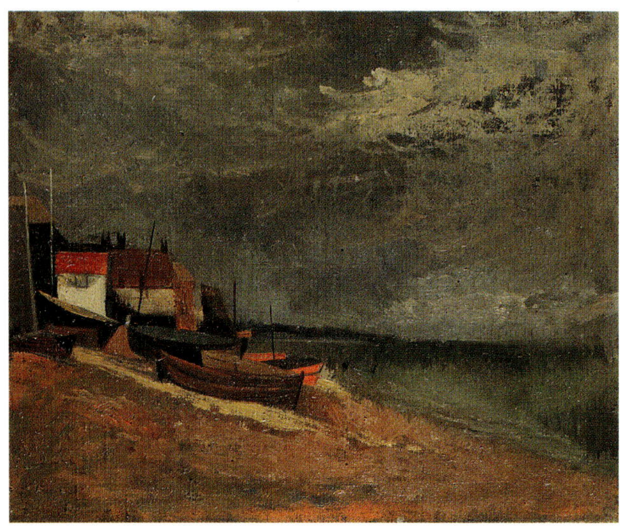

7 *Deal Beach*, 1949
Oil on canvas
21 × 26cm (8.3 × 10.2in)
Private Collection, Kent

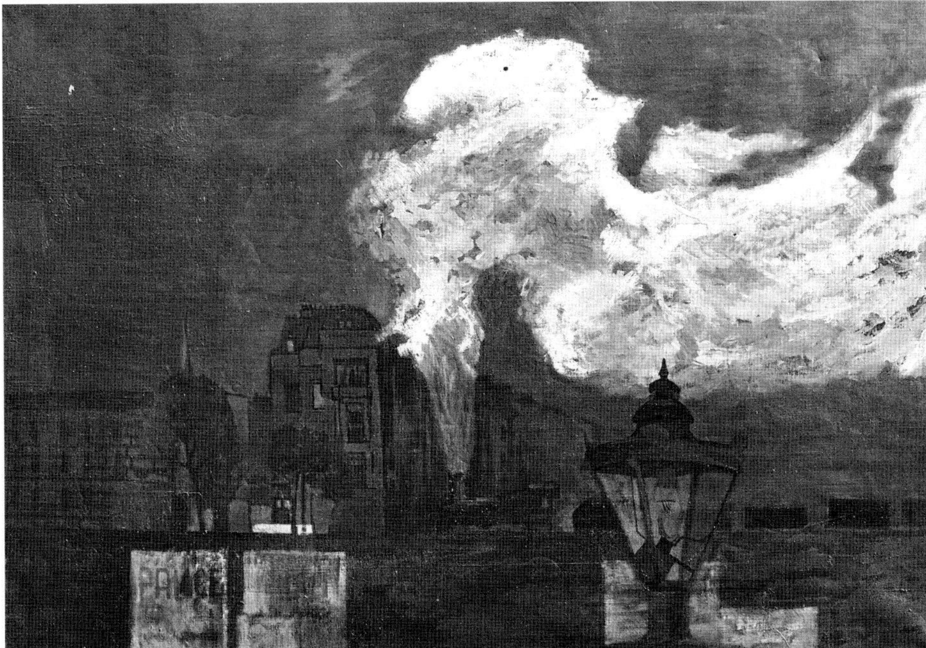

8 *The Train, Battersea*, 1948–9
Oil on canvas
63.5 × 101.5cm (25 × 40in)

Greaves was taught by Ruskin Spear and, to a lesser extent, by Carel Weight and by John Minton, who would draw and paint alongside his students in the life room. Carel Weight was well respected as a serious, exhibiting painter and was helpful in practical ways, offering Greaves free stretchers. Soon Greaves adopted a way of painting, promoted by the college, 'that showed you were serious': 'one could pick up a range of mannerisms from one's tutors' including John Minton's "way with Modernism", Rodrigo Moynihan's "suave portraiture" and Ruskin Spear's "post-Sickertian dabbing and splodging"'.[4] Of all his teachers it was Minton who was of most interest. Greaves respected him principally as a draughtsman, a marvellous, fecund and fluent illustrator, and as a convivial and witty performer, but as a teacher Minton was almost monosyllabic. This was characteristic. Above all, teaching was by example and advice was not necessarily sought, expected or given. Nevertheless, Greaves did find the milieu of the college and his peers stimulating, and he was aware that once he left he would be on his own in the studio. For this reason, both he and Edward Middleditch, having completed their three-year course, applied for a further year, believing that it would allow them to develop their work further: 'We were our own critics. By the end we were a group of students doing it for ourselves. The staff recognised this, that they could only help up to a certain point.'[5]

Common to his teachers was the use of short hog-hair brushes, paint from a tube and the use of a palette, together with a working method predicated on drawing. Greaves, like so many other students, initially followed this lead: he still has the easel he purchased whilst at the Royal College of Art, which had been owned by an old painter in Chelsea and came with an old-fashioned, beautifully polished mahogany palette, complete with thumb-hole. This was a period in which he would do linear drawings as a basis for paintings such as *The Train, Battersea* (plate 8), in which paint was applied a bit at a time in small dabs with short brushes in a post-Cézanne manner. Soon, however, he stopped holding a palette, preferring to place it on a surface to mix his paint, a method that he also soon abandoned in favour of mixing his paint on a table-top or, better still, in cans.

Greaves's ambitions for painting were huge and included epic pictures on grand themes in cinema-screen format. Behind them was surely the excitement he had felt while working on the mural painting at the Junior Art Department at

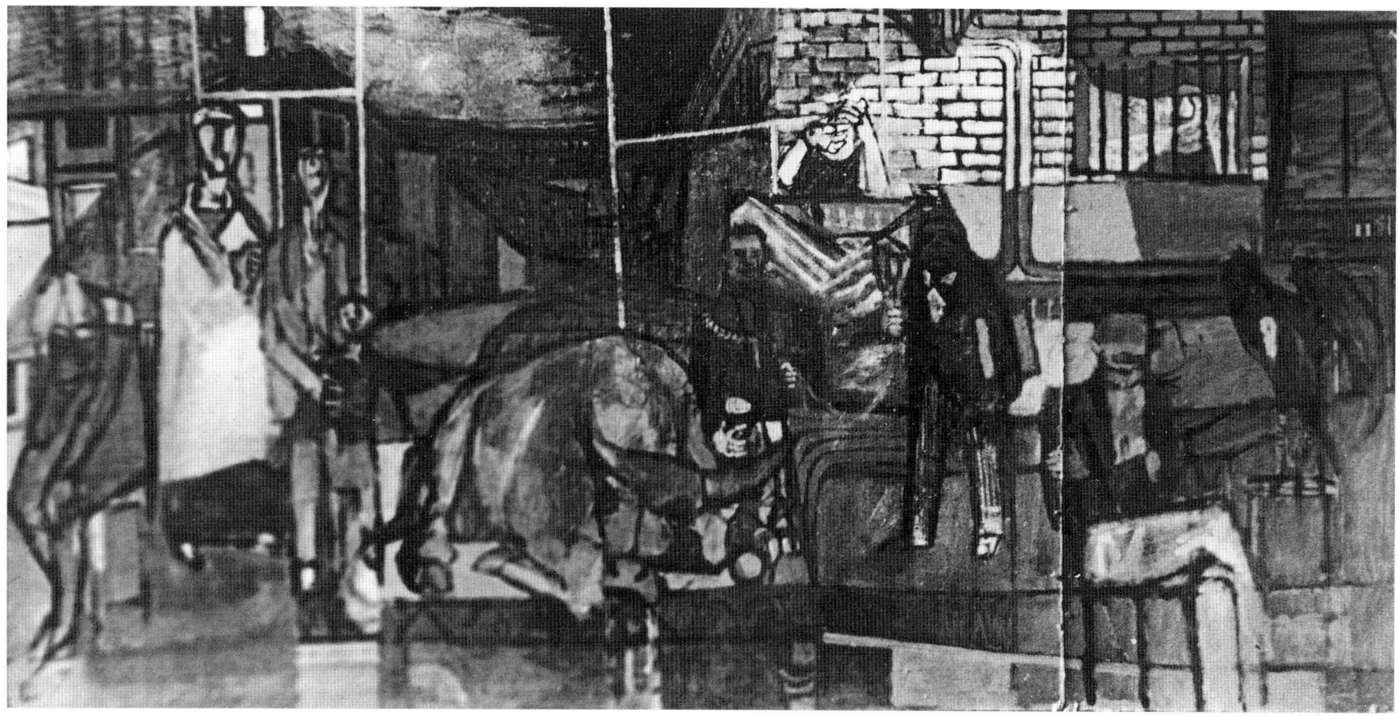

9 *City Life*, 1950
Oil on board
63.5 × 114.5cm (25 × 45in)

Sheffield College as well as his apprenticeship as a sign writer when, besides
painting advertising hoardings, he had also collaborated with day students at
the art school to produce murals for the children's wards of local hospitals.

Corroboration was provided both by the painter Hans Feibusch, whose
celebrated book, *Mural Painting*, was published in 1946, and by what Greaves
saw at the Festival of Britain in 1951. Through its *Sixty for '51* exhibition and
major mural commissions, the Festival did much to encourage artists to think
big and to concern themselves with communicating to a wide public. Greaves
remembers that the Festival as a whole, and its emphasis on design in particular,
had little impact, but he was impressed by murals by Keith Vaughan, Josef
Herman and Leonard Rosoman, as well as large paintings by, among others,
John Minton.

Over 1950–1 Greaves worked on a number of paintings which were conceived
on a public scale. Among these paintings were *City Life* (plate 9), *The Temptation of
St Anthony* (plate 10) and *The Waiting Room* (plate 11). Planned in a conscientious and

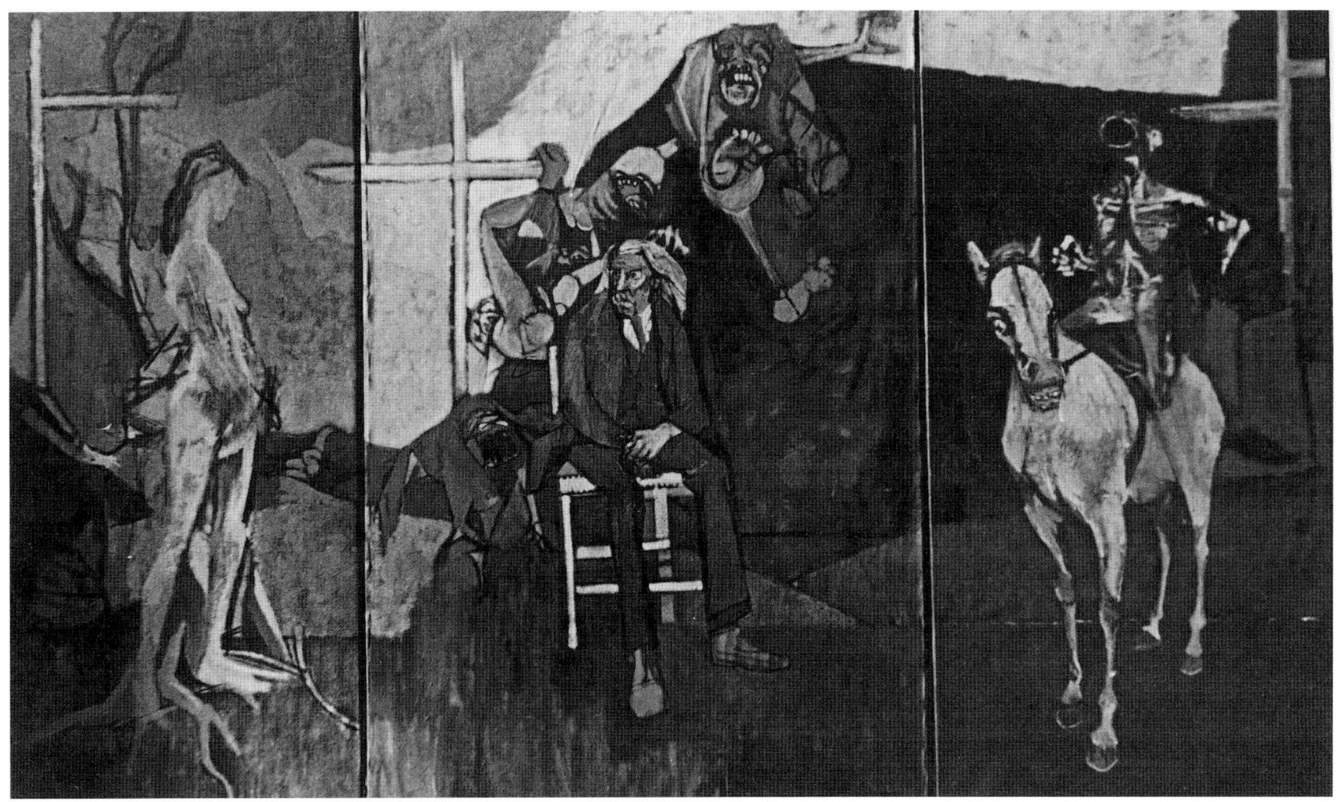

10 *The Temptation of St Anthony*, 1950–1
Oil on board
122 × 183cm (48 × 72in)

conventional manner, from drawings followed by a largish oil study, *City Life* is
a disjointed attempt to combine a city view, presumably of Sheffield, with local
incident. The result leaves one's eyes with no obvious resting point as they
navigate abrupt changes of scale and viewpoint. In comparison, the triptych
of *The Temptation of St Anthony* is almost histrionic with its heightened gestures
and skeletal screaming figures. Whether consciously or not, the result married
Francis Bacon's painful realism with a more explicit narrative that has affinities
with the work of Peter de Francia.

The most successful of these three paintings, and also the most austere,
is the existential tableau, *The Waiting Room*. Gesture is suppressed and space
is simplified. A plain wall runs across the picture-plane and figures are isolated
rather than inter-related. Above all, this is a painting about mood. Individuals
are identifiable (including Greaves's father on the far left and, seated on the
sofa, the artist's first wife, Margaret Johnson, whom he had married the previous
year), but the painting was clearly intended to be read as a larger comment on the
human predicament. This is a painting more inspired by literary than pictorial
sources, stimulated by Greaves's reading of Jean-Paul Sartre's *Huis Clos* and Albert
Camus's *The Outsider*. Looming over the brooding figures is the dominating
presence of a chart of a human torso, a portentous reminder of mortality.

A painting of his home city, *Sheffield Landscape* (plate 13), related not just to
Greaves's childhood but also to a more recent experience. Travelling back to
Sheffield after his first term at the Royal College of Art in the winter of 1949,
Greaves had seen the city as though for the first time. He discovered a dramatic,
stark beauty in the streets. A light snow had fallen and the white lines of
snow on black rooftops had a linear, almost etched quality. Something of this
is discernible in *Sheffield on Sunday* (plate 12), a painting that has certain echoes
of L.S. Lowry's depiction of Salford, which not only included streets teeming with
people but also places totally devoid of them. The road is snowy white and totally
deserted, and the dark roofs and chimneys set up a repeating rhythm. If this is
a Sunday then it must be very early in the morning. What is so striking is how,
from the outset, Greaves eschewed anecdote and swiftly ditched the allegorical
in favour of a matter-of-fact approach that would, with a few notable exceptions,
leave little room for metaphor.

Perhaps the most successful of all his early paintings was a panoramic view
of Sheffield that Greaves completed in 1953. *Sheffield* (plate 14) is rightly celebrated
as one of Greaves's most powerful and distinctive early paintings, and can be

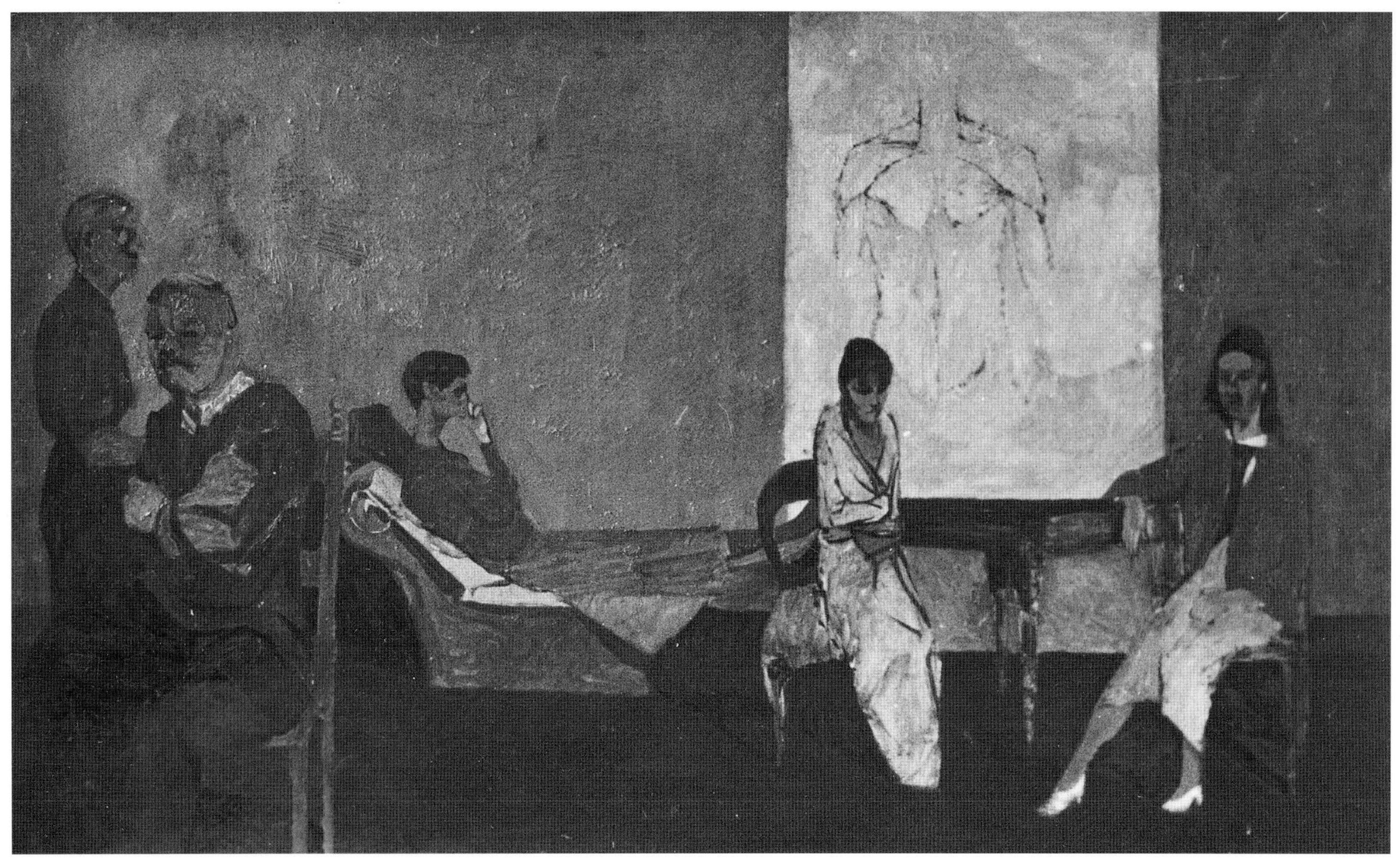

11 *The Waiting Room*, 1951
Oil on canvas
76 × 127cm (30 × 50in)

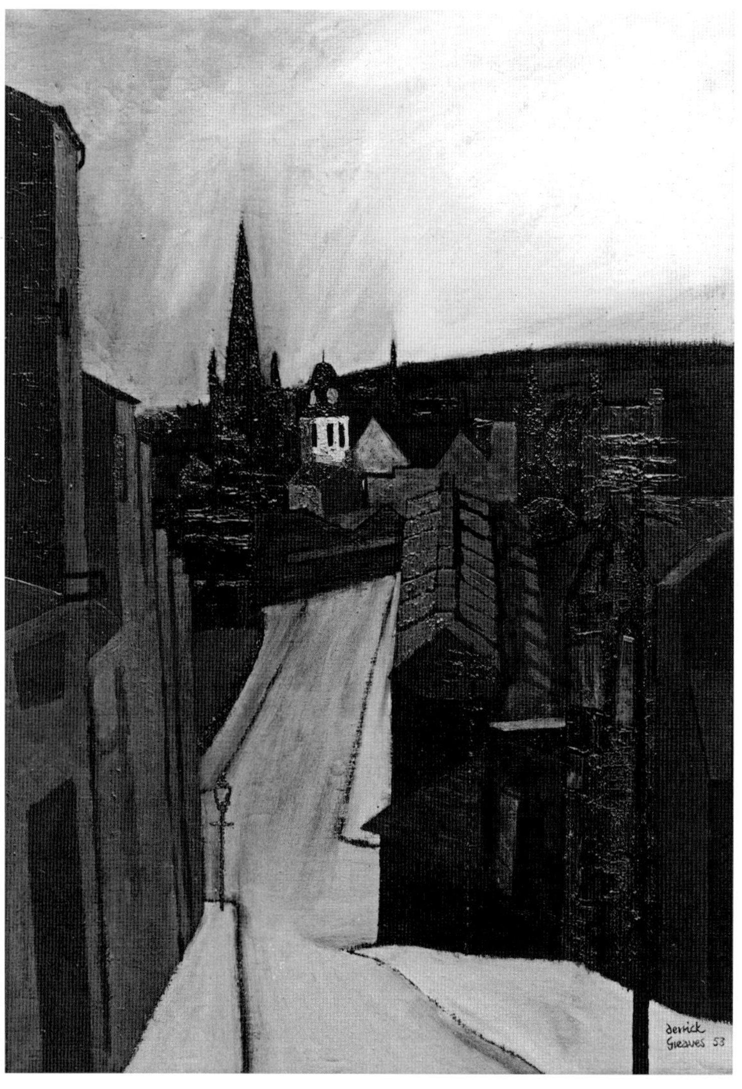

12 *Sheffield on Sunday*, 1953
Oil on canvas
102 × 71cm (40 × 28in)

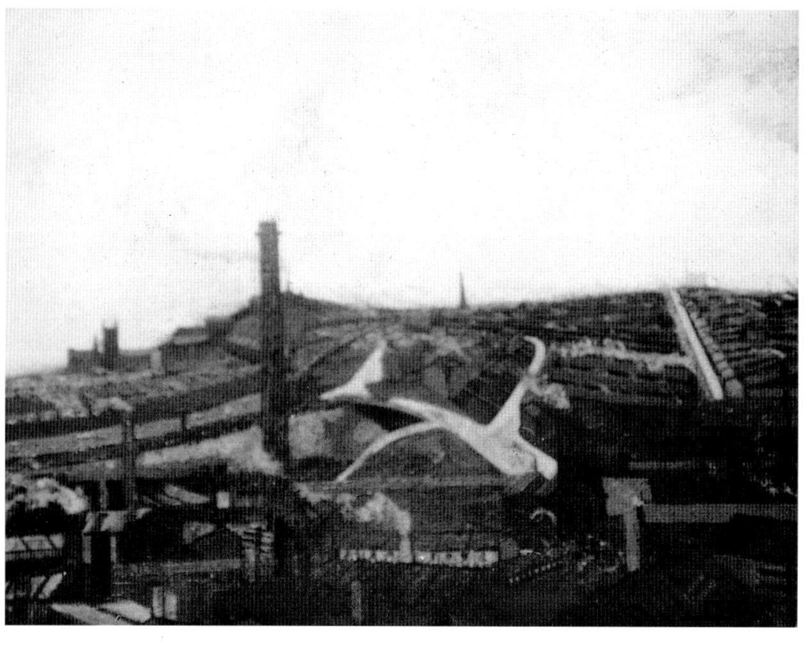

13 *Sheffield Landscape*, 1953
Oil on canvas
76 × 127cm (30 × 50in)

understood best in the light of these earlier works. Interestingly, it was not painted in Sheffield at all, but was executed in a basement studio in Pembroke Road, London.

Greaves's *Sheffield* panorama is richly evocative and lucidly articulated, showing that Greaves had learnt big lessons about economy in terms of both composition and paint. The colours are muted and the mood is elegiac, a farewell to childhood, perhaps. However, what the painting does reveal is that Greaves was still relying heavily on his power as a draughtsman, rather than his facility as a painter, and that although for major statements he consistently adopted a panoramic format, he was not yet entirely its master.

Sheffield is a picture of two halves; a composite image derived from different drawings that whilst being faithful to the topography of the city nonetheless combines different viewpoints. Significantly, *Sheffield Landscape* shows only the right three-fifths of the subject, suggesting that the building that dominates the left of the painting was conceived separately. This factory building has the power of a robust charcoal drawing whilst the houses and industrial buildings on the

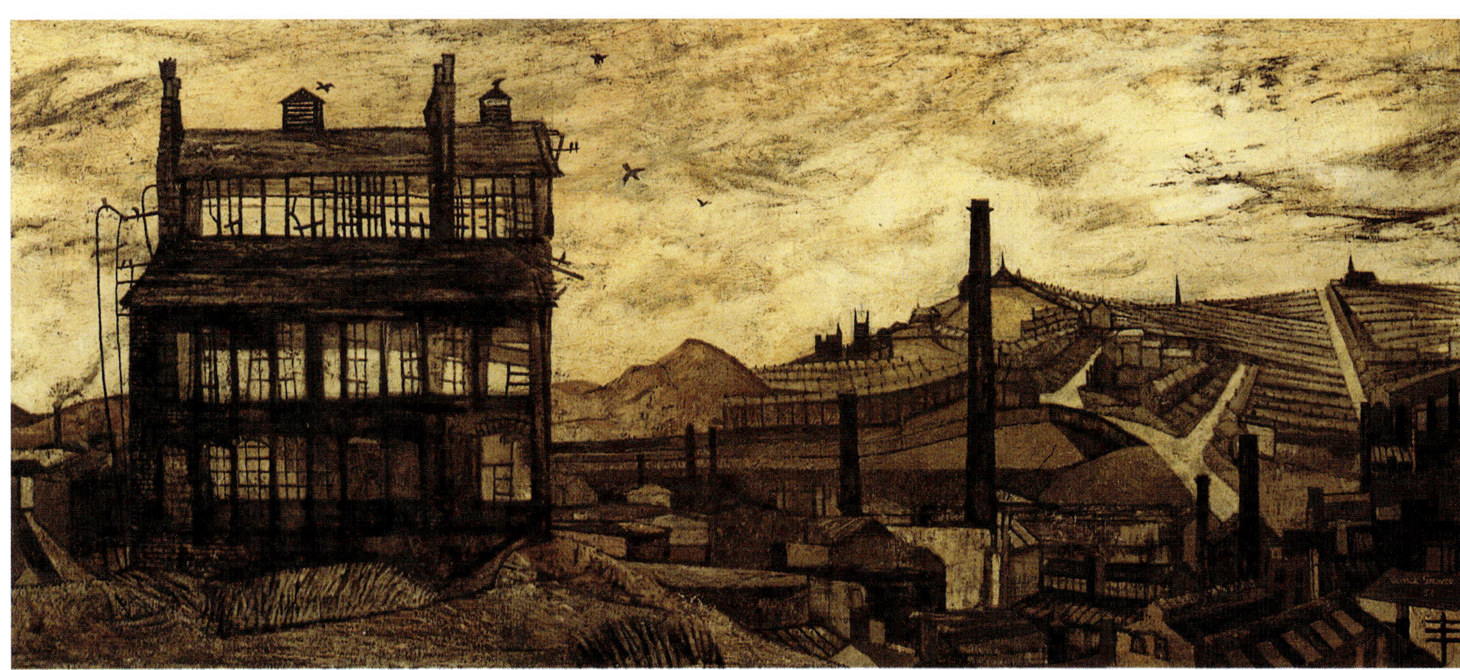

14 *Sheffield*, 1953
Oil on canvas
86.2 × 203.3cm (33.9 × 80in)
Graves Art Gallery, Sheffield

right are carried by line and remain close to their sources – pencil drawings of
Sheffield. Given the size of the abandoned factory building, one would expect the
other buildings to be in the middle ground or distance, yet they too are pushed
to the front of the composition.

In this reliance on draughtsmanship and struggle to conceive on a grand·
scale, Greaves was perhaps simply echoing the strengths and weaknesses of
some of the leading painters around him. He would judge his teacher, John
Minton, to be a more natural illustrator than a painter, an artist who despite
producing some powerful portraits 'had never been hit hard by the core language
of painting', and he felt that Ruskin Spear allowed 'journalism to get in the way'
and 'lacked the quiet density of Sickert'.[6] There is, however, something of Carel
Weight in this view of Sheffield.

Weight's large-scale urban paintings of 1950–3 are arguably the most
powerful paintings that he ever produced. The mood of Weight's *Going Home*
(1950), *The Yellow Wall* (1951) and *The Pre-Raphaelite Tragedy* (*c.*1951), with their
warm brickwork and glowing skies, surely lies behind Greaves's *Sheffield*.
Both teacher and pupil present the subject at sunrise or sunset and the mood
is nostalgic. In each case the canvas format is an extended horizontal and the
resulting sweep is emphasised by the frontal presentation of the architecture,
especially the brick walls that run across the picture plane. However, Greaves's
depopulated city replaces Weight's highly personalised storytelling with a
more universal romanticism.

Greaves's views of Sheffield illustrate post-war reformulations of a national
tradition through ideas of the uniqueness of place, the *genius loci*, in which
prominence was given to an artist's intimate response to a specific part of Britain.
In the isolationist years of the 1940s, this found focus on the rural with Paul Nash
in Dorset, Ivon Hitchens in Sussex, Graham Sutherland in Pembrokeshire, John
Piper in north Wales and Peter Lanyon in St Ives.

However, by the early 1950s, not least through the writing of John Berger,
there was an identification of tradition with realism, and realism with urban
experience, that trod a path from the caricature of William Hogarth to Sickert
and Camden Town painting, through Euston Road School reportage to a new
generation of 'Kitchen-Sink' painters. True, Berger would admire responses to the
land from Peter Lanyon's St Ives to Sheila Fell's Cumbria, but he also celebrated
responses to the urban world in Ruskin Spear's Hammersmith, Lowry's Salford,
Prunella Clough's docklands and Greaves's Sheffield.

Significantly, despite his years at the Royal College of Art, London is almost
completely absent from Greaves's work. In contrast to elders such as Minton,
Spear and Weight and contemporaries such as Edward Middleditch, Frank Auerbach
and Leon Kossoff, London held little appeal as a subject as he felt that it was already
teeming with artists.

Following his ambitious early paintings, Greaves's works of the mid 1950s
would demonstrate his heightening powers as a painter as well as his innate
strength as a draughtsman.

Notes
1. Derrick Greaves, unpublished
journal entry, undated.
2. Derrick Greaves, undated note
to James Hyman, July 2006.
3. Courtney, tape 1, side 1.
4. Courtney, tape 7, side 1.
5. Courtney, tape 11, side 1.
6. Derrick Greaves, interview with
James Hyman, 14 December 2005.

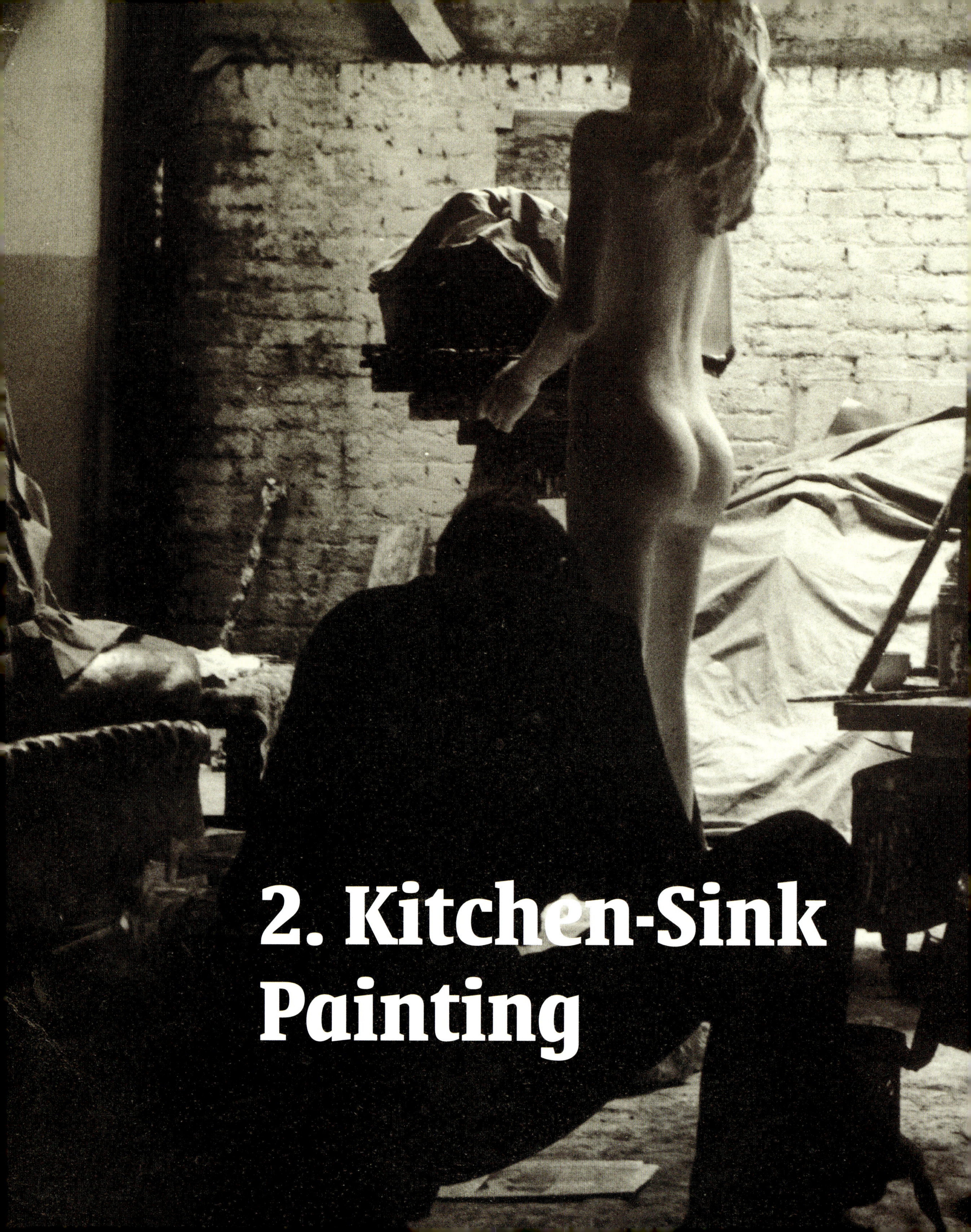

2. Kitchen-Sink Painting

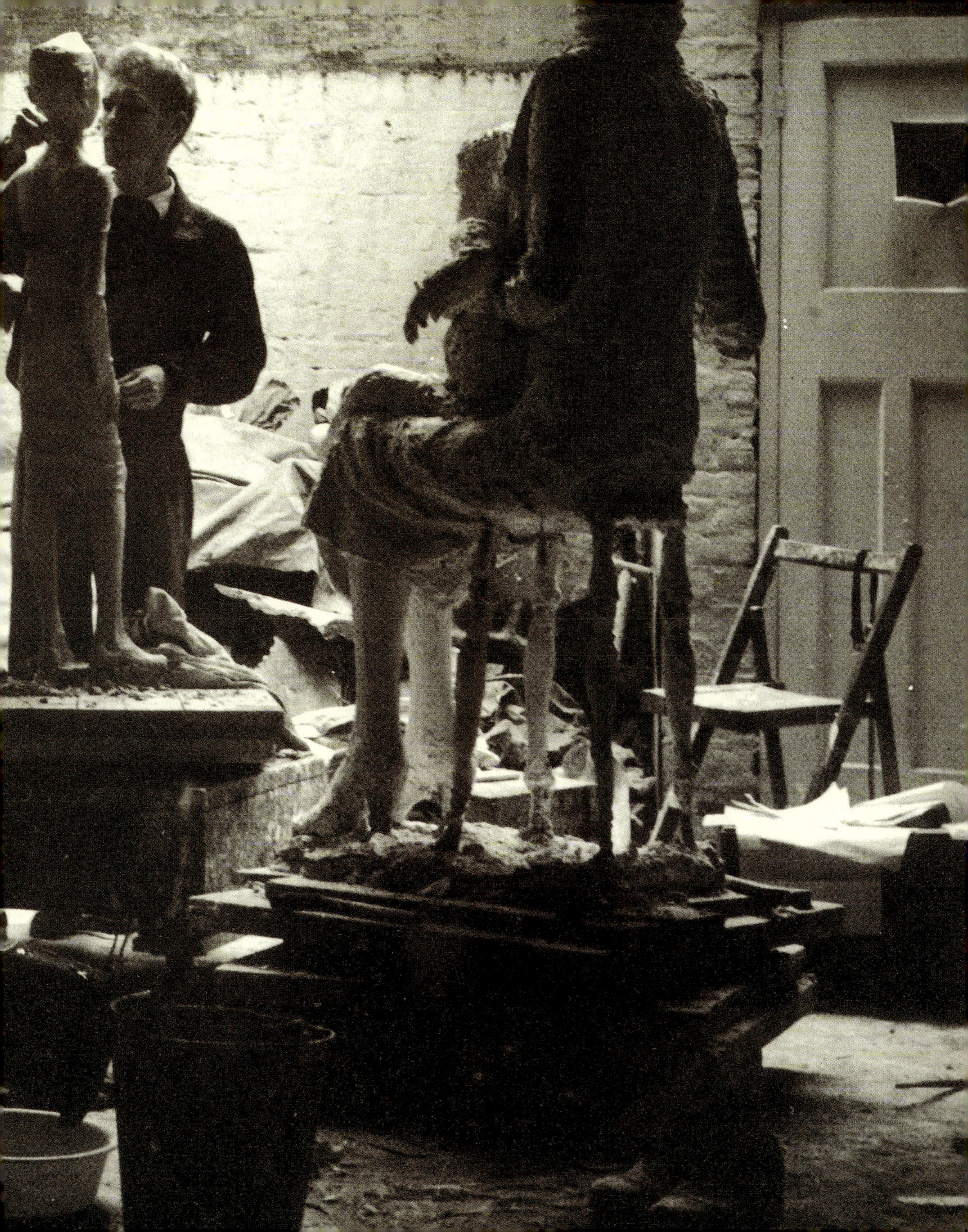

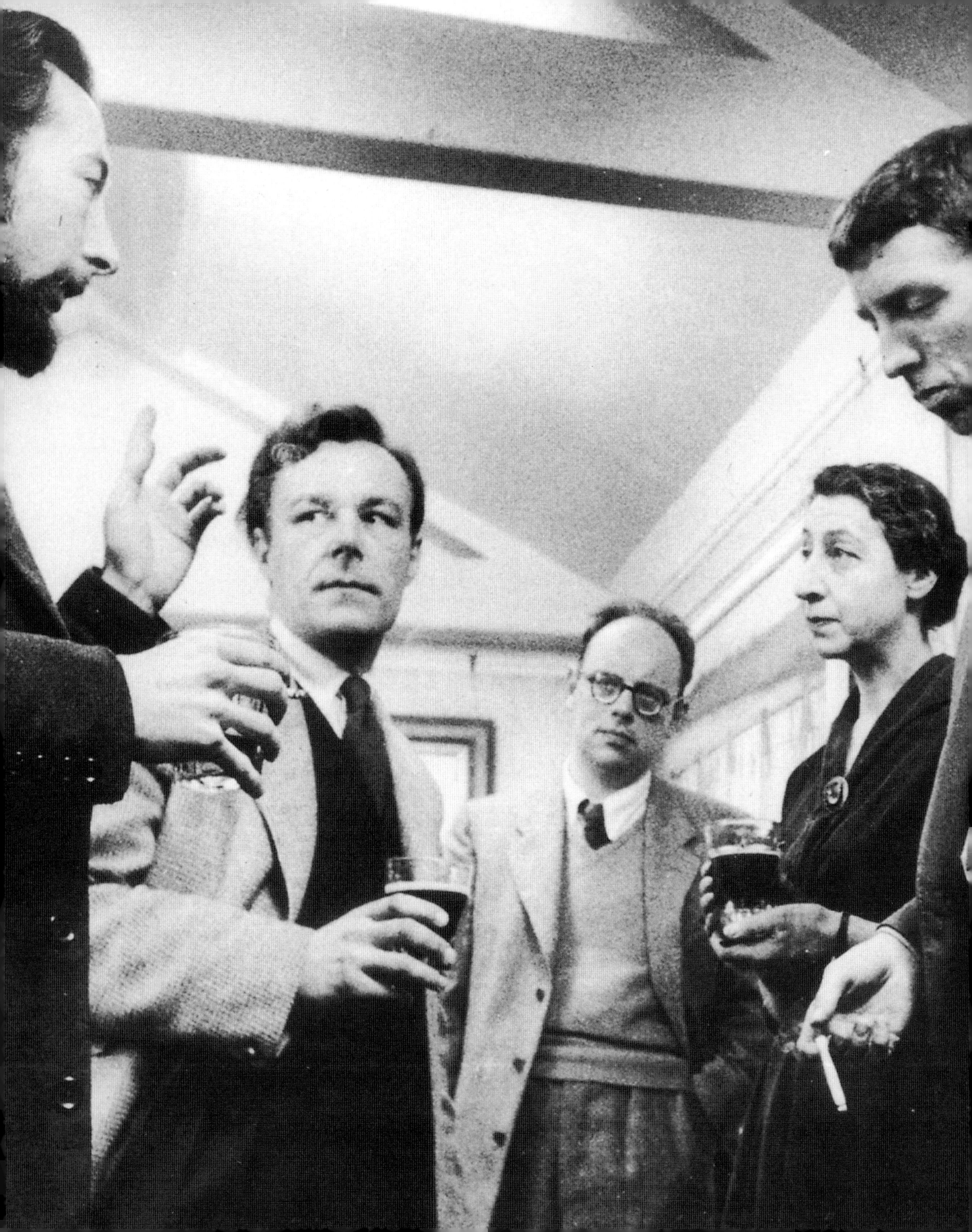

2. Kitchen-Sink Painting: Derrick Greaves and Social Realism

It should be stressed that they themselves never had any intention of forming a group, nor of inscribing themselves under any particular faction … The more one studies these four young painters, the more different they appear. One has to take the trouble to appreciate individuals individually. Short cuts by classification are superficial.

Helen Lessore, 1955[1]

From the outset, the 'Kitchen-Sink' painters (or 'Beaux Arts Quartet', as Derrick Greaves, John Bratby, Edward Middleditch and Jack Smith were also known) were grouped by expediency, not ideology. True, they studied at the Royal College and exhibited at the Beaux Arts Gallery, but there was no shared aesthetic or common manifesto. If they shared anything it was a suspicion of elegance and a dismissal of Henry Tonks and Randolph Schwabe's legacy of polished drawing that had taken root at the Slade School of Fine Art. Instead, their aesthetic was tougher, more robust, exemplified by their preference for charcoal rather than pencil to give a greater forthrightness and engagement: 'We were all discontented, kicking against the pricks. The bit was too tight on the drawing. We wanted to be free.'[2]

With the exception of John Bratby, whom Greaves barely knew and seldom met, there were bonds of personal friendship. From 1949–52, Greaves lived in Earls Court at 44 Pembroke Road, a house that had belonged to Aubrey Beardsley's mother, with friends from Sheffield including the painters Jack Smith and Leslie Duxbury, as well as the sculptor George Fullard. This was extremely enterprising: since the building had been bombed, Greaves and his fellow students were able to secure a long lease on condition that they restored the property. One of Greaves's most powerful early paintings, *Baby in Pram* (plate 17), shows Duxbury's child on the doorstep and a portrait of Jack Smith (plate 18) was also painted there.

Jack Smith had been a friend since childhood when both lived on the same Sheffield street and shared a love of painting and drawing. When both men went to live and study in London, it was natural that they should share digs together. Greaves recalls that Smith had the large back room at Pembroke Road, overlooking the garden, and worked so conscientiously that soon the room was so filled with paintings on board that Smith could barely get to his table to eat. It was a fun and stimulating time. Greaves was also close to George Fullard, whom he recalls as very bright, rather wild and with a lightning mind, and full of songs and jokes. For entertainment on a Friday and Saturday evening Greaves and Fullard would go down the street to the Pembroke Arms pub and sing music hall songs such as *Me and Jane in a Plane*, *The Winkle Song* and *Me and Old Bill Smith were Dusties*.

Around the corner was Edward Middleditch's studio and his close friendship with Greaves dates from this time. They would see each other's work as it progressed, talk intensively about their interests and read many of the same authors, among them Jean-Jacques Rousseau, D.H. Lawrence and Aldous Huxley. Dissatisfied with the work of many of their contemporaries, they sought an art that was tougher and more straightforward. This led them to reject Paris, or at

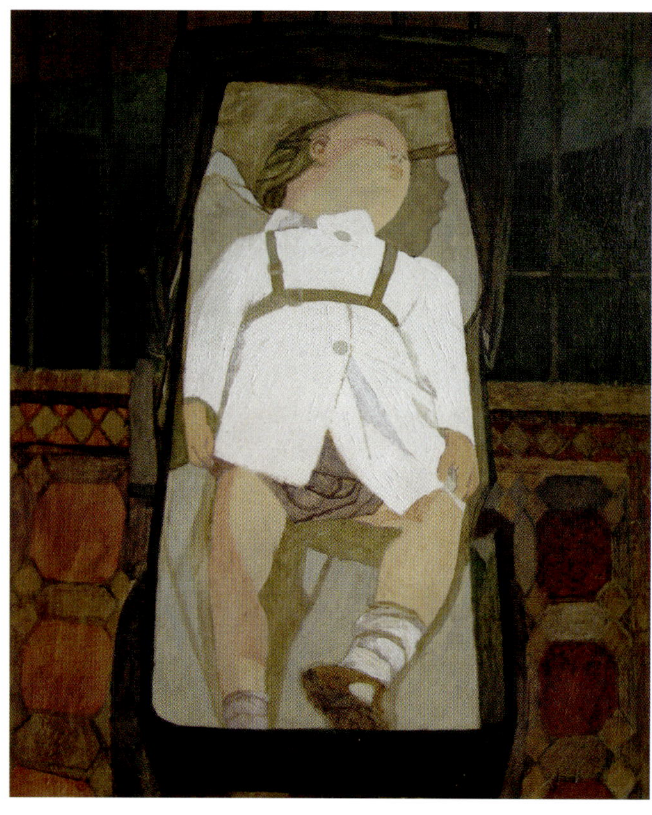

17 *Baby in Pram*, 1949
Oil on board
76 × 81cm (29.9 × 31.9in)
Private Collection, Wales

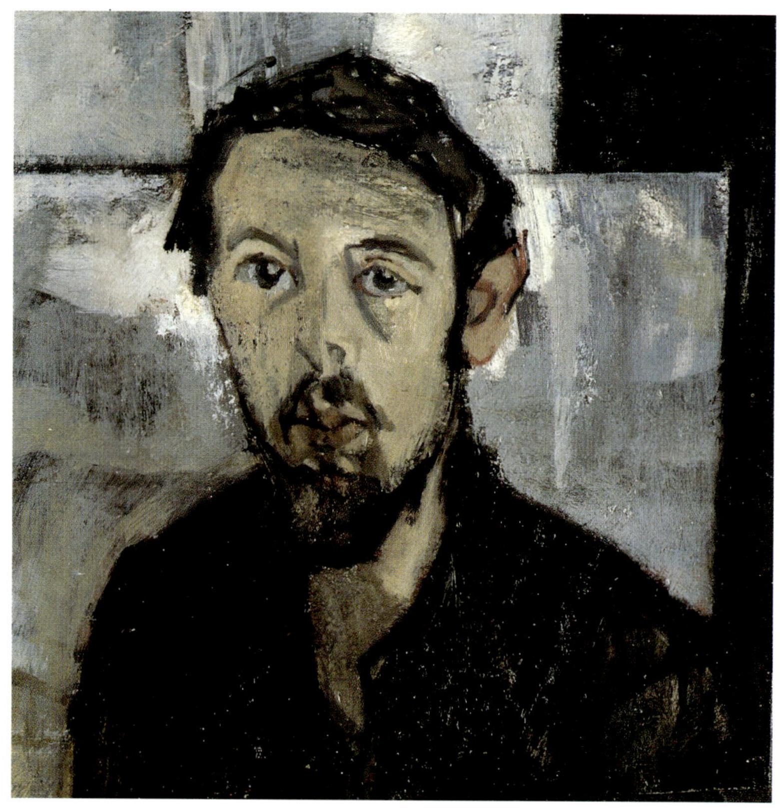

18 *Portrait of Jack Smith*, c.1949
Oil on canvas
28.4 × 27.9cm (11.2 × 11in)
National Portrait Gallery, London

least its younger artists, whom they felt to be imitating the mannerisms of their elders. But their conversation was above all practical rather than theoretical; for example, conversations about paint and colour might turn to their preference for Rembrandt colours, which had a greater range than was offered by the more familiar Winsor and Rowney.

Where Middleditch and Greaves differed was in their response to landscape, a dominant concern for both artists, neither of whom dwelt on city motifs. Greaves loved the romantic idea of the northern landscape running through Wordsworth's Cumbria to W.H. Auden's notion that you can put your ear to the ground and hear water in unseen conduits. In contrast, Middleditch responded to the landscape in more visual terms, not least through his friendship with some of David Bomberg's former students, such as Miles Richmond, who dramatised the bulk of the landscape and the drama of a slope.

Above all, there was a generosity of spirit, a camaraderie in which these artists were more inclined to praise than criticise. What mattered was to do the work. Touting the work around galleries was anathema and the idea that it might sell a distant thought. If there was a 'Kitchen-Sink' group then it was this band of artists living together from 1949–52 in a house of bed-sitters with a shared sink in the kitchen downstairs. This was a period that predated their first one-person shows and coincided with their student years, and it is conspicuous how little this circle of artists ever had to do with John Bratby. What's more, by the time that 'Kitchen-Sink' painting was championed Greaves was not even living in Britain, having won a scholarship to study for a year at the British School in Rome (1952–3), which he then succeeded in extending for a further year (1953–4).

In fact, the critical promotion of a 'Kitchen-Sink' school developed during the mid rather than the early 1950s. In late 1953, the Walker Gallery, an art dealer in London, staged an exhibition entitled *Paintings for the Kitchen*. Just as John Berger presented young social realists as a continuation of tradition, so the anonymous reviewer of this exhibition in *Art News and Review* provided an historical foundation: '… the kitchen has a hallowed place in the history of art … The marmites of Chardin, the flayed chickens of Soutine, the eggs and frying pans of William Scott, are all part and parcel of the great mythology of European art.'[3]

Then, a year later, David Sylvester wrote an essay entitled 'The Kitchen-Sink' for the recently launched journal, *Encounter*.[4] This, too, provided an historical context for the paintings of a new generation of artists, and again addressed painters from across Europe. Sylvester's essay was extremely broad in its historical and geographical references. It used 'Kitchen-Sink' as a characterisation, not as a label, to trace a broad international trend rather than denoting a small British group, and did so without making claims for the realism of these painters. Indeed, the idea that 'Kitchen-Sink' painting constituted realism was a contradiction to Sylvester, whose own existentialist 'realism of the imagination', exemplified by Francis Bacon and Alberto Giacometti, stood in opposition to the 'Romanticism' he deplored in supposed realists such as Paul Rebeyrolle. However, the label 'Kitchen-Sink' stuck and was subsequently applied to just four artists – Bratby, Greaves, Middleditch and Smith – at the centre of claims for a British social realism and Sylvester became credited with giving the quartet its name.

Despite Sylvester's perceived association with the idea of 'Kitchen-Sink' painting, the presentation of a quartet owed more to other writers, not least to John Berger, John Minton and Helen Lessore of the Beaux Arts Gallery. Lessore not only staged the first solo shows for the painters but also arranged their first group show, at Cambridge's Heffer Gallery in 1955, which encouraged critics to seek points in common. Their profile helped Lessore's gallery assume a coherent identity and it quickly became synonymous with social realism by young artists. In 1953 John Berger asserted that 'The Beaux Arts is quickly and deservedly gaining the reputation of being the one gallery where it is possible to see the serious work of young painters'.[5] Quentin Bell observed, in 1956, that 'the Beaux Arts Gallery … is in a sense the spiritual home of social realism in this country';[6] in 1957 Trewin Copplestone described the gallery as the 'group Headquarters' for the Kitchen-Sink painters.[7]

In fact it was not until the 1955 exhibition of the Beaux Arts Quartet at Heffer Gallery, followed a year later by the Venice Biennale, that Bratby, Greaves, Middleditch and Smith were exhibited together as a group. In each case, however, the stress was placed on the individuality of each artist. Indeed, despite the desire to champion a common project, John Berger was sophisticated in the way in which his first reviews of the Beaux Arts Quartet not only placed the work of each artist in a wider national and international context, but also acknowledged individual achievement. In a review of Bratby's first solo show at the Beaux Arts Gallery in 1954, Berger, for perhaps the first time, grouped together the Quartet: 'Bratby's vision has values and qualities in common with Jack Smith, Edward Middleditch and Derrick Greaves. There is the same suspicion of elegance and the same ability to be moved by the commonplace'.[8] However, he also acknowledged its 'intense and personal emotions'. Certainly, Berger made generalisations about the social concerns of the quartet's choice of subjects, but nevertheless he was careful to distinguish between intention and implication. Recognising that 'the motives are not directly social or political', Berger argued that 'they all paint without protest but with great sympathy for the few precious possessions of the dispossessed'.[9] Indeed, the consistency he perceived in their subject matter encouraged Berger to believe that the quartet did not simply present what was in front of them but had a conception of what was an 'appropriate' subject.

A prevalent theme was that of a mother and baby. Reflecting both personal circumstances and a post-war baby-boom, these prosaic images were an anti-dote to Henry Moore's lofty idealisation of the subject as a universal symbol of maternity. Edward Middleditch's rare depiction of a person, *Baby* (1952), Jack Smith's iconic *Mother Bathing a Child* (1954) and Greaves's *First Steps* (plate 19) are paintings of privation conveyed in muted tones that are at best distantly related to Moore's well-fed families. Greaves had married a nurse, Margaret Johnson, in 1950 and in 1956 she gave birth to their first child, Simon, soon to be followed by Julia and Daniel. Images of his wife and oldest son would dominate his work of 1956 and its presentation in exhibitions in London that year.

However, critics quickly recognised the fissure between critical aspiration and artistic practice, which grew ever wider as the work of the individual members of the Beaux Arts Quartet became more subjective, hermetic, romantic and even abstract. Their former tutor at the Royal College, John Minton, who perhaps felt that their fame was eclipsing his own, satirised this in an essay of 1956 entitled 'Three Young Contemporaries'. Referring to 'three of the most notable painters who have left the Royal College in recent years', namely Greaves, Middleditch and Smith, to whom he referred by initials only, he ridiculed the gap between the lofty aspirations of the critic and the pragmatic concerns of the artist:

> *No painter wears his heart on his sleeve and no painter explains himself except by his painting. Set a questionnaire he will do everything to lose it … Is that the ageless Venice, Mr G? Are you a social realist, Mr M? Is that the Child of Europe, Mr S? … Is it valid? Does it relate? Is it socially significant? The critics cry and in answering themselves fill their columns. Giving the painter time to get the nose drawn right, the foot reshaped, the foreground redrawn, the middle-distance reconsidered. Yes, but isn't it too descriptive? Or not descriptive enough? Or too theatrical? No, but I mean, is it timeless? And the painter has time to buy more paints, to catch the train, even for a short delay in the station bar, and he is away…*[10]

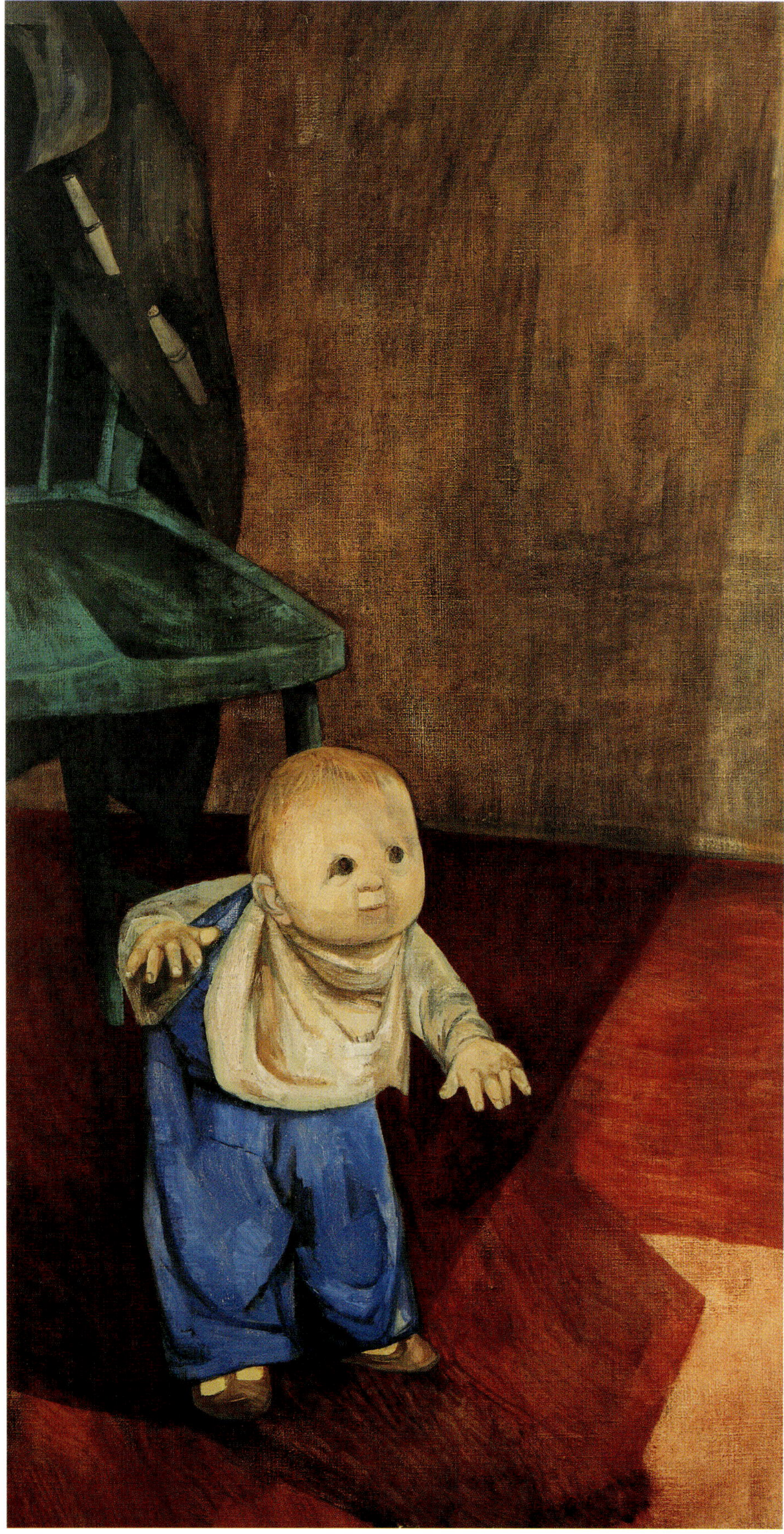

19 *First Steps*, 1956
Oil on canvas on board
143.5 × 76cm (56.5 × 29.9in)
Private Collection, London

Elsewhere their individuality was celebrated. One of the leading British art journals, *Art News and Review*, published a front page profile on Derrick Greaves in November 1956 that not only confirmed how quickly his reputation had become established, but also provided one of the most prescient characterisations of his concerns. In it the art critic Pierre Rouve wrote that:

> *Stubborn attachment to whatever the devalued term 'realism' may mean is all too often a shield for creative impotence. With Derrick Greaves it is above all an act of humility. It is the refusal of a man deeply immersed in the vicissitudes of the human adventure to transform his art into some kind of shop window for the wares of egocentric fetishism.*[11]

By this time Greaves was routinely included in London's institutional and commercial galleries. His first significant exposure had come in group exhibitions of young painters at the Lisle Street gallery of the Left-leaning exhibiting society, the Artists International Association (A.I.A.) in 1949 and 1950;[12] at the R.B.A. Galleries in 1950; and then at the Whitechapel Art Gallery in the seminal group exhibition of social realism, *Looking Forward* (1952).[13] From such exhibitions Greaves received his first attention from the press.

The most important of these exhibitions was *Looking Forward*, a manifesto exhibition of social realism curated by John Berger, which was explicitly conceived to attract a large public audience and to be accessible to the working class. Berger wrote that the exhibition was intended to provide 'the raw material of a socialist art', for which 'the new patrons will be trade unions, democratic local councils, community centres, etc.'[14] The exhibition catalogue provided a bold characterisation of Berger's realism:

> *Realism is not a method but an attitude of mind ... the realist always starts from the particular and from this beginning tries to deduce a typical truth ... the realist is fundamentally optimistic because he accepts the world – not necessarily as it is – but as it can be, according to the potentiality of its own laws of development ... The realist attitude breaks down the studio wall and projects the artist into ordinary life.*[15]

The materiality of the thick paint married to social concerns led Greaves and several of his contemporaries to be presented by critics as followers of Gustave Courbet, especially in the wake of a major exhibition of the artist at the Marlborough Gallery in 1953. Prominent among these champions were John

Berger and Nevile Wallis. In his review of Berger's exhibition, *Looking Forward*, Wallis singled out for praise Arthur Hackney, Edward Middleditch and Derrick Greaves, whom he characterised as 'Cousins of Courbet'.[16] This relationship was also at the heart of Berger's praise of artists as individual as Prunella Clough and Josef Herman.

Following *Looking Forward*, Greaves's public career took off, although characteristically the artist was diffident about this success. In 1953 he had the first of his two solo exhibitions at Helen Lessore's Beaux Arts Gallery. In contrast to Michael Andrews, for whom the gap between being offered a show by Helen Lessore and its realisation was six years, Greaves had just three weeks between Lessore's visit to his studio and the staging of his first show at her gallery. Greaves recalls that she visited twice, explaining that she never decided after a single studio visit: 'then to my terrible surprise she said "can you be ready in three weeks?" So I showed what I had.' This included canvases he had rolled up and brought back from Rome and recent works of Sheffield. But Greaves never saw the show, having by then travelled back to Italy for the second year of his Abbey Major scholarship in Rome.

Greaves sold everything at his first one-person show at the Beaux Arts Gallery. As the artist later recalled:

I was surprised at the success, but I was just getting on with things in Italy … John Berger wrote about me regularly after that, but it was as though it was happening to somebody else. It's journalism. All painters know what the value of their paintings are. The fact that they may be used to justify this, that and the other is not to do with them really. I felt that you couldn't ever really expect to make a living out of painting and didn't really want to court the publicity. I didn't really know what to do with it. Bratby wanted us to be known as a group, but the rest of us felt the job was to be an individual. Be responsible for your own thing. It all happened in parallel to what I was doing.[17]

Greaves's exhibition attracted enthusiastic support. Stephen Bone, writing in the *Manchester Guardian,* proclaimed that this was 'one of the most promising first exhibitions that has been seen in London for some time', praising 'a strong and individual personality'. John Russell, meanwhile, declared in the *Sunday Times* that the exhibition, 'with its ease and natural breadth of manner, foretells a distinguished career'.[18]

Then, from November to December 1955, Greaves held his second show at

the Beaux Arts Gallery, this time coinciding with Sheila Fell's first exhibition
at the gallery. Given the large size of the paintings, just eight were shown,
accompanied by a portfolio of drawings. Some of his most ambitious paintings,
these works were nonetheless attacked in *The Times* for an 'obsessive concern
with detail at the expense – particularly in some large work – of an interre-
lated design'.[19]

This was criticism that John Berger directly refuted in a lengthy paean of
praise: 'The privilege – and I mean that in all modesty – of describing these
works for the first time presents formidable difficulties; their originality, which
manifests itself not in their novelty but in their profound obviousness, excludes
all ready references.' What Berger identified and stressed was a literal, mimetic
quality, a direct relationship between Greaves's handling of paint and the quality
of the thing depicted: from the smoothness of a baby's skin to the roughness of
a worker's hands. Arguing that 'Greaves has rejected every precept of academic
teaching', Berger praised the way that 'the arbitrariness of any one moment of
life comes before the imposed pattern of any composition'. Hence the fact that
the largest painting on show, *A Sicilian Subject* (plate 45), eschews a conventional
composition and gives each object its own autonomy and individuality, not so
much a breakdown of the composition as a way of showing respect for each
distinct element: 'Indeed each object is separate. If a man has only ten possessions, he tends to count them separately.'[20] This separation, already identified
in this review of 1955, would be a central aspect of Greaves's presentation of
objects in the decades to come.

Inclusion in group exhibitions consolidated his reputation and status as a
leading realist. In 1955, Greaves was included in *The Artist's View of an Industry*,
which laid stress on the work of young artists invited by Shell Oil to make works
on the subject of the oil industry. Greaves and Middleditch each produced pictures
of a distillation unit at Shell Haven refinery in Essex (plate 20), suggesting that
the two friends had made a joint visit. The following year, Greaves was one of
the younger exhibitors in the Institute of Contemporary Arts (I.C.A.) exhibition
of landscape painting (January 1956) and included in the Arts Council's *Six Young
Painters* (1957), which also presented figurative paintings by Michael Andrews,
John Bratby, Harold Cohen, Martin Froy and Philip Sutton. Internationally, Greaves
also appeared in major exhibitions in Russia and Italy. Then, at the year's end
and coinciding with Rouve's aforementioned profile, Greaves had work included
in exhibitions at the Adams Gallery and the Piccadilly Gallery, both in London.

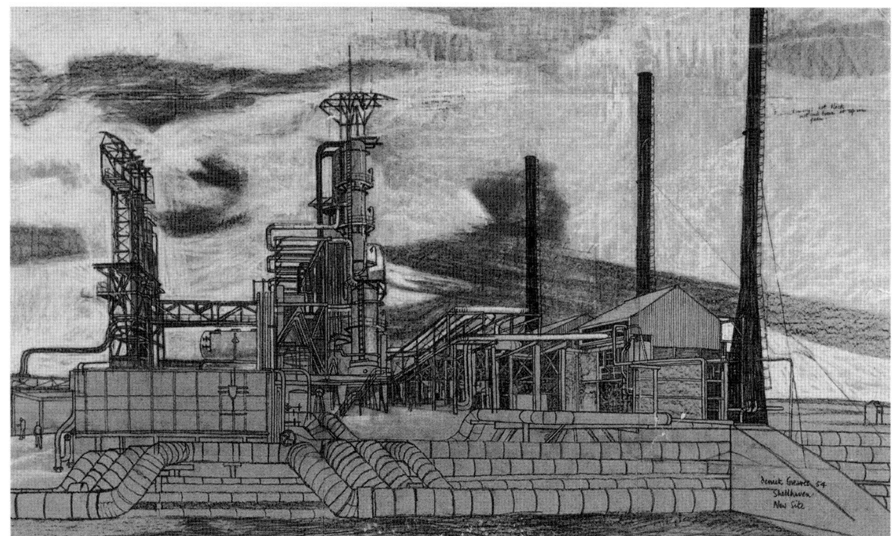

20 *Distillation Unit (Shell Haven Refinery, Essex)*, 1954
Ink and charcoal
76 × 102cm (30 × 40in)

By now drawings and paintings of a mother and child had become a key theme for the artist and were brilliantly evoked in an essay by John Berger on the Kitchen-Sink painters that reproduced Greaves's painting, *Mother and Child* (plate 21):

When he paints the hand of a mother holding her child, he tries to suggest all that has made that hand what it is. The cooking, the sewing, the caressing, the clenching in anger, the scrubbing, the way it's been held by her lovers. And then he contrasts all this with the baby's hand — the baby who is just beginning to learn through his hands to distinguish one object from another.[21]

In precise working drawings of the mid 1950s the form would be carried by line alone, as in *Baby – Finger in Mouth* (plate 22), the sparseness of which anticipates the economic use of line in Greaves's later work. Greaves would convey his tenderness towards the subject, as in *Mother and Child* (plate 24), by using soft pencil, but he would also make robust pencil and charcoal drawings, such as *Baby, Bath and Dog* (plate 23), for exhibition. The paintings of his children that resulted, such as *First Steps* (plate 19), *Simon Martin Greaves* (1958) and *Anna Julia Greaves* (1958), used paint in a post-Cézanne way, with colours mixed on a palette or plate and dabbed on a bit at a time. *First Steps* is characteristic of the period, although its delicacy contrasts with contemporaneous, thickly impasto paintings in which forms were painted to suggest the weight of the subject and light used to model their volumes. *First Steps* was included in one of the most important international exhibitions of British art of the 1950s, *Looking at People*.

Looking at People toured Britain during 1955–6 and was visited by 250,000 people, before travelling to Russia where it was the first show of Western art since the Russian Revolution in 1917. Initially including work by just three artists – its instigator, the illustrator Paul Hogarth, the painter Carel Weight and sculptor Betty Rae – by the time it reached its final British venue, the South London Art Gallery, the exhibition had been expanded with the inclusion of Greaves as well as Edward Ardizzone, Alistair Grant, George Fullard and Ruskin Spear. It was this expanded version that travelled to Russia and was at that time one of the largest exhibitions of contemporary British art ever held outside Britain: the catalogue lists 156 works.

Spear, Hogarth and Greaves travelled to Russia for the exhibition, cutting the tape at the opening at the Pushkin Museum of Fine Arts and speaking on Moscow Radio. In a speech at the opening ceremony, Hogarth told of the idealism behind the show: 'We have been moved by the fact that artists as well as statesmen can and are able to contribute to international understanding.'[22]

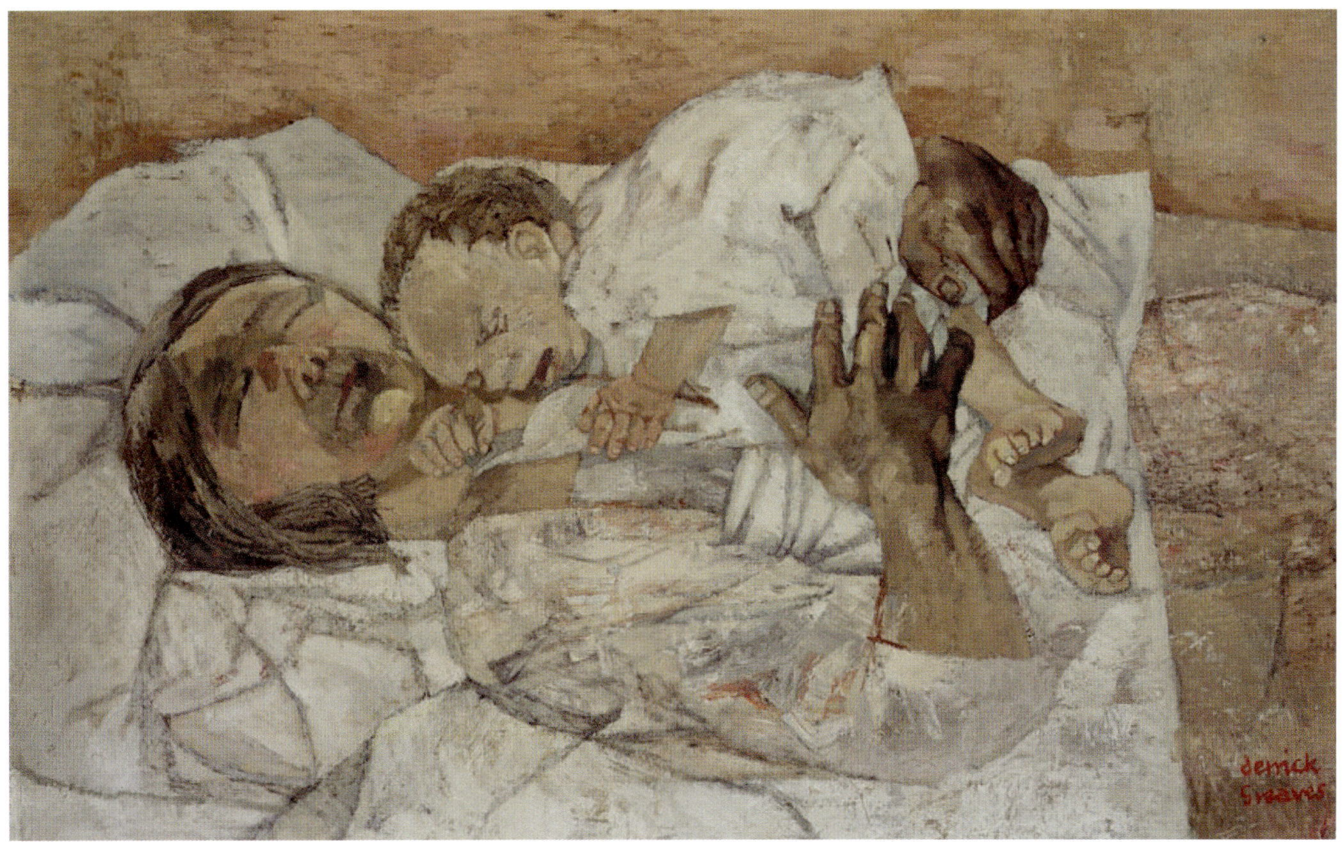

21 *Mother and Child*, 1956
Oil on canvas
71 × 91.5cm (28 × 36in) approx.
The Berardo Collection, Museum of Modern Art, Sintra, Portugal

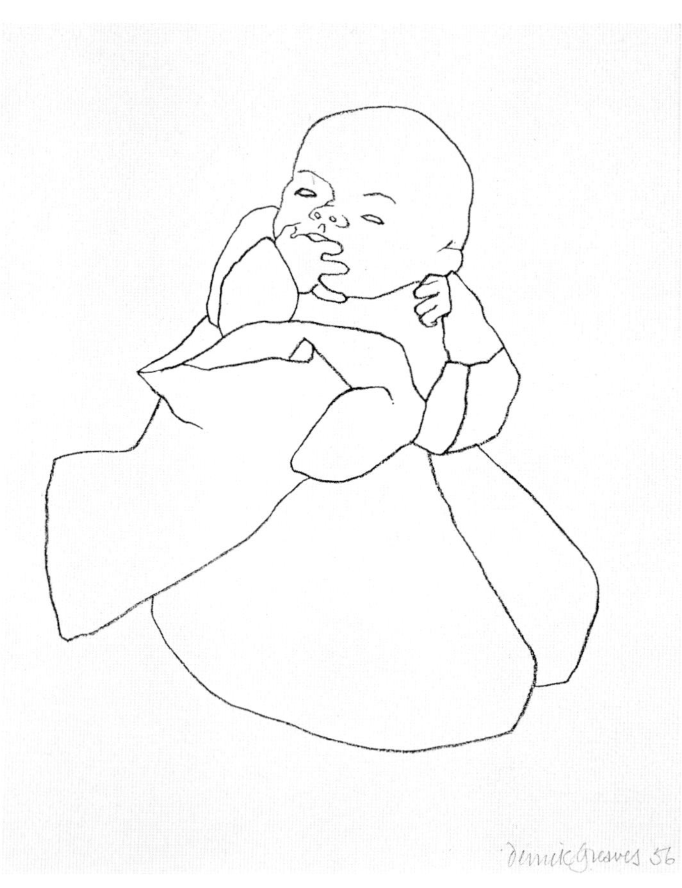

22 *Baby – Finger in Mouth*, 1956
Charcoal on paper
30.5 × 25.5cm (12 × 10in)

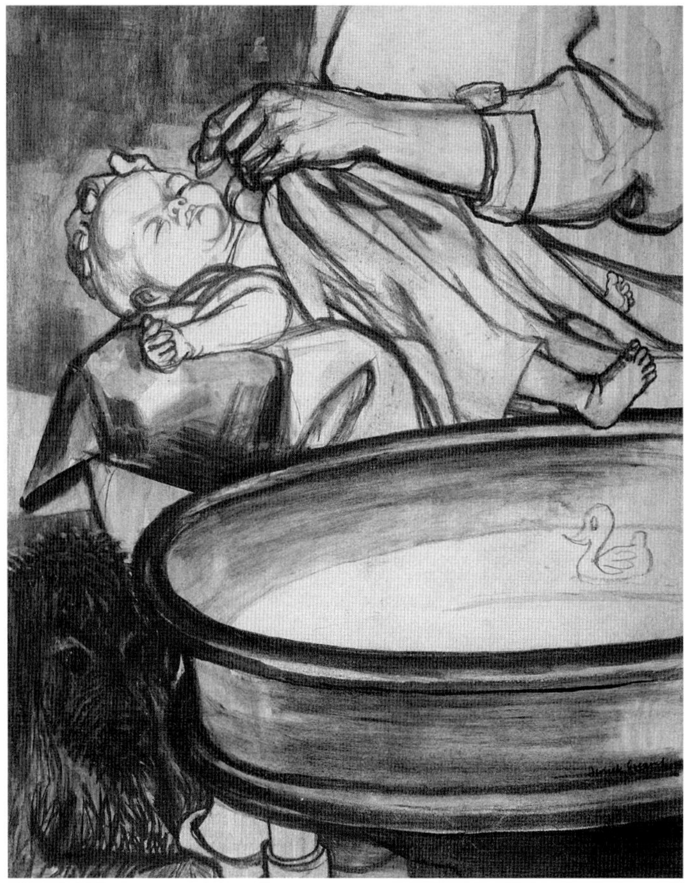

23 *Baby, Bath and Dog*, 1956
Charcoal on paper
61.5 × 49.5cm (24.2 × 19.5in)
Private Collection, London

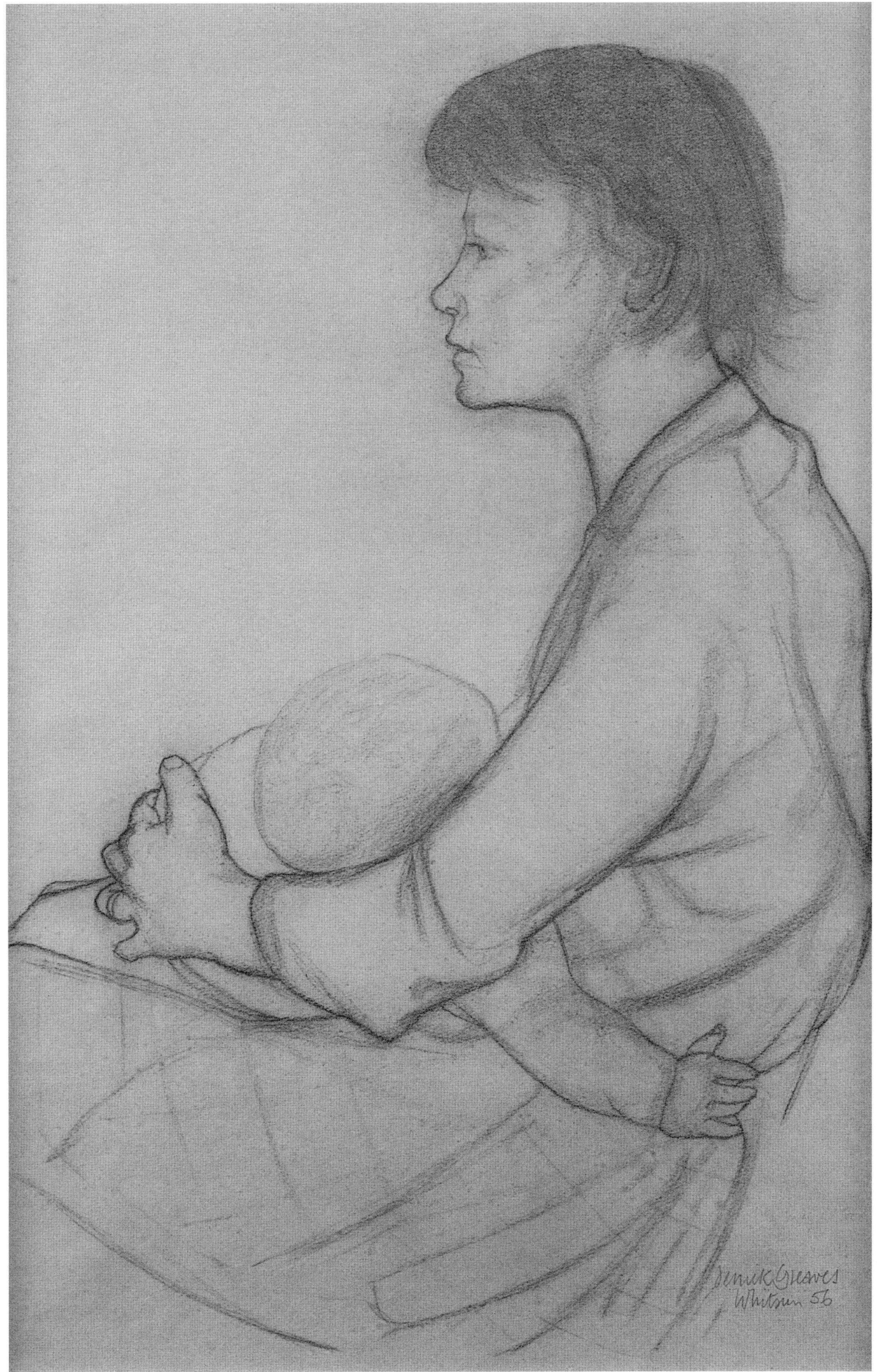

24 *Mother and Child, c.*1956
Pencil on paper
55 × 37.5cm (21.7 × 14.8in)
Claire and James Hyman, London

However, this exhibition of British social realism received limited support, and the proposed staging of *Looking at People* at a second venue, the Hermitage, was cancelled.[23]

Whilst there, Greaves also travelled through the Soviet Union under the auspices of the Union of Soviet Artists, meeting artists in each town, and visiting studios and workshops where he was able to talk freely with the artists. He also travelled to Armenia and produced a series of large monotypes which he later showed in London (plates 25 and 26).

He found Soviet art to be figuratively competent to the point of slickness, but very worn and out-of-date by that time. Ilya Repin, for example, he disliked for his rhetoric, whilst recognising his confident proficiency. What he did admire were Russian icons and Andrei Rublyov's 6–7ft (2.4–2.8m) figures, the memory of which has stayed with him ever since. Meanwhile, in the Hermitage, works by Picasso, Matisse and Raoul Dufy made a lasting impression. Little was to be seen of modern Russian art as it was kept hidden away in the basement storage areas

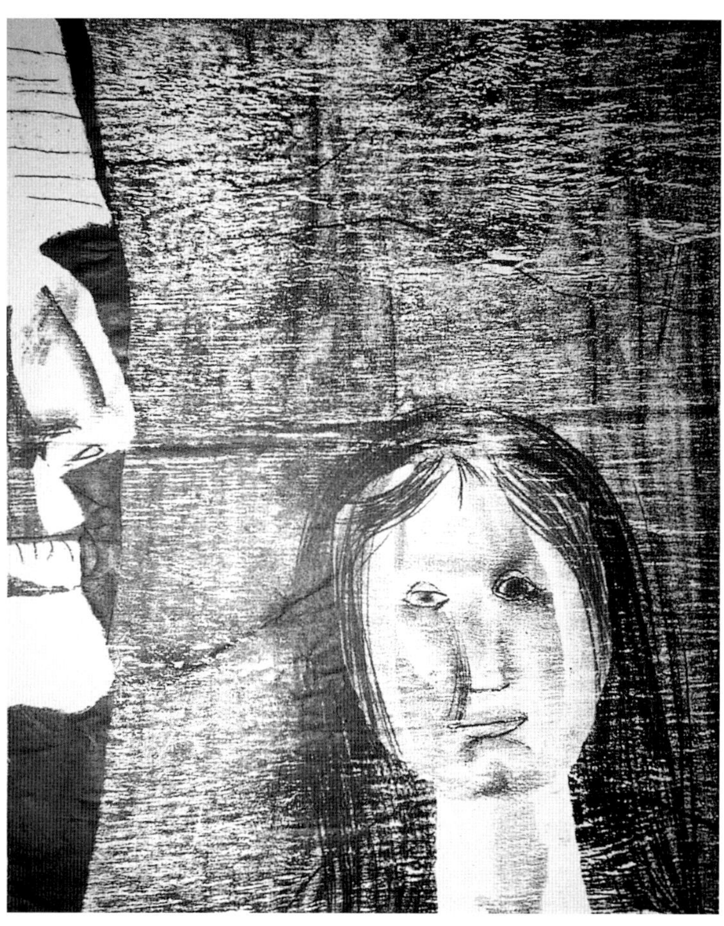

25 *Armenian Monotype I*, 1957
Oil on paper
61 × 48.2cm (24 × 19in)
University of Wales, Aberystwyth

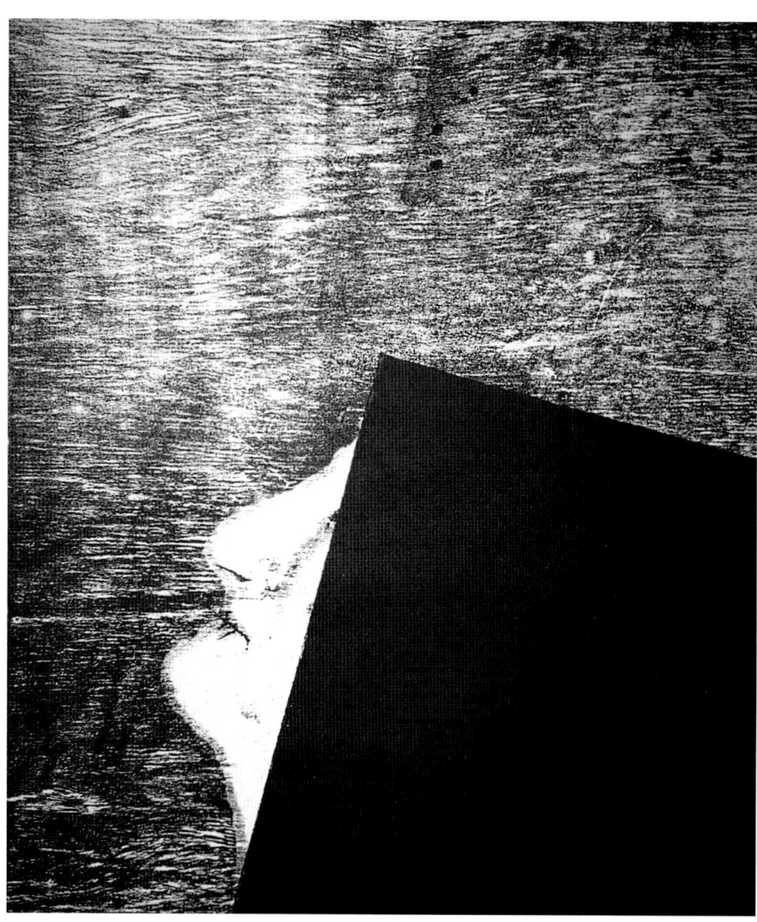

26 *Armenian Monotype II*, 1957
Oil on paper
61.5 × 48.2cm (24.2 × 19in)
University of Wales, Aberystwyth

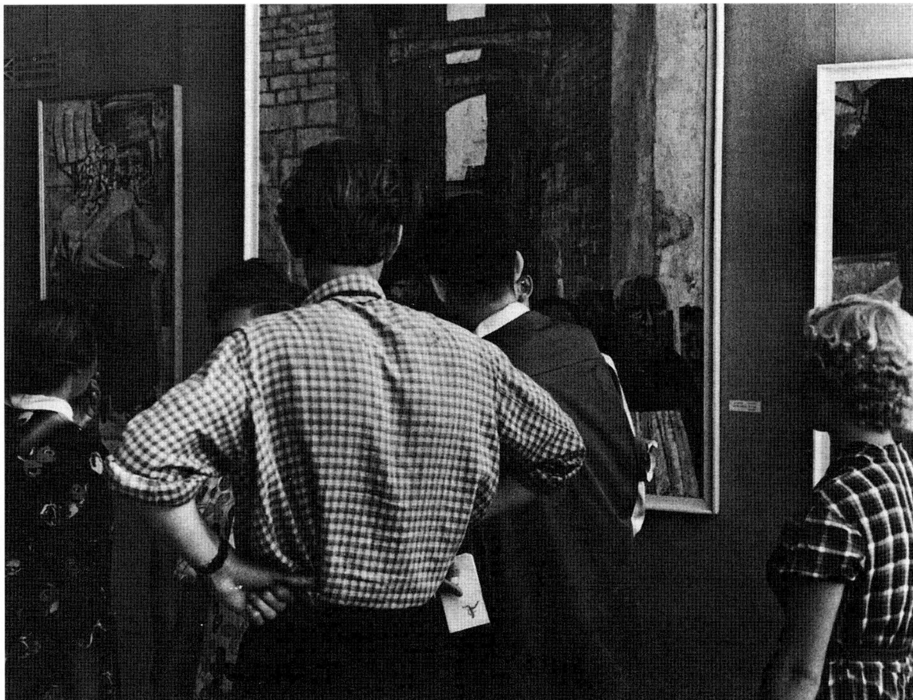

27 *Looking at People*, Pushkin Museum of Fine Arts, Moscow, 1957

of the Tretyakov Gallery and other museums. This was frustrating to Greaves for he had hoped to see work from Marc Chagall's Vitebsk period and paintings by Kasimir Malevich and Natalia Goncharova, but none was to be seen.

At the end of 1956, the impression of a social realist context for Greaves's painting was reinforced by two extremely focused group shows at the Adams Gallery and the Piccadilly Gallery. *Three British Painters* at the Adams Gallery presented just Greaves, Middleditch and Peter de Francia. All but two of Greaves's paintings were studies of a baby and the others were of a pregnant woman, and 'owe their immediacy of feeling to a realist's true concern for the dignity and pathos of the human condition'.[24] For Alan Clutton-Brock, reviewing the exhibition in the *Listener*, Greaves's 'series of pictures of babies show an advance in vigour and precision of statement; the best of these works have an undeniable if alarming vitality'.[25] For John Golding 'the exhibition ... makes one aware of the extent to which the new English realism is becoming a conscious school ... all [three] take the same blunt, rather grim view of life, and all work on a large-scale in a direct and uncompromising technique'.[26]

At Christmas 1956, the Piccadilly Gallery showed drawings by three artists: Greaves, Middleditch and Alistair Grant. This time Greaves presented no less than

14 drawings on the theme of maternity, gaining an ecstatic review from critic
Pierre Rouve:

> *This is drawing almost at its very best – an art that does not aim at black and
> white substitutes for luscious pigments and relies on a concision of line and
> candour of emotion. Here the draughtsman is what he should always be – a truth
> teller … With an impressive economy of means and with a vigilant eye for the
> basic impact of his graphical idiom he avoids the twin traps of academic
> verisimilitude and expressionist rhetoric. Through the elimination of the
> superfluous he achieves that overwhelming immediacy without which drawings
> lose their autonomy to become mere stand-ins for a painting to come. With
> Greaves, drawings are stars in their own right – for his art, bred on simple
> integrity becomes more and more a decisive denial of artfulness.*[27]

The immediacy and clarity that Greaves now demonstrated as both painter
and draughtsman owed much to what he had learnt in Italy.

Notes

1. Helen Lessore, 'Introduction', *Bratby, Greaves, Middleditch, Smith*, Heffer Gallery, Cambridge, February–March 1955.

2. Courtney, tape 11, side 1.

3. Anonymous, 'Paintings for the Kitchen', *Art News and Review*, 12 December 1953, vol.5, no.23, p.2. This was a review of pictures by a Mr Lawson-Dick.

4. David Sylvester, 'The Kitchen-Sink', *Encounter*, December 1954, vol.3, no.6, pp 61–4.

5. John Berger, 'The Young Generation', *New Statesman*, 25 July 1953, vol.156, no.1168, p.101.

6. Quentin Bell, 'Round the London Galleries', *Listener*, 12 April 1956, vol.55, no.1411, p.399.

7. Trewin Copplestone, 'Not Drawn to Scale', *Art News and Review*, 15 February 1957, vol.2, no.2.

8. John Berger, 'John Bratby', *New Statesman*, 25 September 1954, vol.48, no.1229, p.358.

9. John Berger, 'John Bratby', op. cit.

10. John Minton, 'Three Young Contemporaries', *Ark*, 1955, no.13, pp 12–14.

11. Pierre Rouve, 'Portrait of the Artist – Derrick Greaves', *Art News and Review*, 10 November 1956, vol.VIII, no.21, p.1, p.11.

12. *Young Painters Working in Britain*, A.I.A. Gallery, Lisle Street, June–July 1949. As well as Greaves, those exhibited included Prunella Clough, Robert Colquhoun, John Craxton, Josef Herman, Robert MacBryde, John Minton, William Scott, Jack Smith and Keith Vaughan. In a review in *Art News and Review* (S. John Woods, 'Young Painters in Britain', vol.I, no.10, p.6), Greaves was one of just four young artists singled out as 'worth noting', the others being Jack Smith, Henry Mundy and Gillian Ayres. *Paintings by Contemporary Artists*, A.I.A., January 1950, included *Pinch O'Snuff* by Derrick Greaves.

13. Berger has confirmed that it was during the preparation of the show that he became aware of Greaves's work (John Berger, letter to James Hyman, 12 April 1993). Derrick Greaves recalls that it was only after his return from Italy in 1953 that he met Berger (Derrick Greaves, letter to James Hyman, 8 February 1994).

14. John Berger, 'Dear Enemy …', *Tribune*, 26 September 1952, Whitechapel Archive.

15. John Berger, 'Foreword', *Looking Forward*, Whitechapel Art Gallery, London, 1952.

16. Nevile Wallis, 'Cousins of Courbet', *Observer*, 5 October 1952, Whitechapel Archive.

17. Courtney, tape 12, side 1.

18. *Sunday Times*, 1953. Artist's Archive.

19. Anonymous, 'Two Interesting Painters: Grim and Brooding', *The Times*, 6 December 1955. Artist's Archive

20. John Berger, 'Greaves and Hogarth', *New Statesman*, 10 December 1955, vol.50, no.1292, p.792.

21. John Berger, 'The new realists at the Venice Biennale', *Vogue*, July 1956, pp 58–9, 109.

22. Paul Hogarth, *Drawing on Life*, David and Charles, Newton Abbot, 1997, pp 50–1.

23. In 1960 another exhibition of British art was brought to the Pushkin. Entitled *Painting from Britain 1700–1960*, it used a national tradition to contextualise recent achievement and its timing reflected a relaxation under Nikita Khrushchev. Again, reaction was mixed. In a review in *Iskusstvo* (no.2, pp 47–53, 1960), attention was focused on those who had shown in 1957 including Betty Rea, Hogarth and Greaves, who was praised for showing the influence of Guttuso, although concern was expressed about his 'deformations'.

24. Anonymous, 'Realists All: British painters at the Adams Gallery', *The Times*, 8 November 1956. Artist's Archive.

25. Alan Clutton-Brock, 'Round the London Galleries', *Listener*, 8 November 1956, vol.LVI, no.1441, p.762.

26. John Golding, *New Statesman*, 10 November 1956, p.586.

27. Pierre Rouve, 'Trio in Black and White', *Art News and Review*, 10 November 1956, vol.VIII, no.21, p.10.

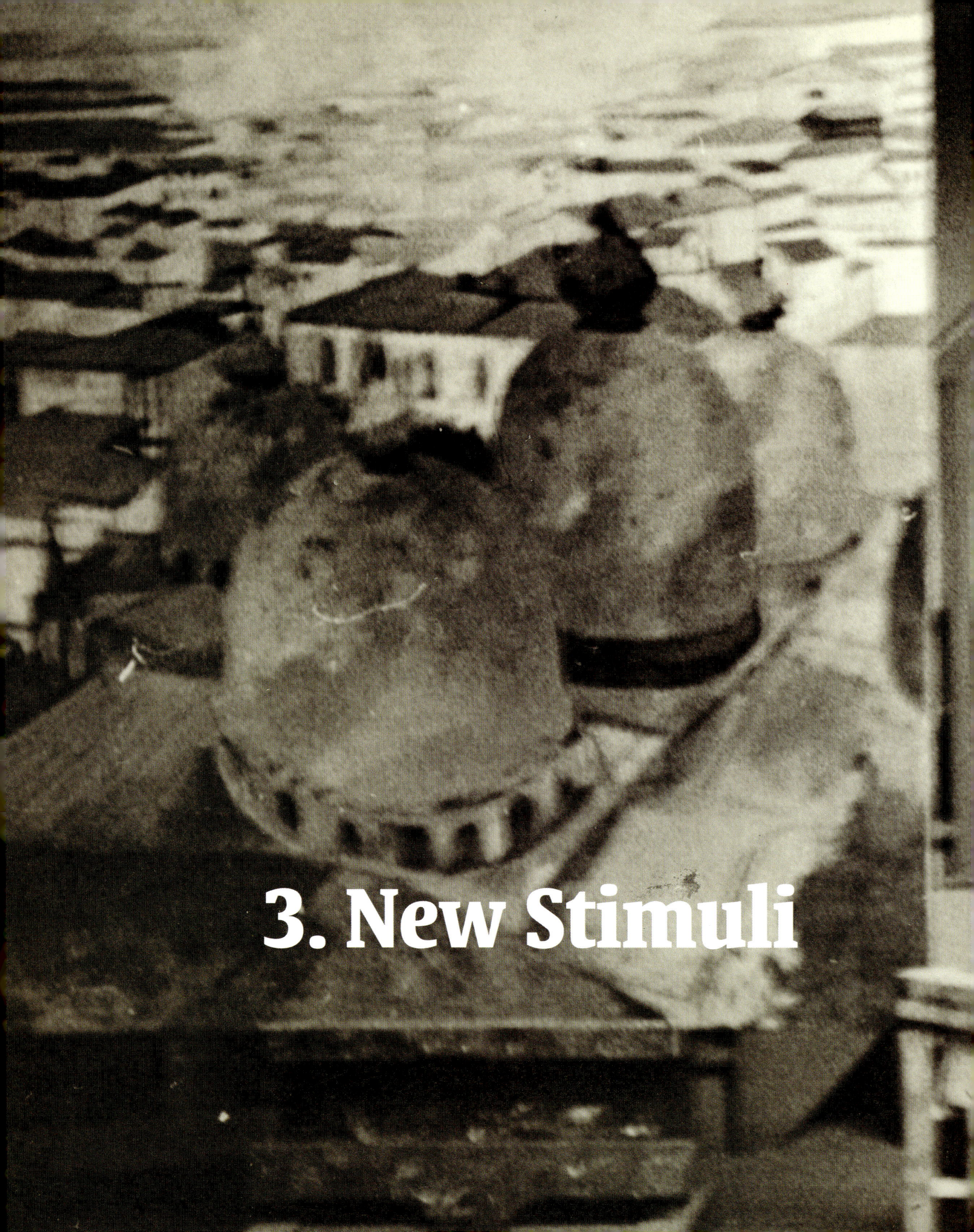

3. New Stimuli

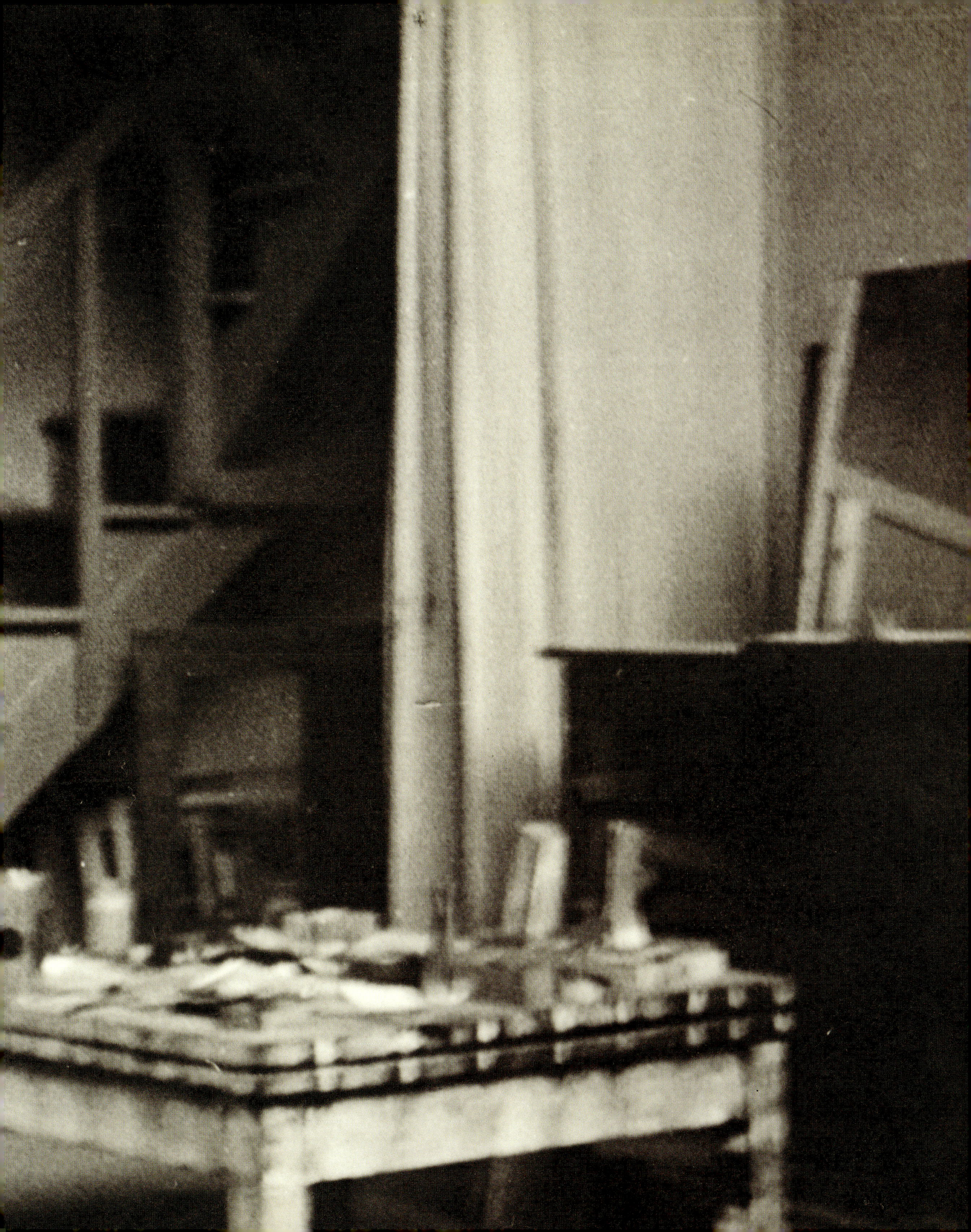

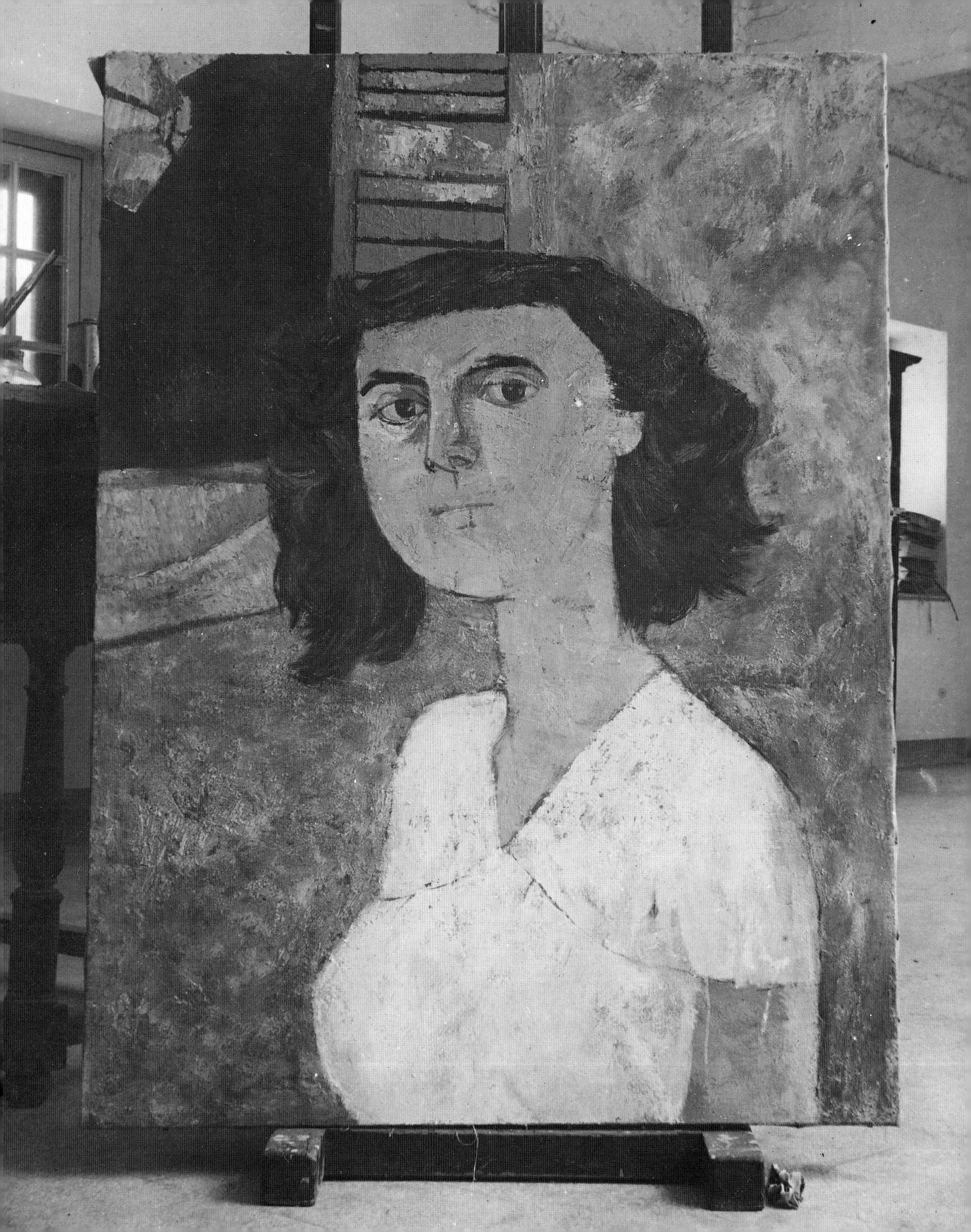

3. New Stimuli: Derrick Greaves and Italy

Painting has an almost magical quality. Sometimes it can be prophetic. It's risky and rather dangerous. It's a visual world, which can have a vivid parallel reality to your life. Like writers and poets and composers you can dissolve your ego into your own activity. There is a life in a painting, which transcends me or you. Italy changed my direction and approach.

Derrick Greaves, undated[1]

The two years that Greaves spent in Rome from 1952–4 were seminal for the development of his work. They may not have represented a complete break from the past, but were certainly a great leap forward. Greaves had travelled to Italy for the first year of his Abbey Major scholarship, clutching a folio of drawings that included studies for *The Waiting Room* as well as for other allegorical, angst-ridden pictures. These were soon replaced by works inspired by blue skies, sunshine, good food and wine and beautiful frescos – 'replaced', literally, for as Rome grew chilly, Greaves burned the drawings he had brought from London in the studio stove to keep warm. This would be the first of many therapeutic bonfires of rejected works that have punctuated key moments in the artist's career.

The journey to Rome, via Paris, with his wife was stressful for Greaves, but when he did finally arrive by train at Turin, gone midnight, he found a restaurant, relaxed immediately and felt completely at home with Italy. They then travelled down the coast, inland through Perugia and Tuscany and on to Rome. After the privations of England, the food and wine made a big impression. Appropriately one of Greaves's most powerful early works is a large charcoal drawing, *Spaghetti Eaters* (plate 30).

What especially impressed Greaves was the indivisibility of life and art. Art was not confined to museums and galleries. It was all around. Churches and civic buildings contained frescos, there were mosaics on the floor and statues in the streets. He was particularly struck by a visit to the Campo Santo in Pisa where the frescos were being restored and he was able to see, first hand, the *pentimenti*.

Previous page:
28 *Domes of Venice* (1953–4)
in the painter's studio, Rome,
1953

Facing page:
29 *La Romana* (1953)
in the painter's studio, Rome,
1953

This under-drawing, although rough, showed how even at a relatively late stage alterations were being made by the artist in response to the surface on which the fresco was being painted. He was excited by the immediacy of it all: 'When I heard that Giotto was a joker and deliberately dropped paint on apprentices below, I could imagine that, having been a sign-painter!'[2]

Reproductions had given him no sense of the works in their setting or their scale: 'At the Royal College I thought of painting as easel painting … In Italy pictures filled whole walls: horses, dogs, figures were life size. The difference between size and scale affected me profoundly.'[3] He also felt there to be a visual togetherness between people and place, a harmony brought about by the continuation of the past into the present. This was a quality Greaves recognised but did not himself feel in England, hence the fact that his scenes of people outdoors were almost exclusively painted in Italy.

Greaves's handling of paint was still thick, dusky and Courbet-like in the weight given to each form, but it was also increasingly straightforward and

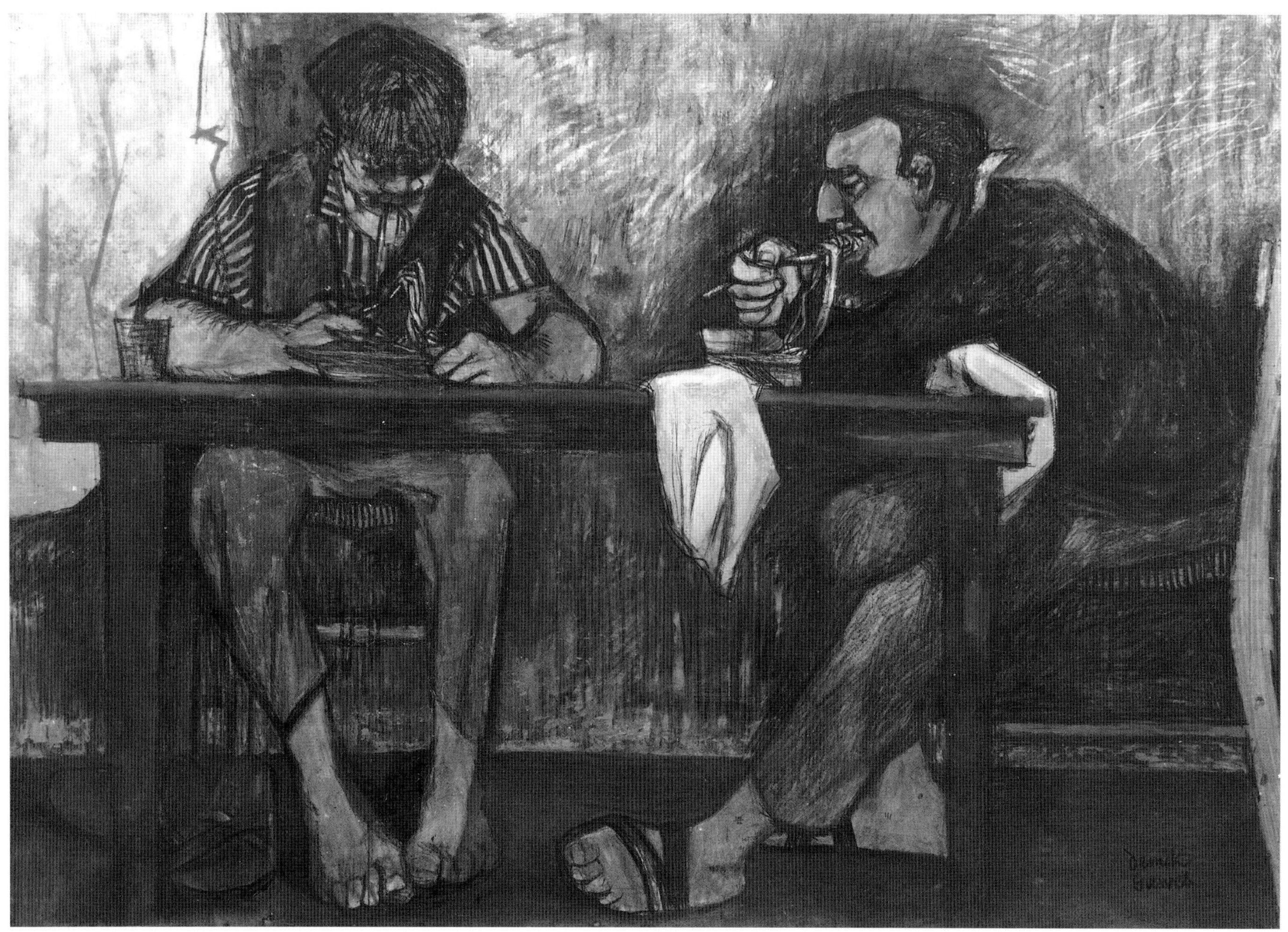

30 *Spaghetti Eaters*, 1953
Mixed media
91.5 × 142.2cm (36 × 56in)
Private Collection

unmannered. His first Italian pictures show that he was building on what he had learnt from paintings such as *The Waiting Room* (plate 11) and *Sheffield* (plate 14), but also reveal that he was seeking to compose works in which he no longer over-burdened the picture with incident, as he had in *The Temptation of St Anthony* (plate 10). His first large-scale Italian painting, *Portovenere* (plate 31), points the way with its bold simplification of form and flattening of space so that the lines of steps merge into the layers of brickwork of the distant church and the sky seems to possess the same materiality as the land. Then in *Peasant Interior, Sicily* (plate 34), a painting that can be read as a more sophisticated reprise of ideas first explored in *The Waiting Room*, Greaves depicts a humble room that is almost completely deprived of furniture and dominated by expanses of scumbled wall. There are two bare chairs, a simple table, a bowl and some plain clothing, but otherwise the room is empty. Perhaps, above all, what draws the eye is the left-hand section of the work, where a doorway is shown leading to a corridor. No people are shown and it is as though we ourselves are in the room, waiting

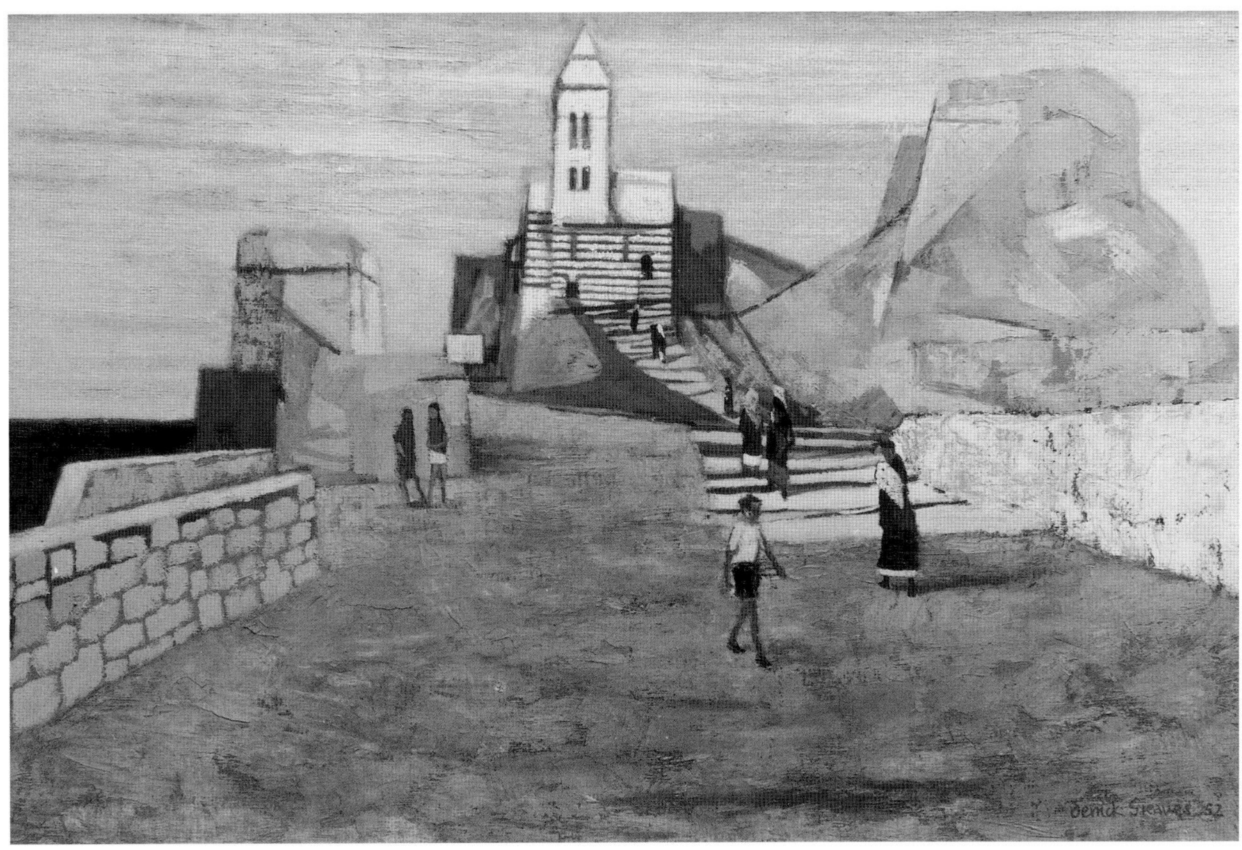

31 *Portovenere*, 1952
Oil on canvas
51 × 76cm (20 × 30in)
Private Collection

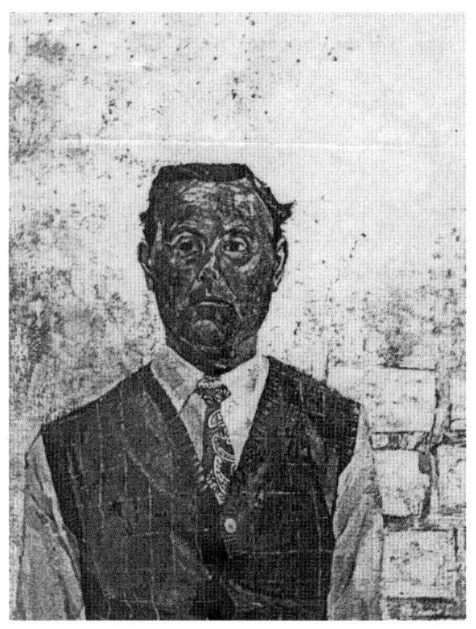

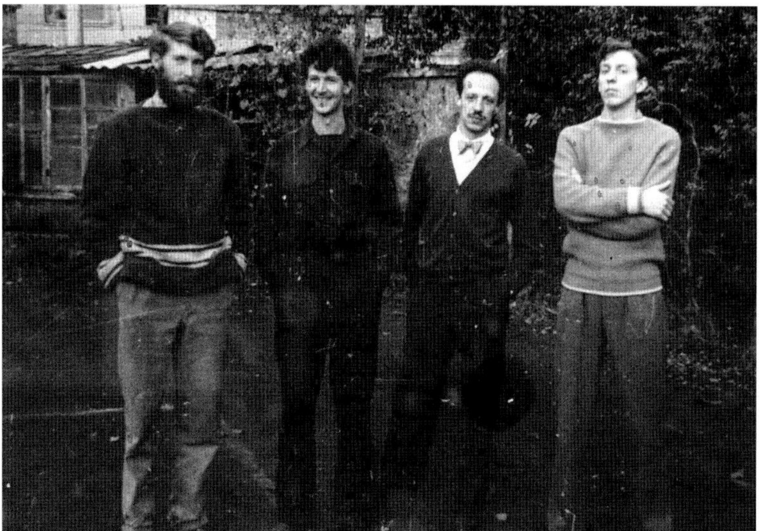

32 *Portrait of Derek Hill*, 1953
Oil on canvas
Whereabouts unknown

33 Peter Branfield,
Michael Andrews,
Heinz Inlander and
Derrick Greaves,
British School,
Rome, 1953

expectantly for someone to arrive. But the existential overtones are less heavy
than before – to live so simply might be a joy and not a burden, an aspiration,
not a sentence. The painting also illustrates that the best of Greaves's early
paintings, and indeed many of those that followed, have a stillness, a sense of
quiet calm: life is simple, objects are distinct and the presentation is direct.

Derek Hill, Head of Painting at the British School, was one mentor. When
it was time for Greaves to travel to Rome for his second year at the School, Hill
offered him a lift by car. The journey included a week's stop-off in Paris, where
Hill had a portrait commission. Paris was freezing, the hotel room was cold and it
was difficult to sleep with inadequate blankets. Greaves had left the little money
that he had with his wife in England, so he couldn't even get warm with good
meals. This was a melancholy time. Greaves wandered the streets and sought
warmth in the museums. Once more, arrival in Italy brought renewed vigour.
Through Hill, Greaves was introduced to a new social circle. Hill seemed to
know everyone and he would invite the great and the good, from Anthony Blunt
to Martha Graham, to the British School for dinner. In Rome, another new friendship was with the leading Italian social realist, Renato Guttuso, whose influence
overlaid what he had learnt at the Royal College of Art. As Berger recognised,
the result was that Greaves's work revealed a fruitful coexistence of British and
Italian qualities: 'Their subject matter, their light and colour, are all Italian, their
understatement and bound-in passions are very English ... Greaves is no longer
promising: he is, whether recognised or not, a European artist.'[4]

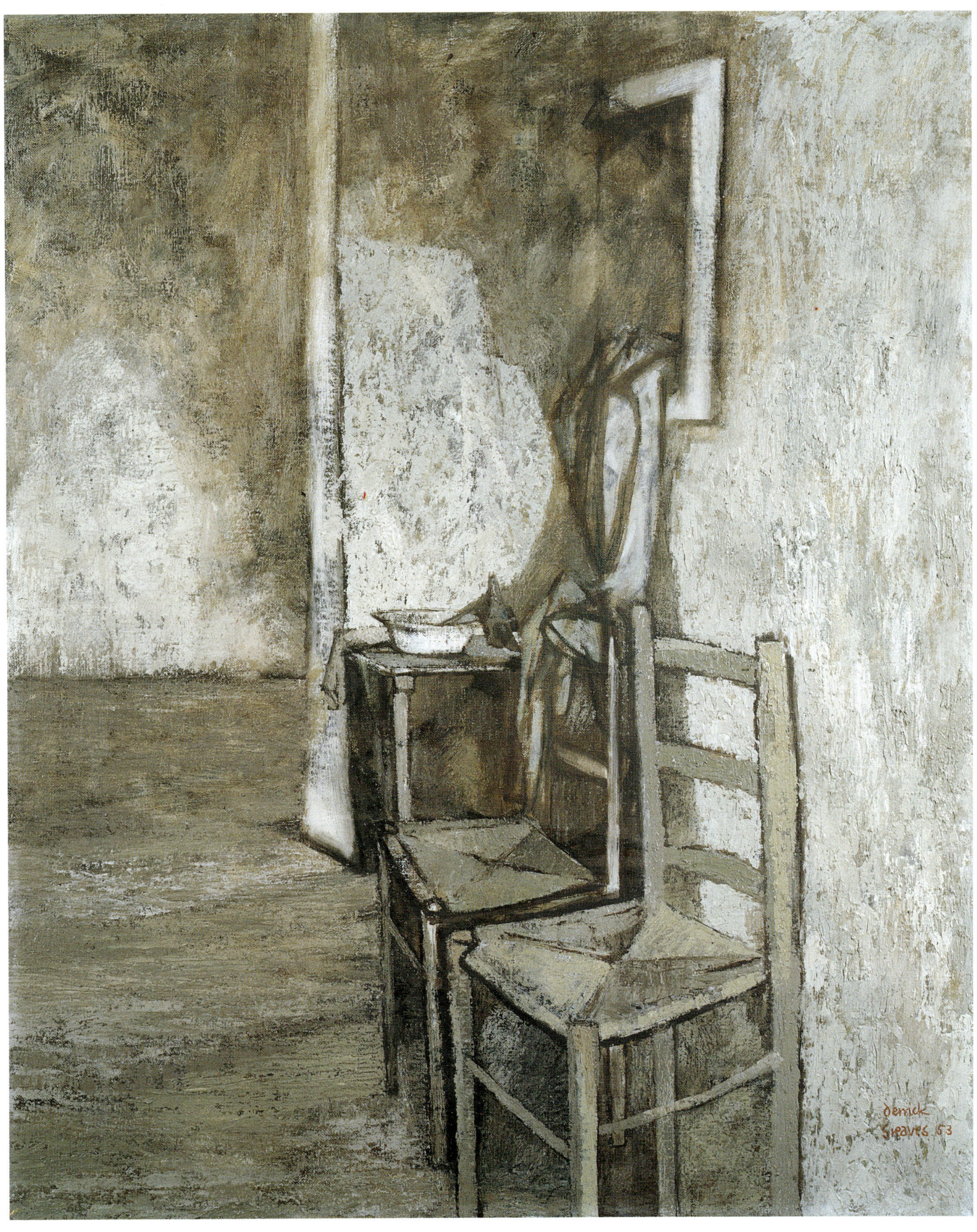

derick
Greaves 53

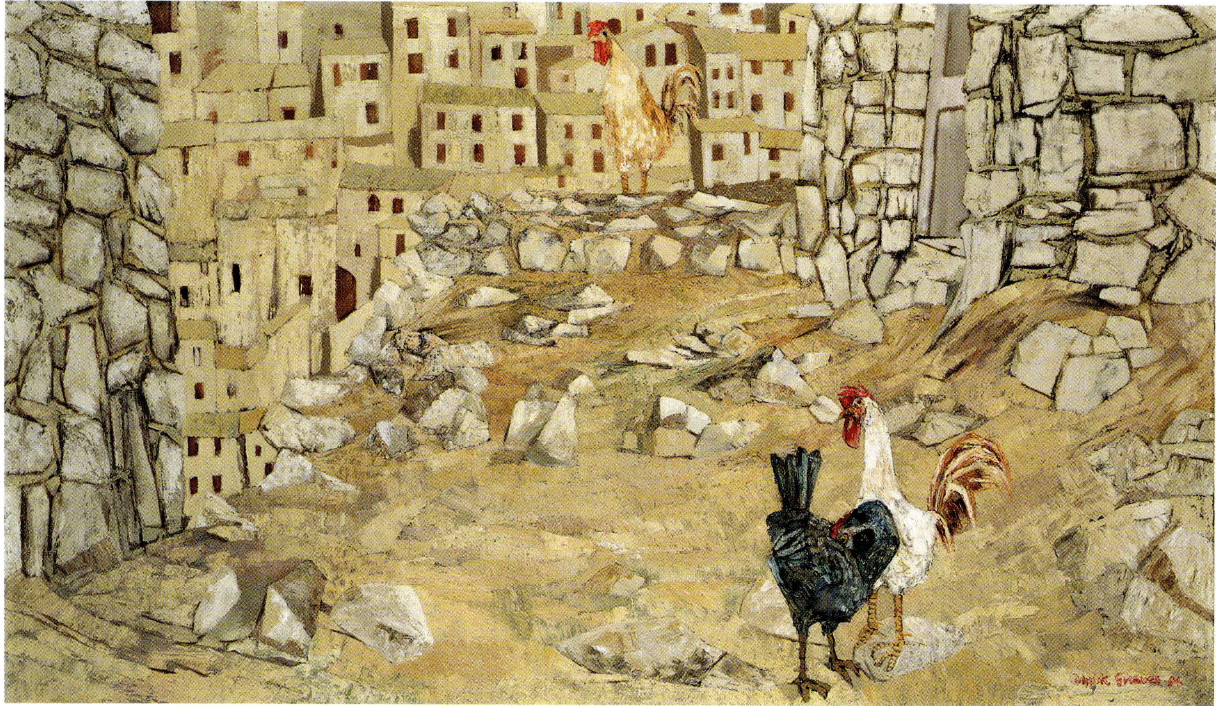

The scale of Guttuso's paintings must have reinforced Greaves's existing
interest in painting big, whilst the use of heightened colour surely encouraged
his move away from a muted palette and relatively tonal approach, but the
emotive, expressionist dimension of Guttuso's work repelled him. Nonetheless,
their friendship is encapsulated by a party Greaves held for Guttuso and his wife
on the occasion of the Italian's 1955 visit to London. The guests included George
Fullard, Edward Middleditch, Leslie Duxbury and Alfred Daniels.[5] Greaves's own
background also paralleled that of many of the Italian artists celebrated by Berger.
In an essay entitled 'Italian Artists of "La Colonna"', and elsewhere, Berger made
much of the artist having a practical function: as mentioned, Greaves had spent
some time as an apprentice sign writer before entering the Royal College of Art.
The artists of 'La Colonna' were also regular writers on art, and this is echoed by
the contributions made by Greaves as a broadcaster and writer.[6]

The impact of Guttuso's work on Greaves was transmitted principally
via the Englishman's visits to Italy rather than the example of what he saw
in exhibitions in England. It is perhaps clearest in the Mediterranean motifs
presented by Greaves, such as images of leisure and work. The dry surfaces of
paintings such as *Road in Anticoli Corrado, Italy* (plate 35), *Children on Steps* (plate 36)

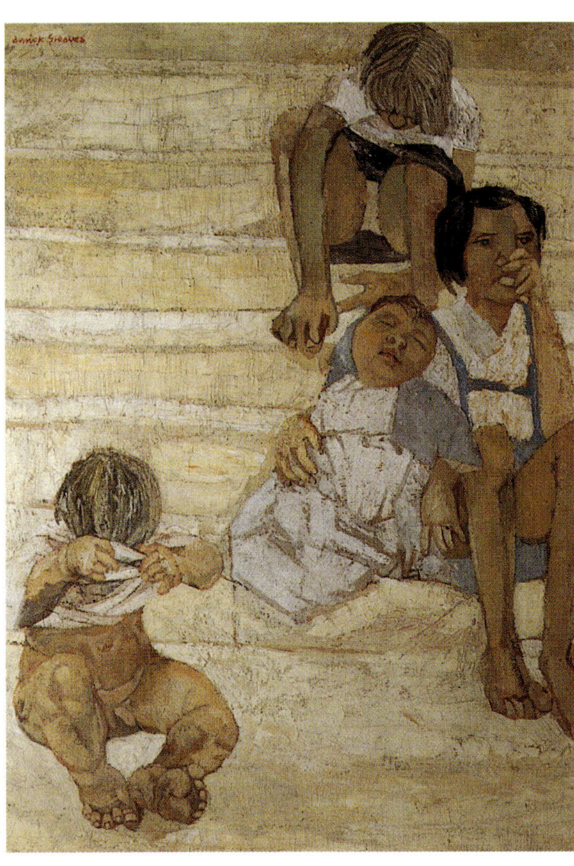

36 *Children on Steps*, 1956
Oil on canvas
121.9 × 91.4cm (48 × 36in)
Leeds City Art Gallery, Leeds

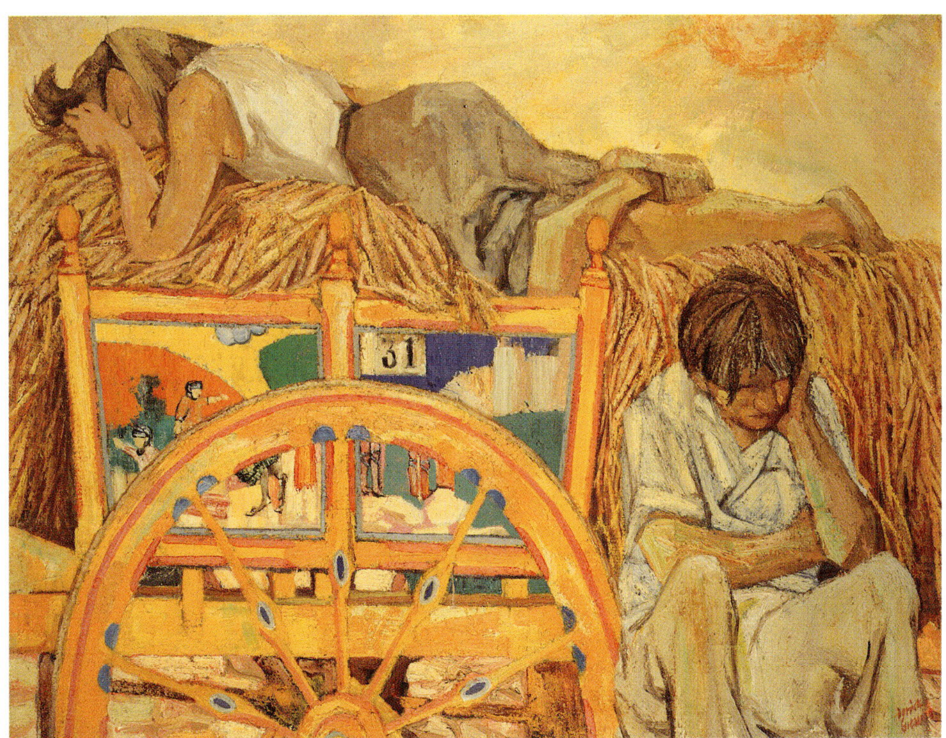

37 *Sicilian Peasants Resting*, 1956
Oil on canvas
91.4 × 121.9cm (36 × 48in)
Private Collection

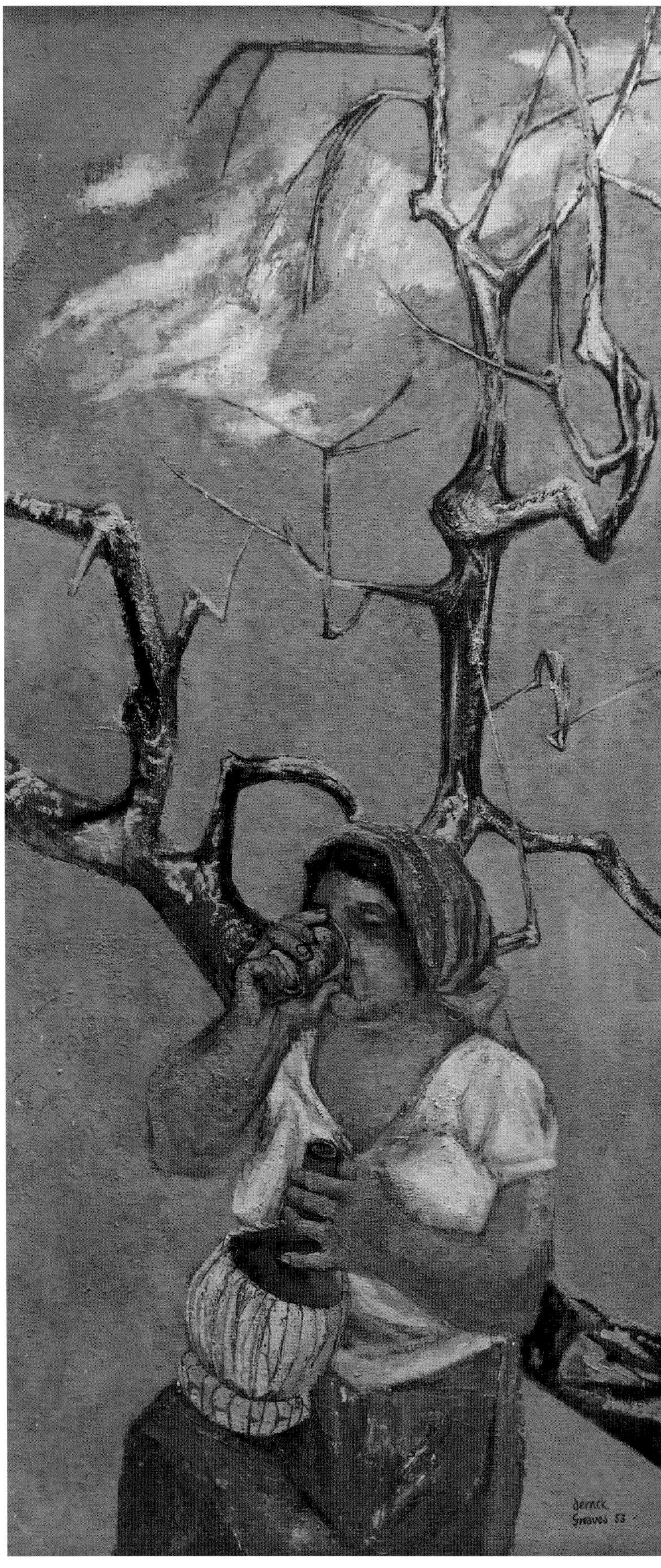

38 *Woman Under an Olive Tree*, *c.*1953
Oil on canvas
152.4 × 68.5cm (60 × 27in)
Private Collection

and *Sicilian Peasants Resting* (plate 37) echo an omnipresent feature of British painting of the 1940s. However, in contrast to the nacreous surfaces of Ben Nicholson or the luminosity achieved by John Piper, Greaves's surfaces often resemble the tempera of a medieval Italian mural painting. In colour, texture and subject matter, Greaves's *Sicilian Peasants Resting* also reflects his admiration for paintings on the sides of the Italian carts used by the agricultural workers. Greaves saw such carts when he visited Guttuso's birthplace, Bagharia in Sicily, and recognised their influence on Guttuso in both their colour and presentation of narrative.[7]

Italy led to a change in light and in colour. In *Woman Under an Olive Tree* (plate 38), there is a robustness to the woman, whose powerful body is matched by the roundness of the wine bottle she clasps and contrasts with the spiky angularity of the olive tree: a humble equivalent of one of Graham Sutherland's greatest portraits, *Portrait of Somerset Maugham* (1949), which was similarly inspired by the Mediterranean sun. This formal contrast between the tree and the woman would subsequently contribute to the power of one of Greaves's most significant diptychs, *In The Garden* (plate 77). Dogs were another recurrent theme, from the 1950s onwards, and their scruffy presence is evident in some of Greaves's most powerful Italian pictures, such as the Arts Council owned *Dog* (plate 43) and *Men and Dogs in a Landscape* (plate 44).

The artist also learnt much from the British visitors and students in Rome, among them Peter Lanyon, Tom Monnington and Michael Andrews. Admiring Lanyon's toughness, directness and courage, Greaves nevertheless argued with him over his response to landscape. On a walk in the Abruzzi mountains, Lanyon discerned heads in dry river beds, whilst Greaves simply saw rocks and tree roots. The prose of Greaves's matter-of-fact approach clashed with the poetry of Lanyon's more metaphoric response. Monnington, meanwhile, admired a new painting by Greaves in his studio at the British School, praising its use of the golden section (where a rectangle is divided into two unequal but proportionate parts). It was an unconscious sense of proportions on Greaves's part, so Monnington drew diagrams to explain what he meant. This lesson led Greaves to re-evaluate this aspect of picture-making, and to this day has had a profound impact on the structuring of his compositions. Greaves went with Monnington to see the Signorellis at Orvieto Cathedral and Piero della Francesco's *Flagellation* in Urbino. Meanwhile, he found Michael Andrews to be a charming companion, but realised that for Andrews London held greater delights than Rome.

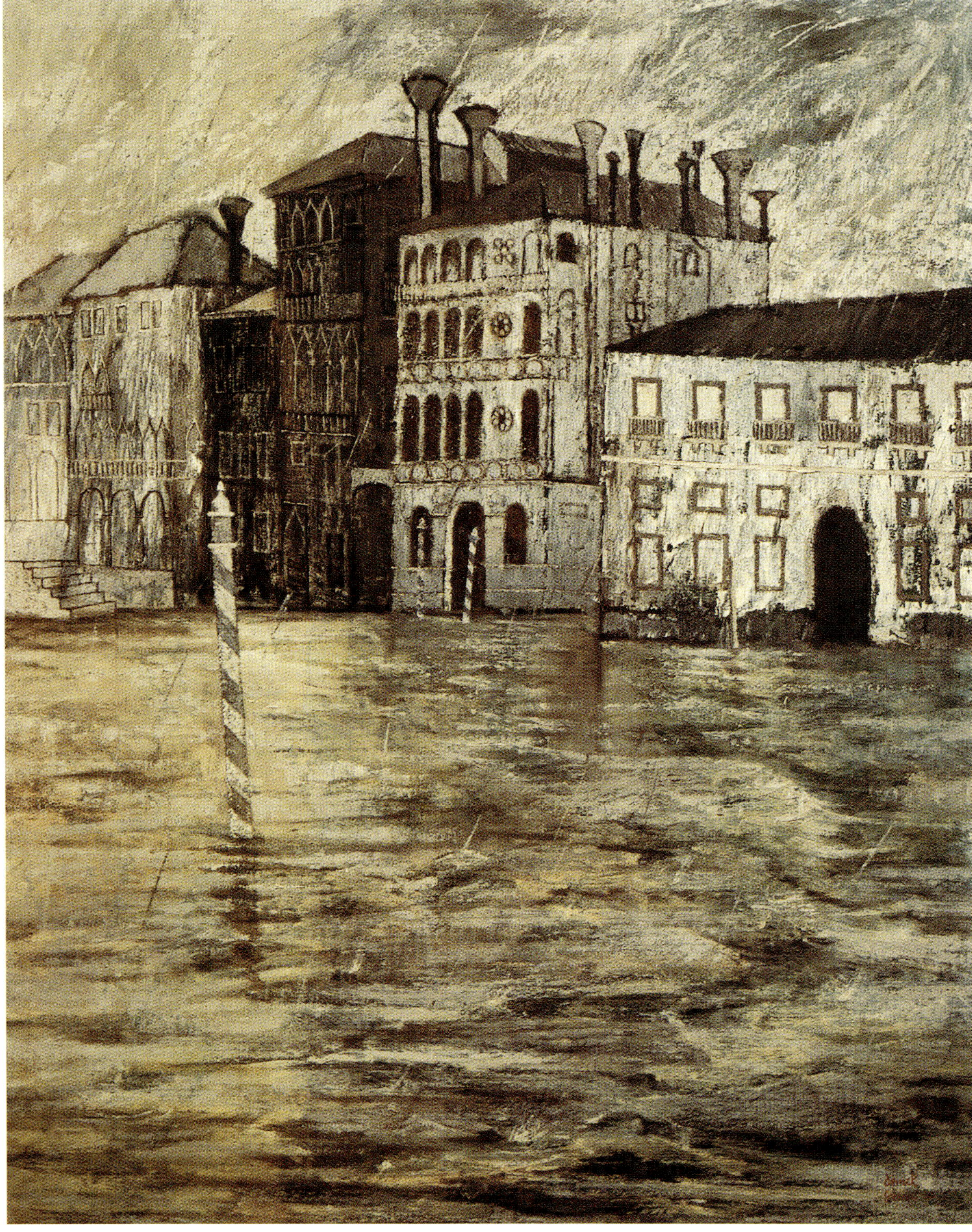

39 *Venice in the Rain*, 1953
Oil on canvas
126.7 × 101.4cm (49.5 x 39.6in)
Graves Art Gallery, Sheffield

Although he was based at the British School in Rome, during January and February 1953 Greaves visited Venice, a stay that was to led to some of his most significant early paintings. Greaves was struck by the melancholy silvery light of winter as it bounced off the water of the largely deserted canals. *Venice in the Rain* (plate 39) evokes a precarious gondola ride along a choppy canal, whilst in *Venice* (plate 40), the two halves of the panoramic format are perfectly in balance, with the composition being tightened up by the frieze-like background of the façades of the palaces alongside the canal. Above all, it is the stones of Venice that dominate, and the four people standing on a gondola are merely a small, harmonious detail.

Greaves also drew the Piazza San Marco from the Campanile. This provided the source for a large painting that he began in Rome and completed in London. While still unfinished in his studio in Rome, *Domes of Venice* (plate 41) attracted a pertinent criticism from the painter Pavel Tchelitchev – 'you work too much from nature' – an assertion with which Greaves himself would soon concur.

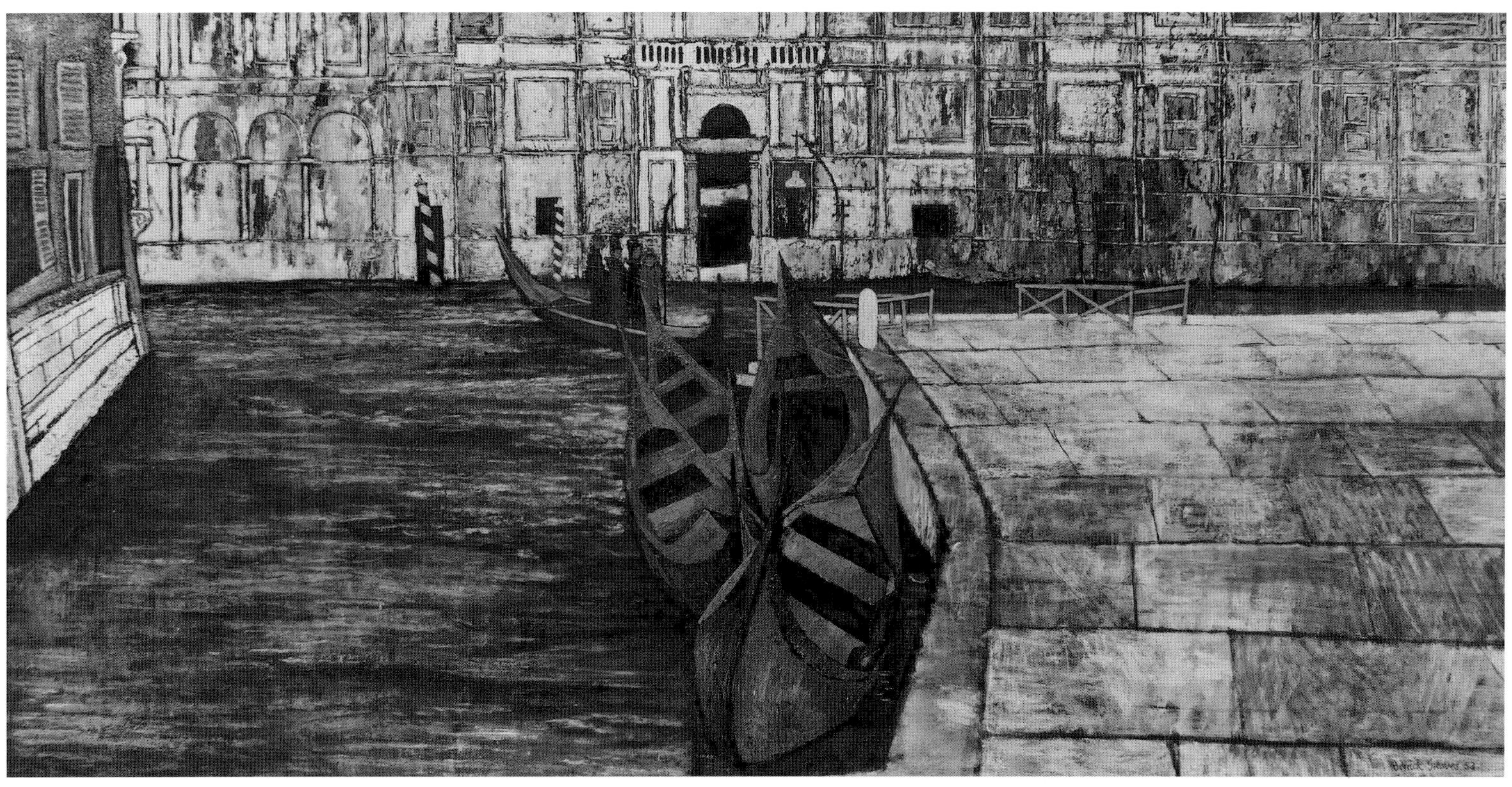

40 *Venice*, 1953
Oil on canvas
91.5cm × 213.4cm (36 × 84in)
Private Collection

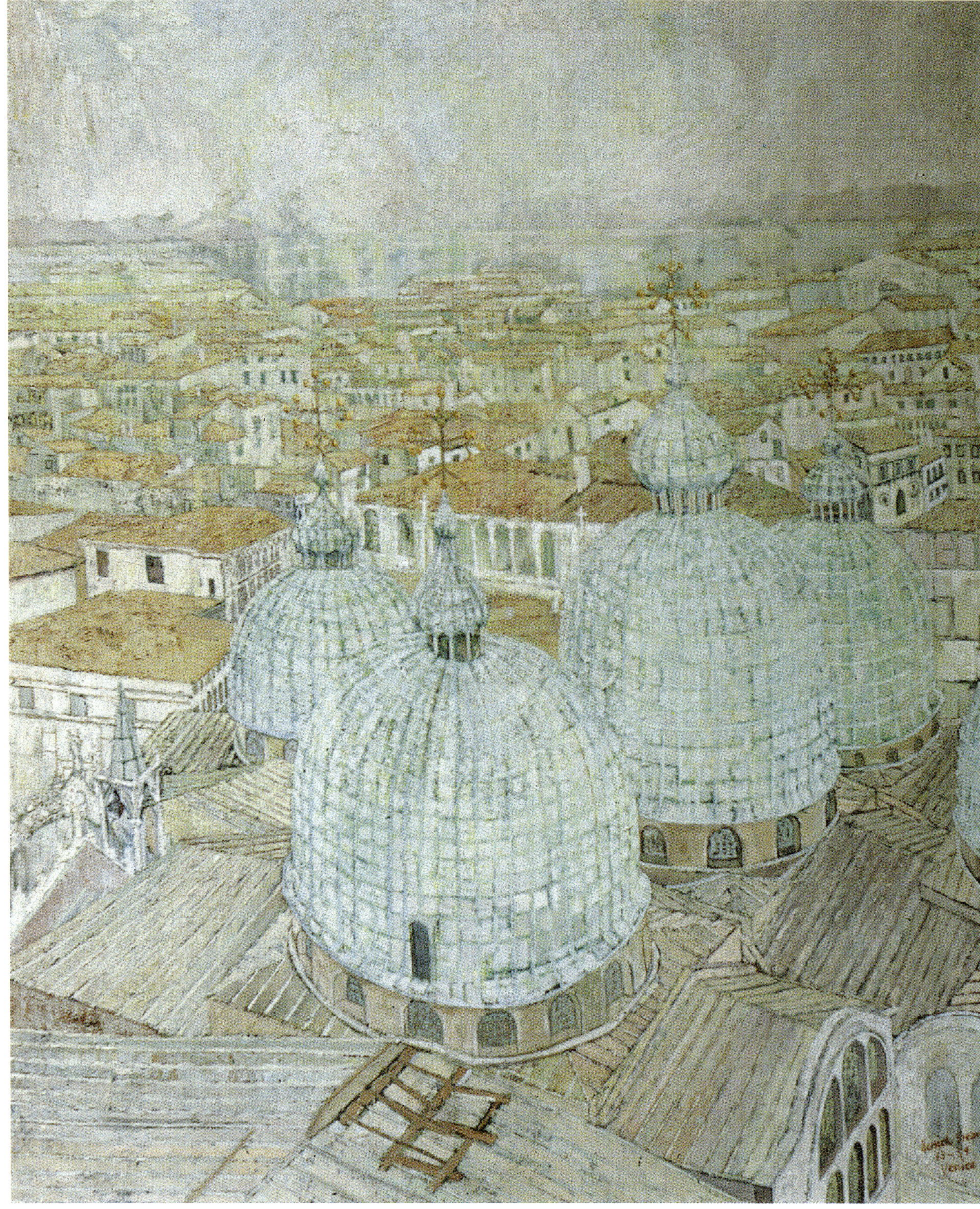

41 *Domes of Venice*, 1953–4
Oil on canvas
184.1 × 154.9cm (72.5 × 61in)
Tate Collection

Appropriately, it was the strength of Greaves's paintings of Italy that contributed to the decision to include him in the British Pavilion at the Venice Biennale of 1956, where he showed four of his Italian paintings. This was the only occasion when the four 'Kitchen-Sink' painters exhibited together outside Britain and was their crowning moment, although it was one that Greaves once again missed, since by then he had returned to England and the British Council did not have the funds to send the artists to Venice.

Greaves recalls that Lilian Somerville, Director of the Fine Arts Department of the British Council, paid a visit to the studio that he shared with George Fullard with a distinguished group that included the eminent art critic, Herbert Read. So dusty was the studio from all the sculptor's bags of plaster that Fullard would swill it down each evening and when Herbert Read took off his hat, Greaves did not feel that it was out of deference. When asked about one of Greaves's paintings, Read declared it to be a good exhibition picture, damning it with faint praise. It would be the two men's only encounter.

As with the precedent of the recent Heffer Gallery show of the four Kitchen-Sink painters, the idea of a coherent group was undermined by the selection and installation of the pictures as well as by the catalogue. The artists were simply referred to as 'Four Young Painters' and the selection of pictures by Herbert Read highlighted each artist's differences through the choice of subject matter by which each artist was represented. It demonstrated that the Quartet was moving away from the prosaic English subjects and settings that had first gained them acclaim, in Greaves's case towards the sun, light and colour of the Mediterranean. Greaves was represented by four sunny outdoor scenes made in Italy. In *A Sicilian Subject* (plate 45), an epic scale, extended horizontal format and emphasis on the front plane results in a clear and colourful image that recalls a wall painting. Making apparent its allegiances to Italian social realism, it presented a Mediterranean motif, employed a range of sunny yellows and included a cart, typical of the farmers of Guttuso's Sicilian homeland.

The installation of these paintings allowed each artist his own wall space, whilst collectively their work provided a visual counterpart to Ivon Hitchens, the more senior painter with whom they shared the British Pavilion. Particularly dramatic was the contrast between the hot reds and yellows of Greaves's Italian paintings and the fresh blues and greens of Hitchens's English landscapes in the gallery beyond. The accompanying catalogue text by J.P. Hodin followed Lessore's precedent by declaring that 'although they exhibit in one and the same London

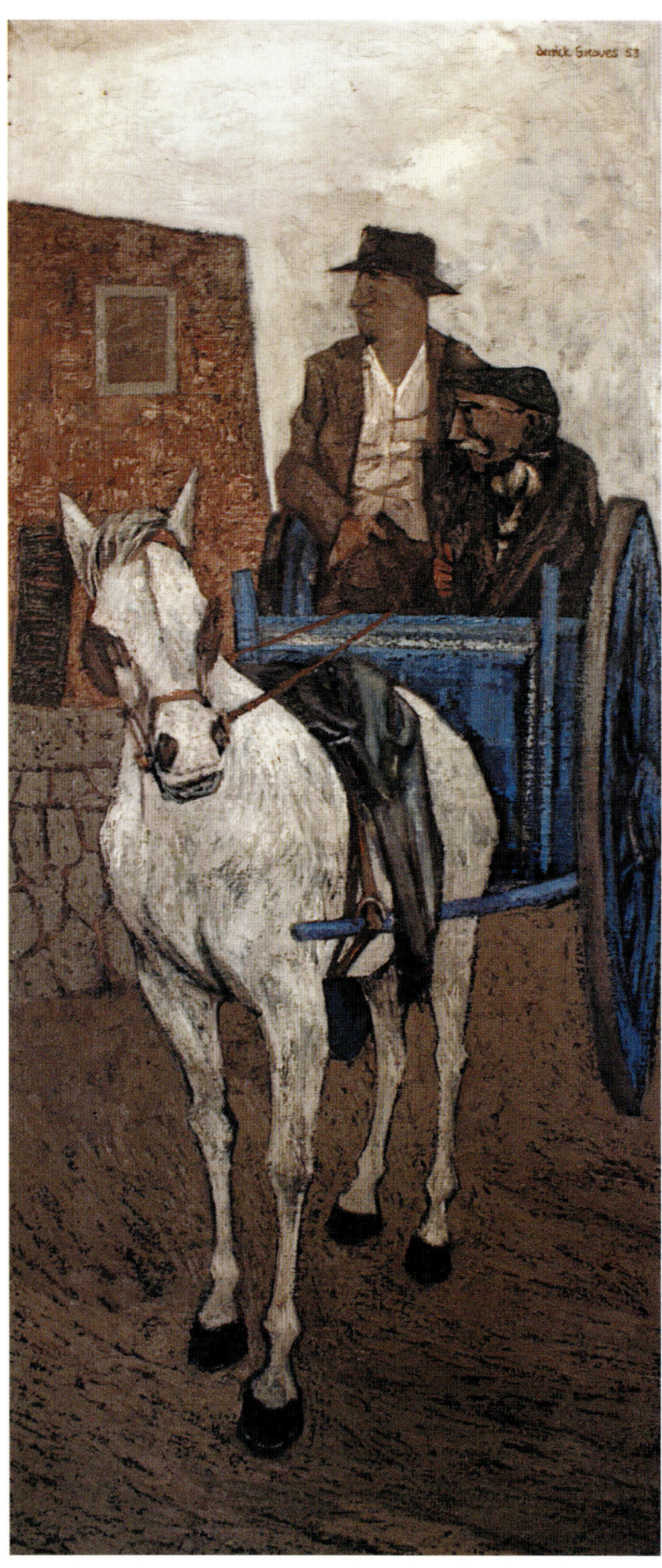

42 *The Cart, c.*1953
Oil on canvas
161 × 77cm (63.4 × 30.3in)
Formerly 'The Collection of Original Works for Children',
Cambridgeshire County Council

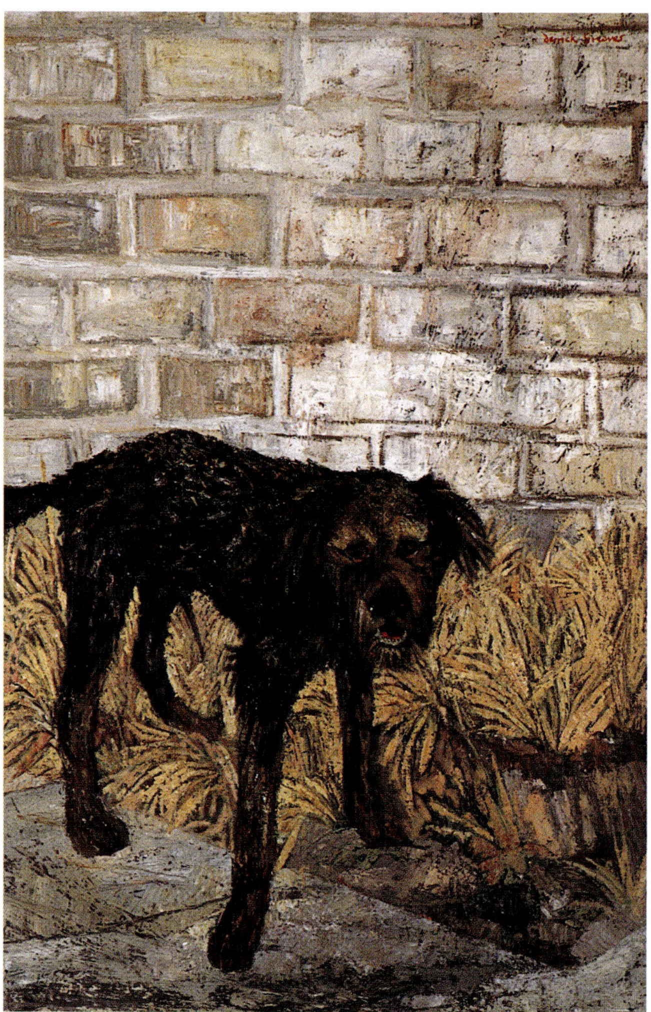

43 *Dog,* 1955
Oil on canvas
118 × 78.7cm (46.5 × 31in)
Arts Council England

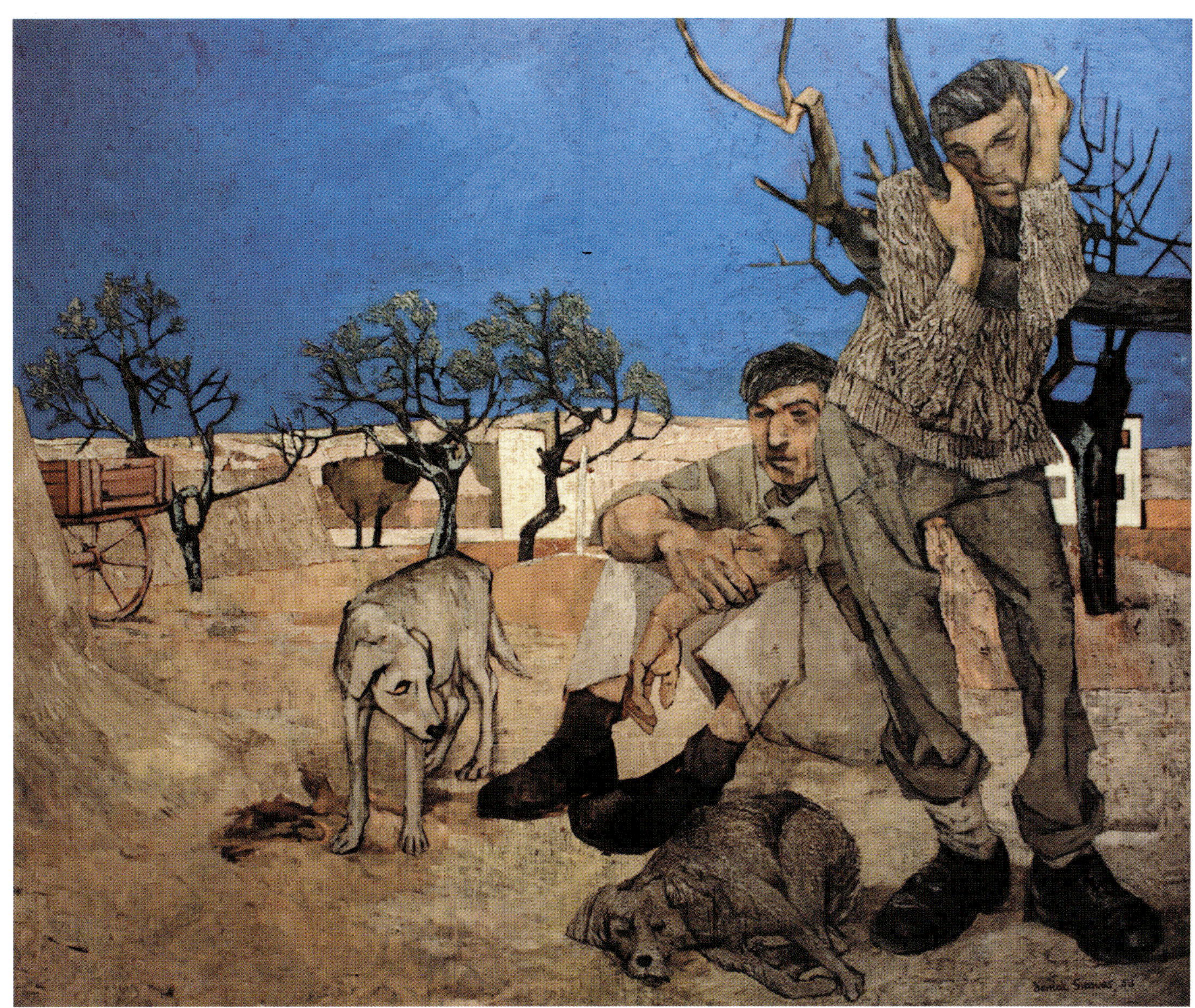

44 *Men and Dogs in a
Landscape*, 1953
Oil on canvas
147.3 × 157.5cm (58 × 62in)
Formerly 'The Collection of Original Works for
Children', Cambridgeshire County Council

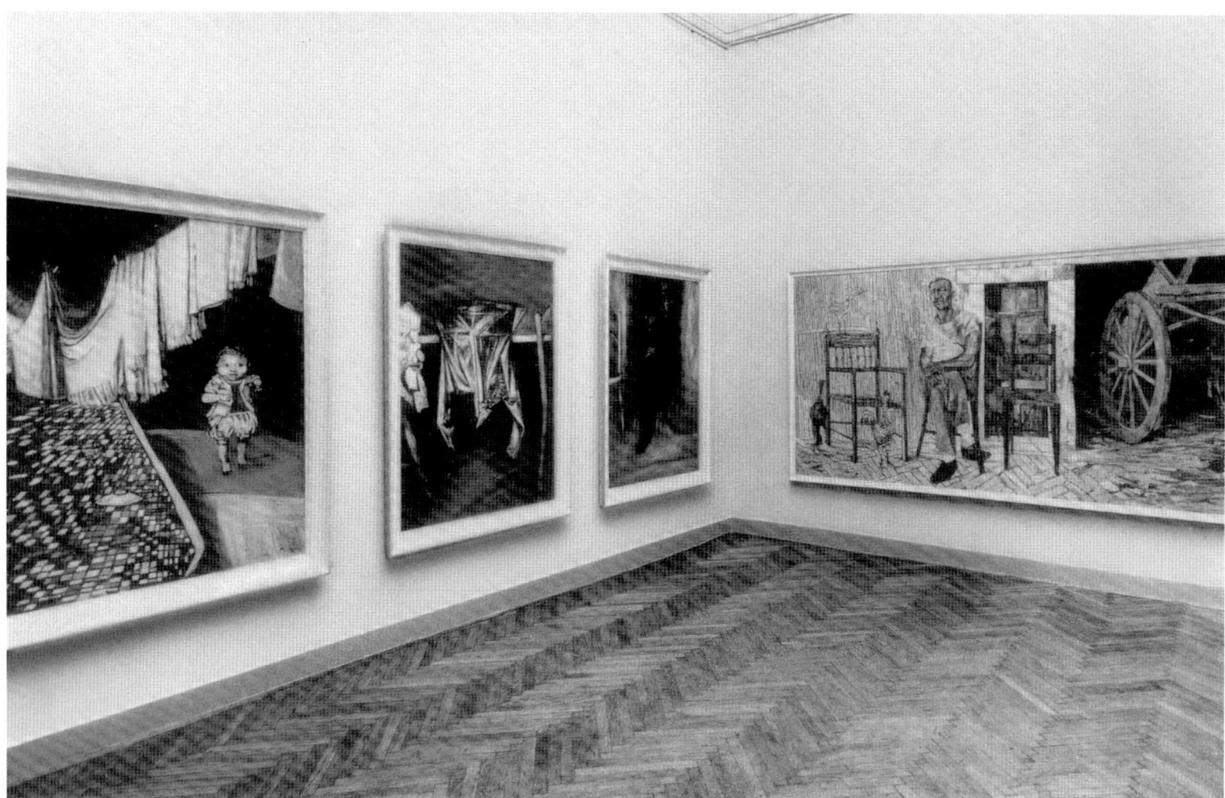

45 Installation views of the British Pavilion, XXVIII Venice Biennale, 1956, including Greaves's *A Sicilian Subject* (1954–5)

gallery, they have neither produced a manifesto nor formed a group'. It then proceeded to discuss the work of each artist separately, reject simple classification and question the presumed realism: 'the frontiers between the objective and the subjective are fluid and it is convenient rather than strictly accurate to call these artists realists'.[8]

Meanwhile, in a review of the Biennale, Alan Bowness addressed the inclusion of these four British painters, seeking to extract them from the term social realist:

The term 'social realist' has been wisely dropped – it might be used for Greaves, but can only damage the others, whose interests, I should have thought, are far removed from the political. One must remember that these painters belong to the same generation as the novelists and poets of the Wain-Amis-Gunn-Larkin group, and they share many of the same preoccupations. Jack Smith seems to possess the writer's brand of humanism to the full; Bratby has done some real Lucky Jim paintings; and Middleditch is the poet among the painters.[9]

Appropriately, too, it was an Italian picture, *Domes of Venice* (plate 41), which would be the first major museum purchase of a painting by Greaves, being acquired in 1955 by the Chantry Bequest for the Tate Gallery.

This, then, was the highpoint for social realism in general and the Kitchen-Sink painters in particular. When the prizes were announced for the John Moore's Liverpool Exhibition in 1957, it was little surprise that the winners were almost entirely figurative painters, that they were predominantly exhibitors of the Beaux Arts Gallery, and that they included Bratby, Smith and Greaves.

Notes

1. Derrick Greaves, undated journal entry.
2. Derrick Greaves, conversation with James Hyman, June 2006.
3. Derrick Greaves, interview with James Hyman, March 2004.
4. John Berger, 'Greaves and [Paul] Hogarth', *New Statesman*, 10 December 1955, vol.50, no.1292, p.792.
5. Information from Derrick Greaves, letters to James Hyman, 8 February 1994 and 4 March 1994. Greaves's qualified enthusiasm for Guttuso contrasts with the response of Jack Smith who 'disliked Guttuso's work very much – too much rhetoric' (Jack Smith, letter to James Hyman, 9 February 1994).
6. Greaves, along with Michael Ayrton, Claude Rogers and Merlyn Evans, was a contributor to the BBC television series *The Artist in Society* (1959), taking part in the first programme. Greaves also recalls taking part in radio programmes recorded for the BBC at Bush House, including a discussion with Reg Butler and Colin MacInnes in the mid 1950s, and an appearance on television with Edward Middleditch and Joan Rodker in which the artists discussed specific examples of their own work and considered society's attitude to painting.
7. Derrick Greaves, interview with James Hyman, 4 March 1994.
8. J.P. Hodin, 'Introduction', in *Four Young Painters*, British Council/Venice Biennale, 1956.
9. Alan Bowness, 'The Venice Biennale', *Observer*, 24 June 1956. Artist's Archive.

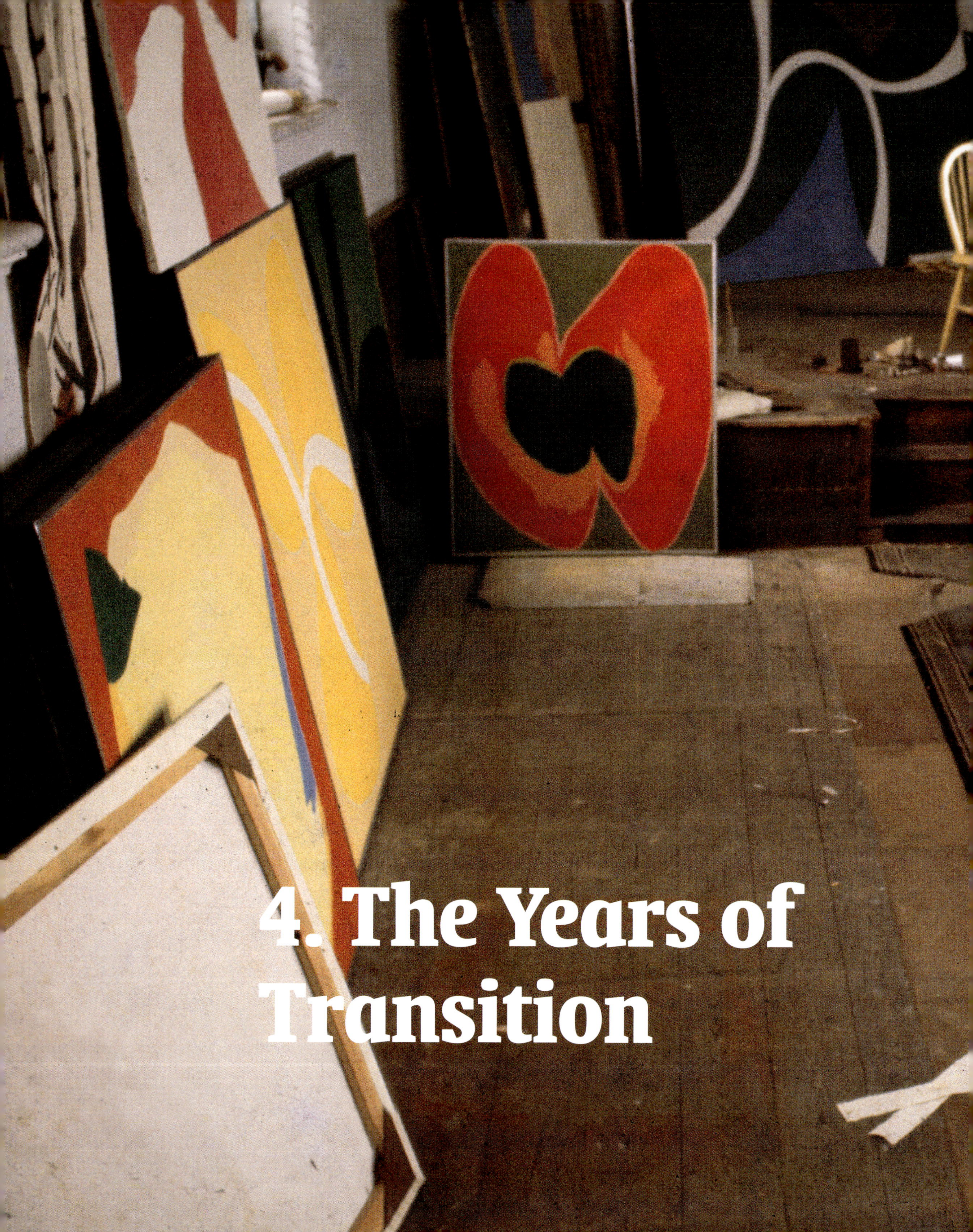

4. The Years of Transition

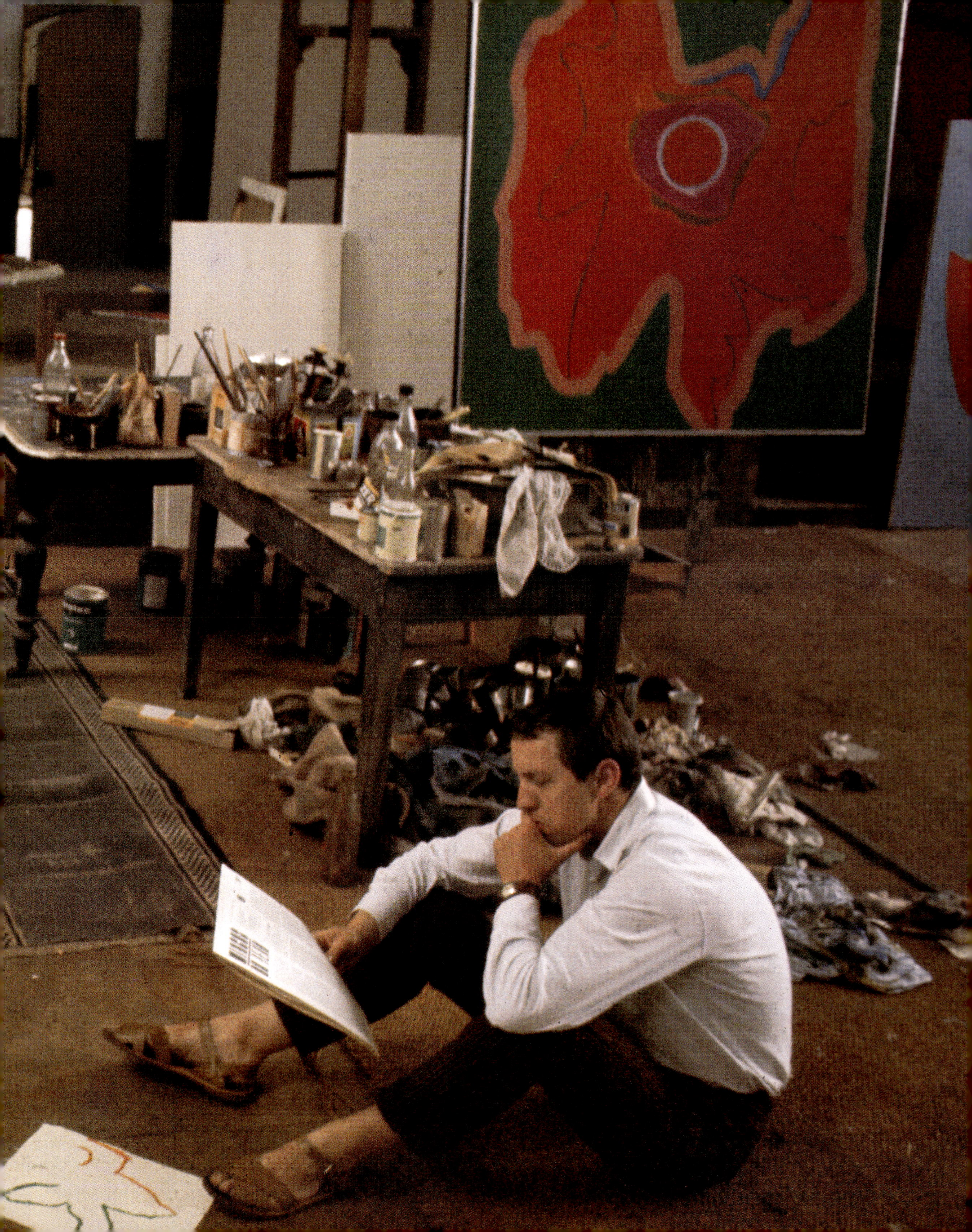

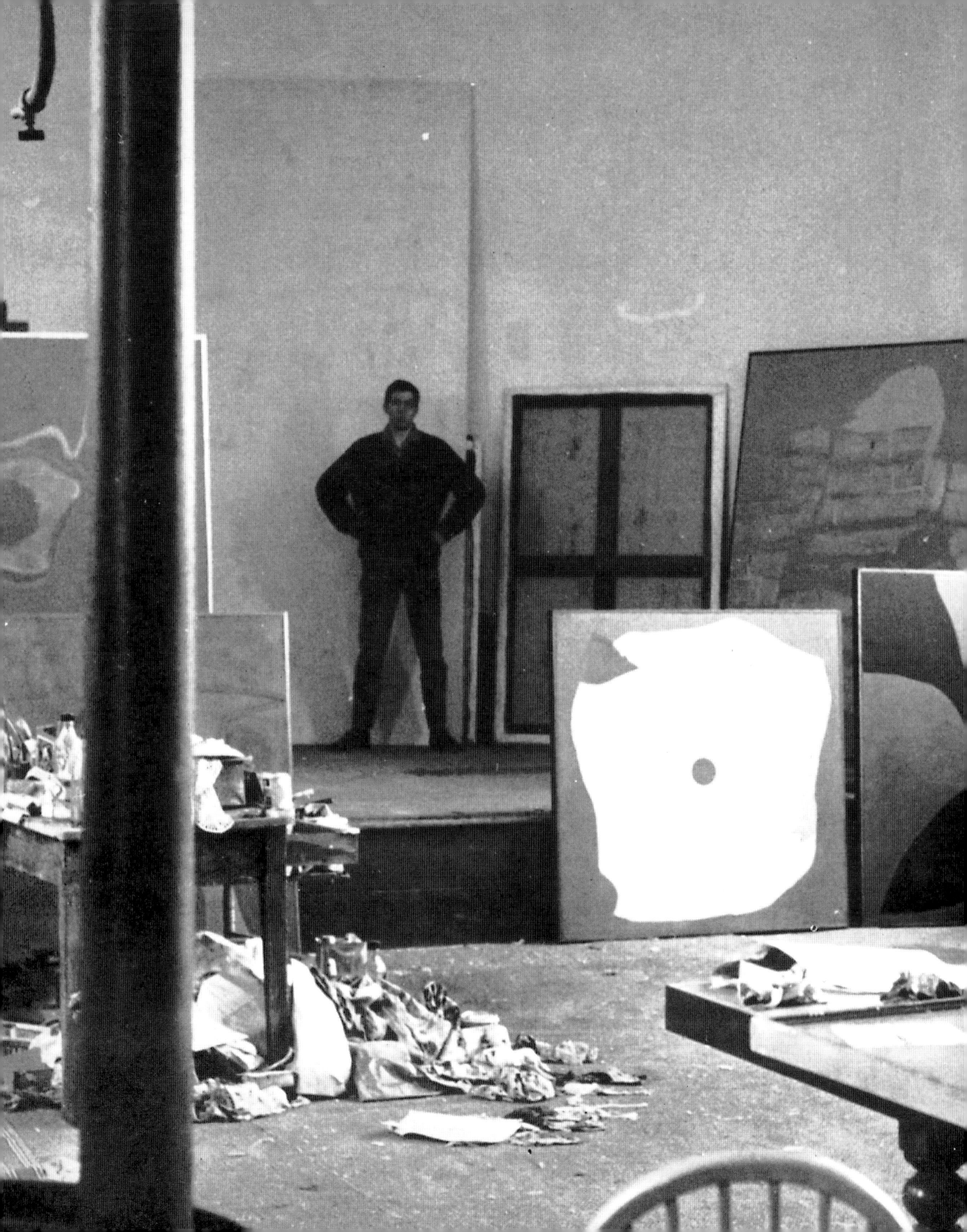

4. The Years of Transition: The Late 1950s and Early 1960s

Greaves has now learned how to involve the spectator in his own reactions and discoveries in more subtle and persuasive ways, to extend his range of expression, to draw out from his material rather than, as often formerly, to impose on it, an emotive force … the assurance with which he now moves from one experience to another is that of a painter who has really found himself, and his vigorous maturity gives the whole collection of work a spirit of elation.

Ray Watkinson, 1958[1]

1956 proved to be a year of triumph and of failure, recognition and disaffection, consolidation and transition. Even as they were acclaimed internationally, at home the weak links that united the Kitchen-Sink painters were being torn apart as youth gave way to maturity. Soon, with the exception of Edward Middleditch, who had always been the closest to Lessore, these artists would disperse from the Beaux Arts Gallery and their work would depart in different directions. The moment is encapsulated by John Bratby's 1956 article, 'A Painter's Credo', the content and tone of which succeeded in challenging Berger, offending Lessore and alienating Greaves, Middleditch and Smith.[2] When, later that year, Bratby asked Greaves for permission to reproduce his work for a subsequent article, Greaves declined, explaining in a letter to Bratby that he and Middleditch were unhappy with his previous writing, which he described as 'ludicrous examples of insensitive egocentricity'.[3]

After just two solo exhibitions at the Beaux Arts Gallery, Greaves moved to Zwemmer Gallery. His first solo show there in 1958 demonstrated how much his work was evolving. The show featured 18 paintings (including Russian subjects), half a dozen drawings and a series of 12 monotypes inspired by drawings done while in Armenia. Characterising the new work in *Art News and Review*, the Left-wing critic Ray Watkinson was full of praise for: 'an exhibition moving in its content, admirable in its accomplishment and exciting most of all for its revelation of a new fluency and ease in a painter whose taut and disciplined draughtsmanship has before often left the riches of paint unexploited …'[4]

Previous page:
46 Derrick Greaves in his Woburn studio *c*.1963

Facing page:
47 Derrick Greaves in his Woburn Studio, *c*.1963

A large collaborative mural that Greaves painted with Edward Middleditch also took him in a new direction. From 1957–9, the families of Greaves and Middleditch lived together in the 'decaying splendour' of a 'dilapidated mansion' at Great Linford in Buckinghamshire.[5] When Middleditch was asked to do a mural for Nuffield College, Oxford he invited Greaves to work with him. The result was a mural entitled *The Four Seasons* (plates 48 and 49) that echoed the massive 'mural' at Cecil Sharp House in London (1950–4) by Ivon Hitchens, with whom they had both recently shared the British Pavilion in Venice.[6] The approach taken by the two young painters was 'free-form' and the only planning was the decision to incorporate certain motifs to represent the four seasons.

The work had Edward Middleditch's stamp on it more than that of Greaves. Middleditch painted cow parsley, meadow grasses and blossom, an equivalent to the pastoralism of Ralph Vaughan Williams's music, whilst Greaves tried to capture the heat of summer, a sleeping figure and a large wagon wheel, pressing old drawings into service.

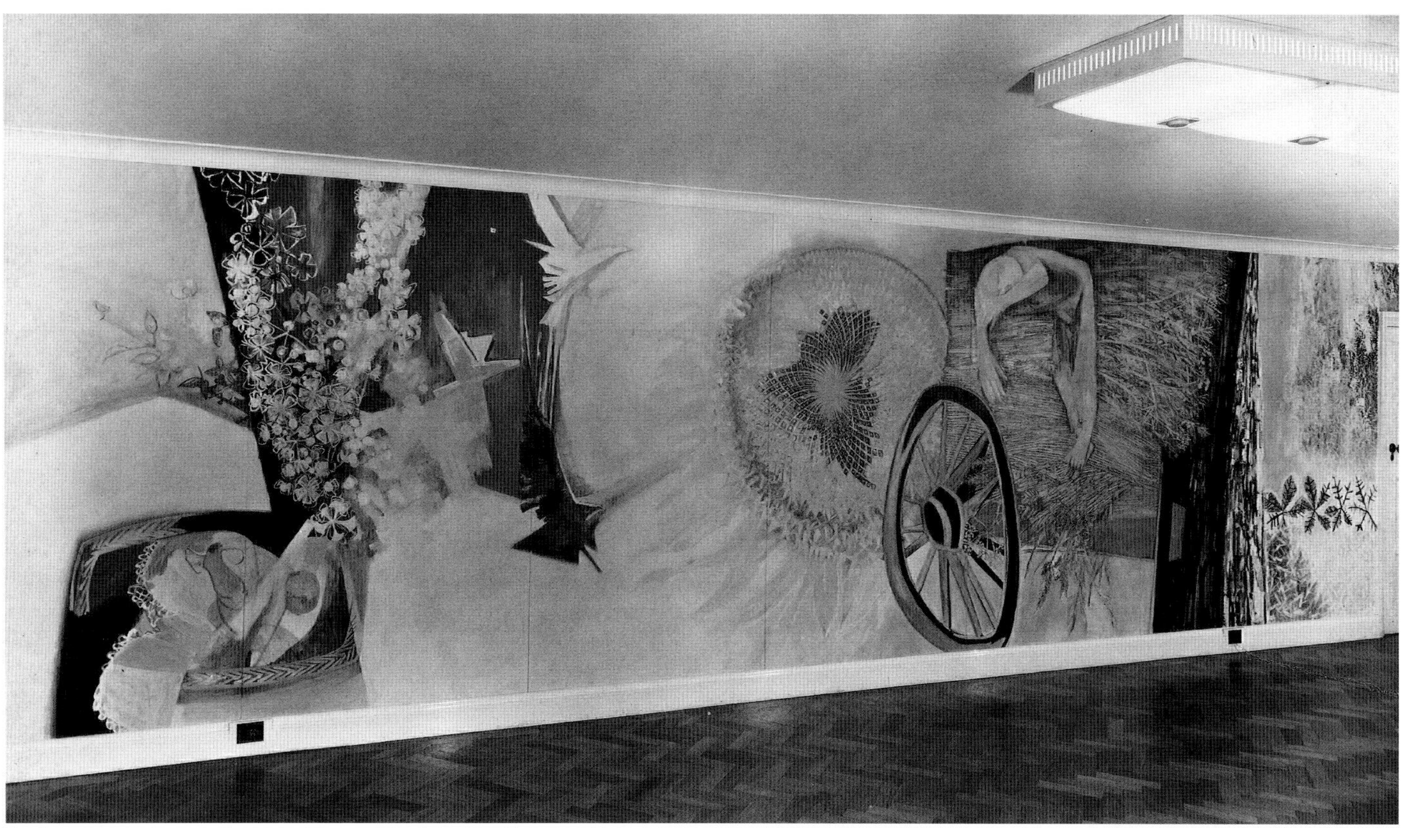

48 Derrick Greaves and
Edward Middleditch,
The Four Seasons mural, 1957,
Nuffield College, Oxford

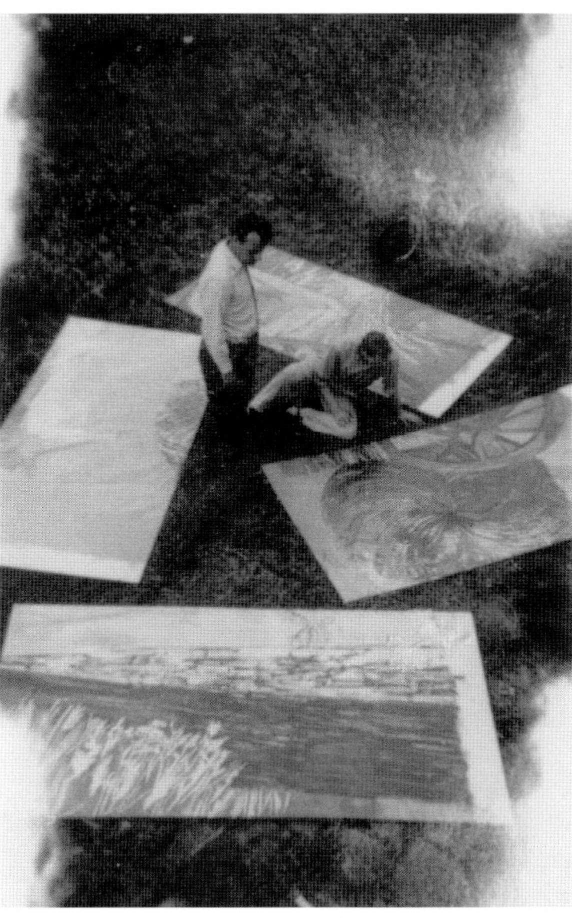

49 Derrick Greaves and Edward Middleditch with the unfinished panels for *The Four Seasons* mural, 1957

The mural was planned as an oil sketch on an 8ft (2.4m) strip of hardboard, rather than through drawings, and was painted on 8 × 4ft (2.4 × 1.2m) boards, totalling almost 60ft (18.3m) in length, in Middleditch's studio. The panels were taken to a halfway stage before being fitted in the library where they were completed 'extempore, like an easel painting on a wall'. This required more effort than intended. When installed the panels did not work in the room, so the two men locked the door and worked on them *in situ*, with paints on a dinner trolley. They went in day after day during the summer vacation, and the work changed out of all recognition. Their only rule was that if they did not like what their friend had done they could paint it out. This 'improvisation' constituted, for Greaves, a sort of 'wall-jazz', and resulted in a work that was quite different from the oil sketch that Nuffield College had initially approved.

Although its subject was apolitical, the fact that this mural was a public and joint endeavour was a source of praise, especially from Berger, who related the success of the project to it having a definite objective and argued that the work of both artists had benefited from such collaboration.[7] However, even the writing of their great champion was now becoming equivocal in tone, and in a backhanded compliment he argued that the mural was 'better than any easel painting which either of them has recently produced. The job presented them with definite objective problems which they clearly had to solve; whereas left to themselves both Greaves and Middleditch, like many other artists, have sometimes tended to forget about solutions and only choose problems.'[8]

In the same summer that Greaves was shown in the British Pavilion at the Venice Biennale, Berger had praised 'Greaves and Middleditch [for] refusing to look back on their success, beginning again'.[9] Two years later, he enthusiastically praised their mural as evidence of this:

It succeeds because, unlike the majority of English decorative mural paintings today, which are either vacuously abstract or quaintly humorous, it has something serious to celebrate. Happiness leaves the mind free not empty, and it is with the freedom attained in this way that one's eye can wander over this wall, delighting in shapes and colours whose meanings are not for one moment denied, but can look after themselves … The collaboration between Greaves and Middleditch has really worked. There seems to have been no conflict of either style or vision. So much for the artist as incorrigible lone hunter.[10]

In fact, Greaves's work was changing fast and the mural had caught him in the midst of reassessing his priorities. Change was fuelled by dissatisfaction with his Italian paintings for being too descriptive: 'I felt there was a lot of received wisdom of the wrong kind in the painting. It was a hard and stony road out of that.' Rebirth was painful. Re-evaluating his vocabulary, Greaves began to feel that in his search for authenticity his painting had become too descriptive of external realities and imitative of surfaces: he would paint a dusty road with dry paint and portray a wicker chair by threading paint as though remaking the chair. As Berger had appreciated in one of his very first essays on Greaves:

An object is what it is because of the way it has been made. Pieces of leather are sewn together to make a shoe. Wicker is woven to make the seat of a chair. An arm assumes its shape and colour as a result of the sum total of the muscular actions it habitually undertakes and the temperatures it endures … Greaves works as an artisan with every brush stroke.[11]

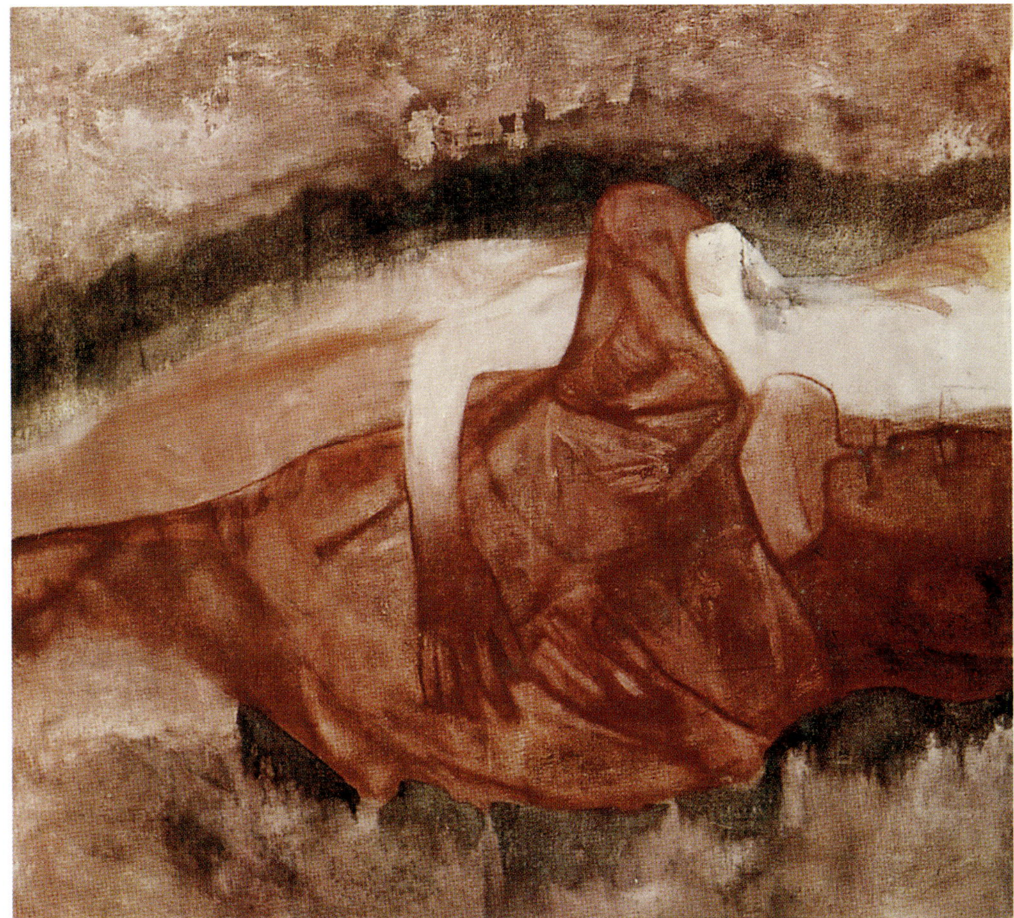

50 *Lovers*, 1958
Oil on canvas
165.1 × 182.9cm (65 × 72in)
Private Collection, London

This mimetic quality was something that Greaves himself recognised: 'Each element was painted in its own way, embodying its unique properties … I was thinking about it all the time. How an apple and a jug each might be painted differently.'[12] What followed were paintings in which Greaves rejected such naturalism; for example, instead of conveying the wetness of water, he would give it the substance of rope, as in *Greece – the Mythic Spring* (1981). In this move away from naturalism, a key painting was *Lovers* (plate 50), a large work that was exhibited in Greaves's Zwemmer exhibition in 1958 as well as with the A.I.A. in an exhibition entitled *Aspects of Realism*, which presented 16 paintings by 16 artists including Greaves, Bratby, Middleditch, Peter de Francia and Joe Tilson. In *Lovers*, two figures melt into each other in an intimate embrace. But this dissolution challenged Berger's promotion of accessible language, objective concerns and typical subjects, leading him to criticise Greaves's work for its lack of explicitness: 'a search for elusive meanings; a kind of dance round their themes, which remain unstated'.[13] In contrast, in an ecstatic review, Nevile Wallis wrote at length about *Lovers*, which for him was

> *the most ambitious attempt to realise the ecstasy of natural union yet given us by any contemporary … The almost swooning mood is heightened by the floating shapes and the deliquescent colour of this image which, in imagination, symbolises the experience that may bring union with the cosmos itself … Greaves reconciles a near-tachiste method with his amorphous yet subtle shapes to communicate an emotional experience which could be conveyed in no other way.*[14]

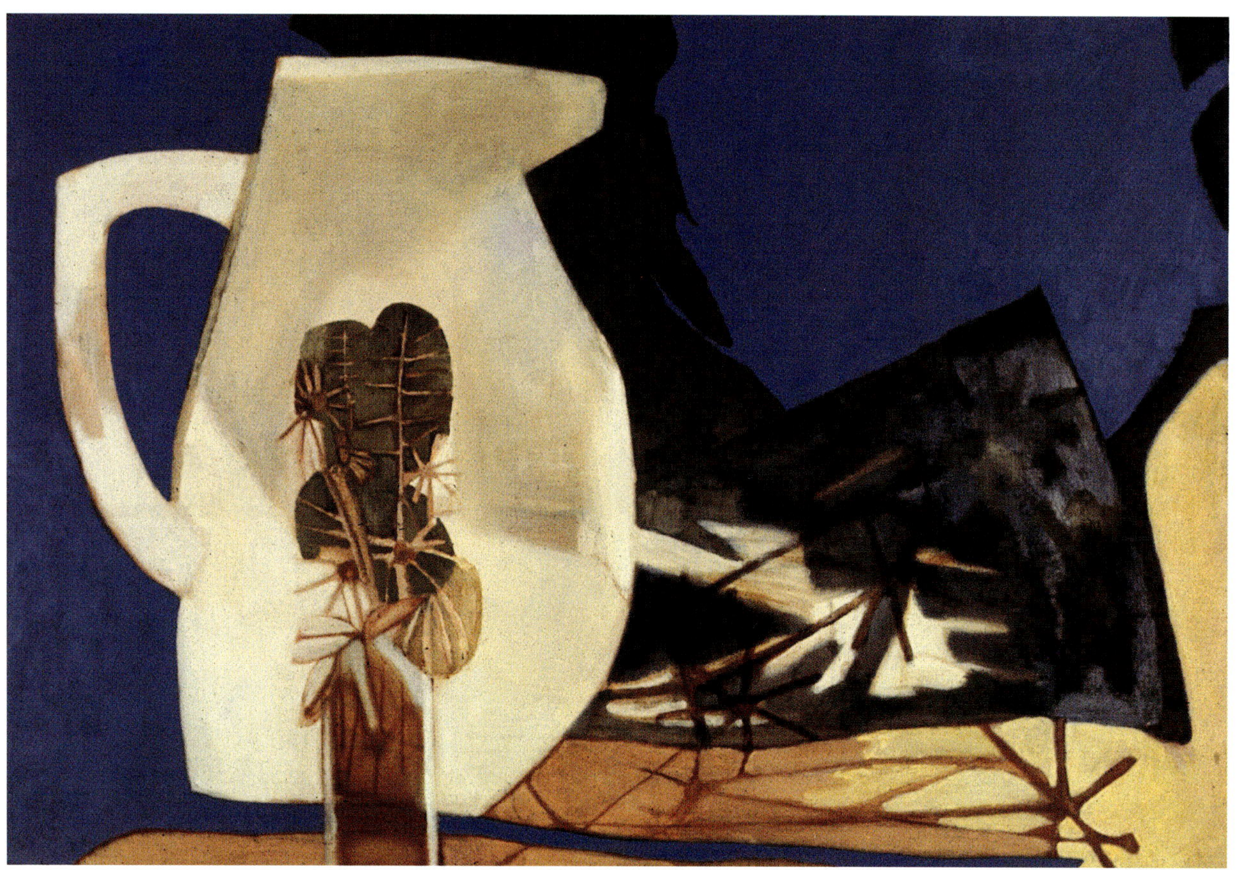

51 *Still Life with Big White Jug*, 1959
Oil on canvas
145 × 213cm (57 × 84in)

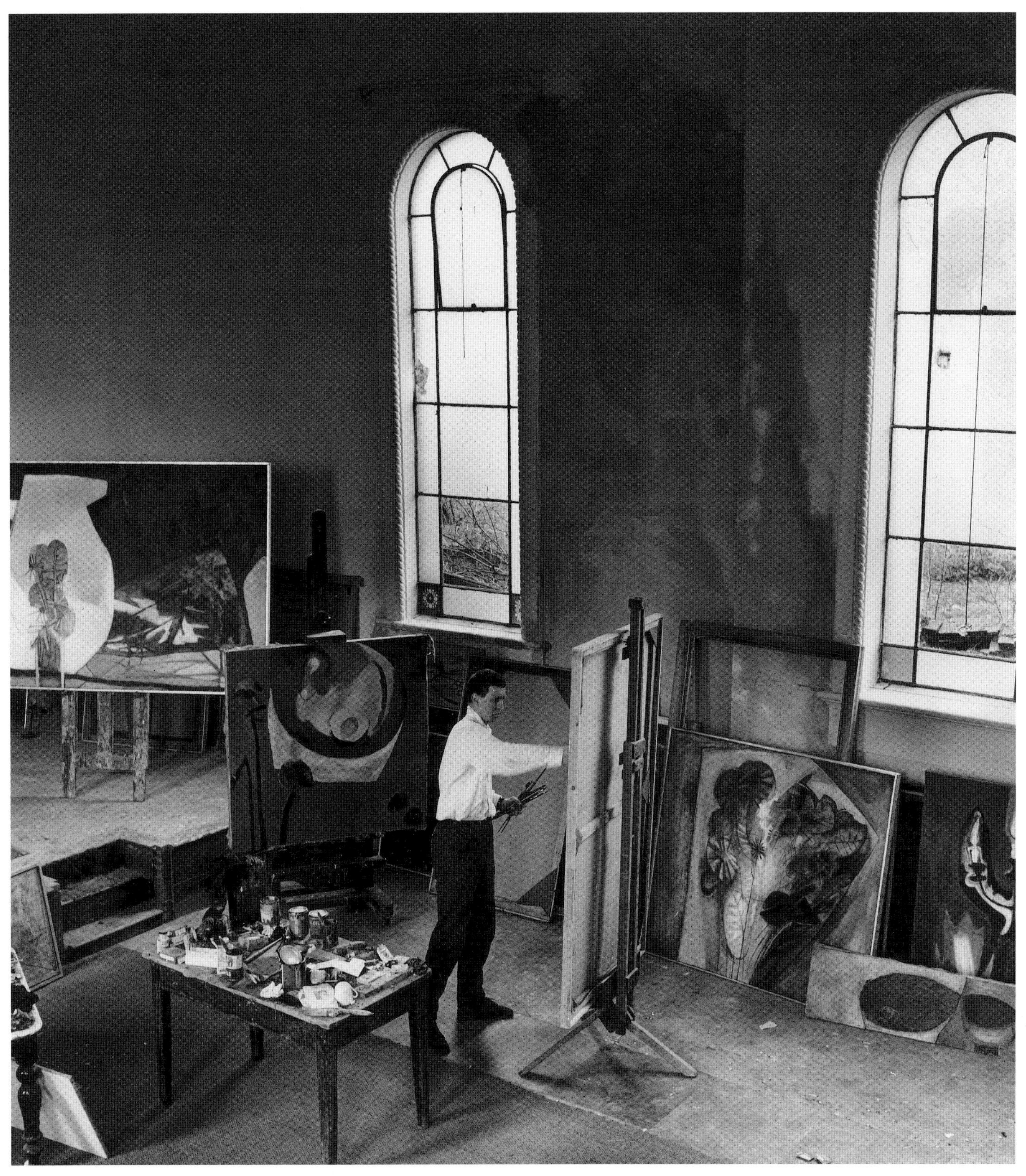

52 Derrick Greaves in his Woburn studio, 1960,
including *Still Life with Big White Jug* (plate 51) and *Still Life* (plate 54)

What Greaves now sought was a painting that was less declamatory and more subtle, less overt and more contemplative. As he asserted in 1960:

Rationalizing, explaining or interpreting a painted image in terms of words is a kind of assassination of the very quality that is its life – namely, its silence. For the painter to attempt such a thing is suicide. Realizing and developing, through a precision of instinct, such images which live visually in their own silence, is my concern, and the only true painting for me.[15]

This was an aspiration that he shared with his old friend Jack Smith, who had also moved to more personal concerns and had similarly gone beyond the paintings that had established his reputation. Smith, interviewed by Basil Taylor in 1960, made a strikingly similar observation: 'I believe that the age of public challenges … is past. Whatever might come out of the next fifty years will be done in a strange kind of silence.'[16]

The following years were filled with exploratory paintings, albeit of a heightened size, which filled Greaves's shows at Zwemmer Gallery in the early 1960s. In marked contrast to what he considered to be Helen Lessore's doctrinaire attitudes and faith in London art schools, Greaves relished Anton Zwemmer's internationalism and openness to the new. Zwemmer had lived in Paris, knew Picasso and presented shows of many of France's leading artists, providing Greaves with a modernist rather than a realist context.

Of these artists, Greaves had a love-hate relationship with Picasso, but his shows at Zwemmer Gallery suggest that he had no such equivocation about a fellow exhibitor, Georges Braque. A major exhibition of Braque's work was staged in London at the Tate Gallery in 1956, a fortuitous moment for Greaves as he sought to develop his work. The exhibition made a big impression, challenging Greaves to reconsider his way of painting and his desire for immediacy. Responding to Braque's *élan*, Greaves recognised that although the work was often very difficult and immensely subtle, it rewarded contemplation and indeed necessitated time to do the work justice. For a young artist who had always sought direct, immediate connection with his audience, this was a challenge and Greaves's paintings of the late 1950s and early 1960s appear to have responded to the questions posed by Braque's late paintings. Greaves's paintings such as *Still Life with Big White Jug* (plate 51), *Fruit Bowl on White Ground* (plate 53), and *Still Life* (plate 54) would succeed and fail for similar reasons.

As in Braque's work, such paintings suggest that, having freed himself from

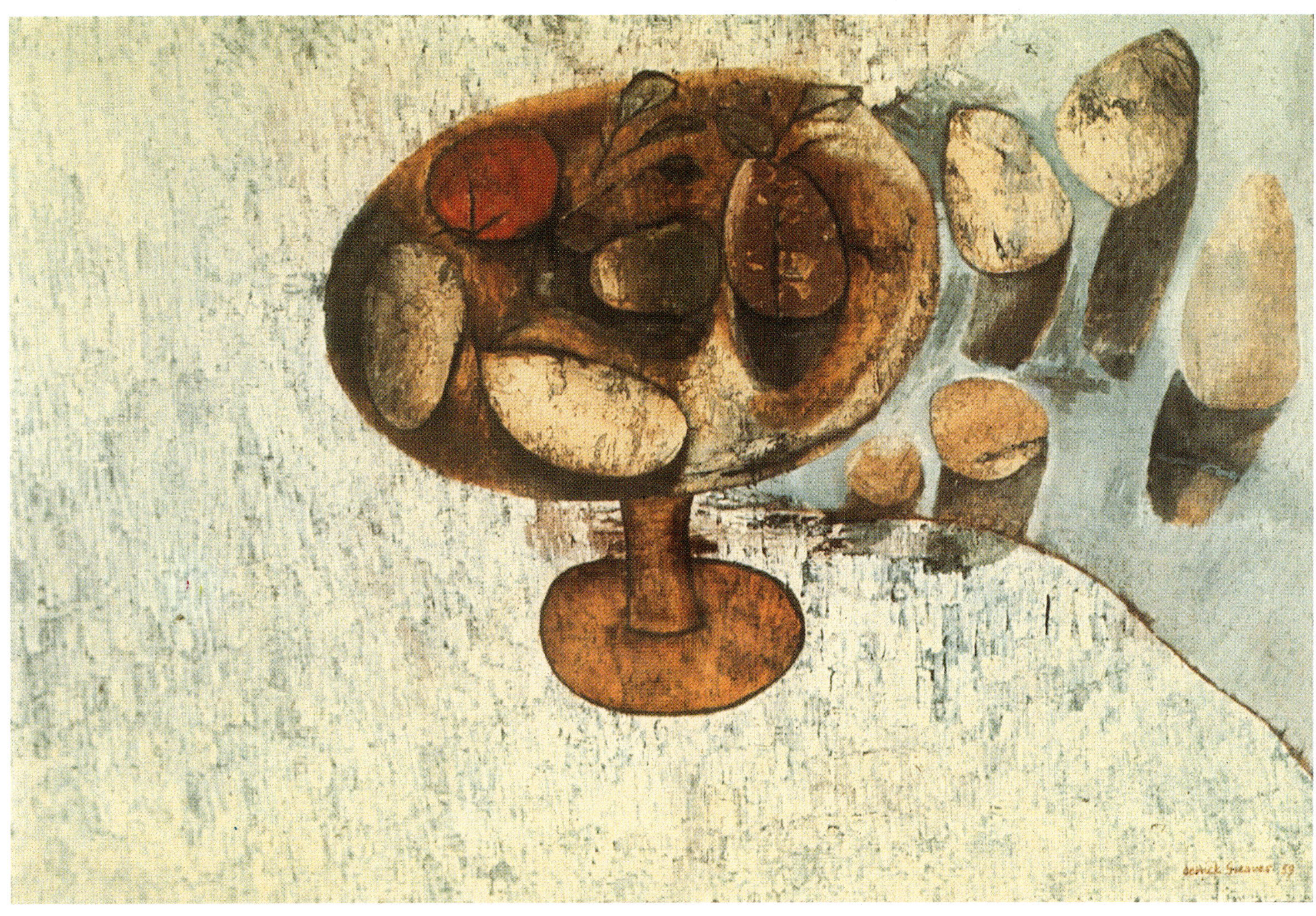

53 *Fruit Bowl on White Ground*, 1959
Oil on canvas
102 × 153cm (40.2 × 60.2in)
Private Collection, London

slavish veneration of the external world, the artist had turned inwards to a more
synthetic process in which objects are reconstituted. For both artists still-life
was the main focus, whether isolated or within a constructed studio setting,
whether derived from observation or from the imagination. Like Braque, Greaves
was criticised for producing work that was too hermetic and solipsistic, leaving
a baffled audience. Also like Braque, paint is handled differently for each object
and different viewpoints, perspectives and scales are combined within a single
pictorial space. The assertive wallpapers that give Braque's grounds such an
emphatic presence also prefigure Greaves's later incorporation of collage grounds
as an active part of the final picture.

Greaves's figure paintings, some of which are visible in studio photographs
from this period (plate 55), also suggest an indebtedness to Braque. Braque's late
figures are surely some of the most peculiar in twentieth-century painting and
those of Greaves from the early 1960s share something of their awkward post-
Cubist reformulation of the body.

Greaves's show at Zwemmer Gallery in 1960 was dominated by still-life
paintings, particularly flowers, and attracted enthusiastic reviews by many of
the leading critics. John Russell praised 'an admirable dignity and integrity' in
Greaves's thorough exploration of 'the possibilities of the still-life', but suggested
that this had a paradoxical effect. While each work was unmistakably by the
artist, 'no two pictures are at all alike: format, subject, handling – all are varied
and renewed from one picture to the next'. The very large size of many of these
paintings led Russell to observe that 'the objects portrayed lose their everyday
identity and become unrecognisable in their majesty, or as the case may be, their

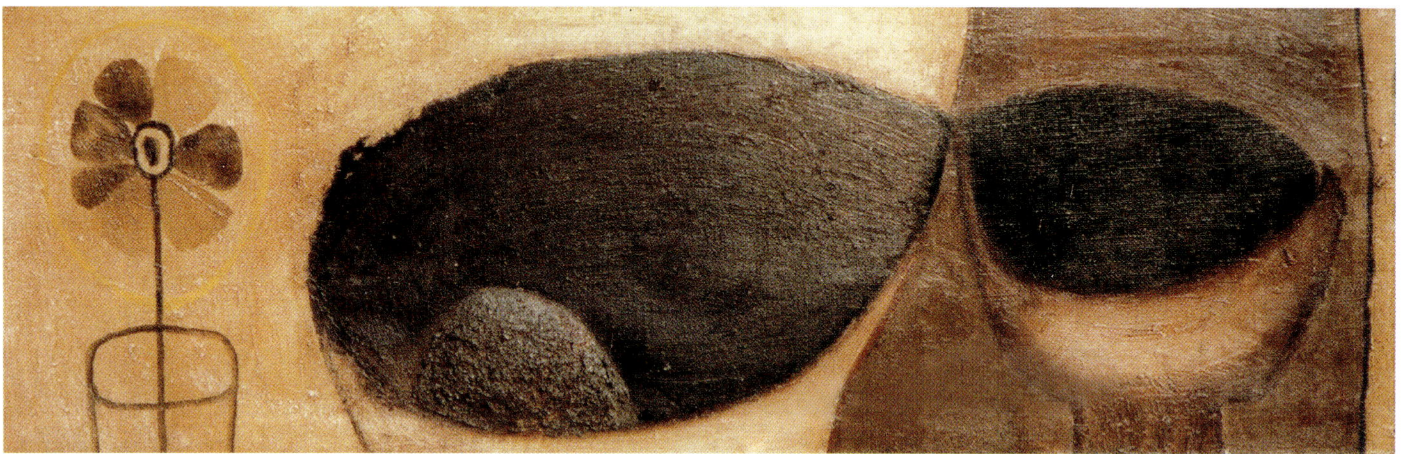

54 *Still Life, c.*1960
Oil on canvas
30.5 × 91.5cm (12 × 36in)
Private Collection

vulnerability and awkwardness'. The otherness of these objects also led reviewers
to reflect on their 'heraldic air', whilst wrestling with their allusiveness.[17]

A review in *The Times* again referred to the size of the oils, suggesting that
the 'lumbering, closed shapes within them suggest that something majestic is
being aimed at without quite being achieved'. Reflecting on *Still Life with Big White
Jug*, the critic addressed the fact that the painting 'conveys a sort of empty
presence … which paradoxically, in view of the way it dominates the gallery, is
not so much an object which is "there" as a space cut out of its blue background'.
He concluded, however, that 'this is nevertheless the exhibition of an imaginative,
searching artist, one with an unusual character that can be blunt and graceful
within the same painting.'[18]

The impact of Braque was discussed not just by John Russell, but also by
Neville Wallis. In his review, Wallis explored the still-lifes on show with reference
to just one other artist, Braque. Writing of Greaves's 'revelatory painting', Wallis
asserted that 'today he might say, with Braque, that he no longer believes in the
immutable reality of anything … In these bouquets and arrangements of fruit
enclosed in outlined shapes one could think of a similar device of Braque's in his
still-life transformations.'[19]

Seeking to remake his vocabulary, Greaves made up quantities of paint in
pots, varying their thickness. This allowed him to judge the relationship of an
area of paint to a line of paint next to it, to juxtapose forms in a valued and
measured way. Encouraged by Braque's example, Greaves now introduced
striking variations in paint thickness and methods of application within a single
canvas, an experiment he would never again repeat.

The paintings of the later 1950s and early 1960s were certainly some of the
most experimental of Greaves's career. Complex and ambitious, they nonetheless
lacked the artist's characteristic clarity of form and concept. Whilst studio photographs emphasise their grand scale and complex spatial construction, the artist's
own dissatisfaction led him to destroy several of these paintings. Paradoxically,
the very quality that Greaves responded to in Braque and aspired to in his own
painting – an artwork of sophistication and subtlety that gave up its secrets
grudgingly over time – was the reason for his impatience with the inaccessibility
of his own paintings.

The mixed critical response to Greaves's 1962 show at Zwemmer Gallery
exposed this problem. Despite aspiring to clarity, Greaves's work had become
more internalised:

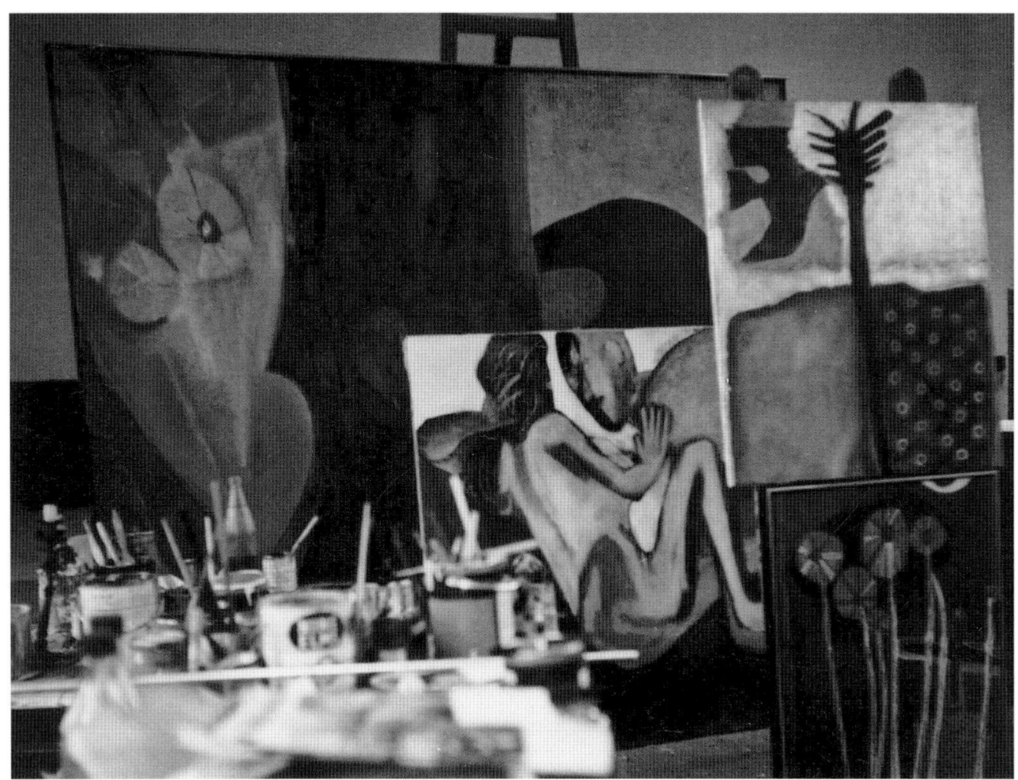

*One of the self-disciplines I have imposed on myself is to make as clear and
clarified an image as I can … I feel a terrible anxiety about the world and the
human situation generally. I am trying to make my pictures articulate about
that. My art has political implications in the broadest sense. I am not painting
pictures primarily about painting … I used to paint the outside world through
my eyes; now I am painting from inside.*[20]

Eric Newton used his review to develop his response to Greaves's previous
show, characterising the 'devices' that Greaves used including 'a tendency to
see everything rather larger than life size' and 'to single out a fragment of the
original visual experience and underlie it by turning it into a pattern (Matisse
did this and there are echoes, though never quotations, from Matisse in his latest
canvases)'. Newton accurately recognised that 'what he is manifestly doing is
to escape from the domination of the observed object, to translate it into paint
by refusing to describe it and to find a formula for giving us an account of his
reactions to it'. Writing of Greaves's 'exceptional intelligence and determination',
he praised his willingness 'to tell a whopping visual lie in order to make a closer

approach to the poetic truth', although he concluded that 'Greaves's journey is not yet complete. The exhibition is transitional. He is still on his way to something that is still a fragment of essential truth based on a visual lie.'[21]

Whilst the journey was praiseworthy, the difficulties it posed for the viewer fill other reviews of the show. The critic of *The Times* admired the certainty yet wrote of the 'absence, relatively speaking, of [a] "way in"' and identified 'a gawky, questing, poetic originality about them … The strangeness of idiom is paralleled by one's uncertainty about how much of the imagery is a translation of the thing seen, how much is invented shape, and at what point the two coalesce.'[22] Meanwhile, in his review Alan Bowness also addressed the awkwardness of these paintings:

> *In a somewhat heraldic style he paints over-lifesize everyday objects – flowers, plants, fruit, kitchen utensils, sometimes the figure. Their forms and colours have, however, become an entirely individual and expressive pictorial language, so that … he can come very close to abstraction without losing any essential qualities. Greaves is an original painter: awkward and graceless to a degree, all the constituents of his art (imagery, composition, texture etc.) lead one towards a feeling of urgent, cosmic unease which no doubt lies at the heart of what he wants to communicate.*[23]

The silence, or rather the lack of declamation or polemic, led to charges of hermeticism in reviews of his solo shows at Zwemmer Gallery in 1962 and 1963. This criticism hit home, touching a nerve for an artist who deep down had remained committed to the importance of communicating with an audience. As he later recalled: 'The paintings had seemed alright in the studio, but once they were in the gallery I realised that they were too hermetic – they didn't mean much to other people and that's important to me.'[24]

The way that his work had turned inwards, was perhaps an unconscious expression of the disillusionment Greaves felt at the failure of social realist painting, including his own, to attract a popular audience. For Greaves there had always been an implicit political dimension to his desire to communicate and it remained, even as his work changed during the 1960s. Greaves had always been 'of the Left': as a young man in Sheffield he attended political meetings and sold the *Daily Worker* in Fitzalan Square. As an activist, he was an early supporter of the Campaign for Nuclear Disarmament, going on 'Ban the Bomb' marches and attending a vigil outside Downing Street in 1959.[25]

Even in the 1960s, when still-life provided Greaves's focus, he incorporated

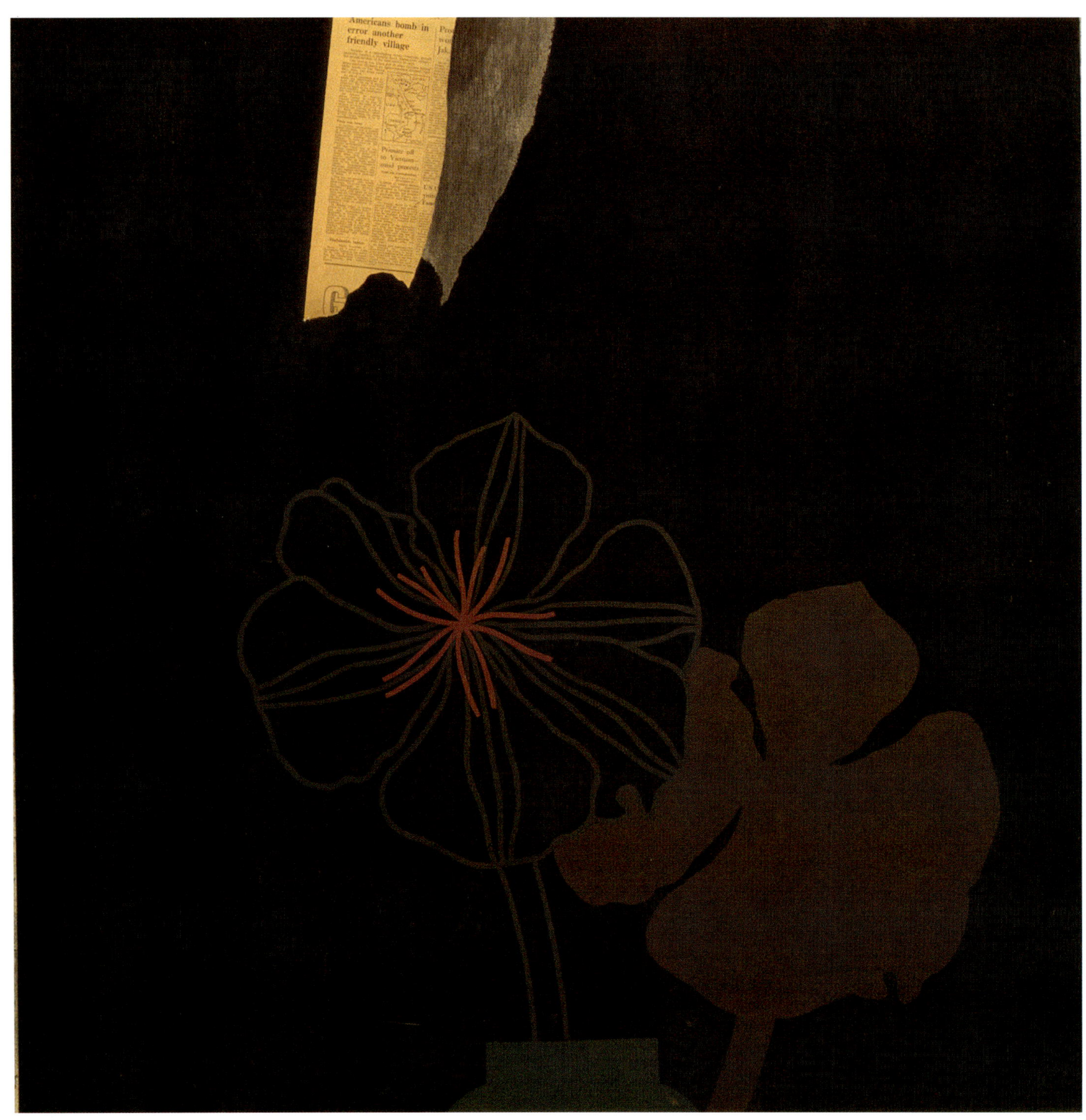

56 *Flower and Collage*, 1968–9
Oil on canvas
130.2 × 130.2cm (51.3 × 51.3in)
Graves Art Gallery, Sheffield

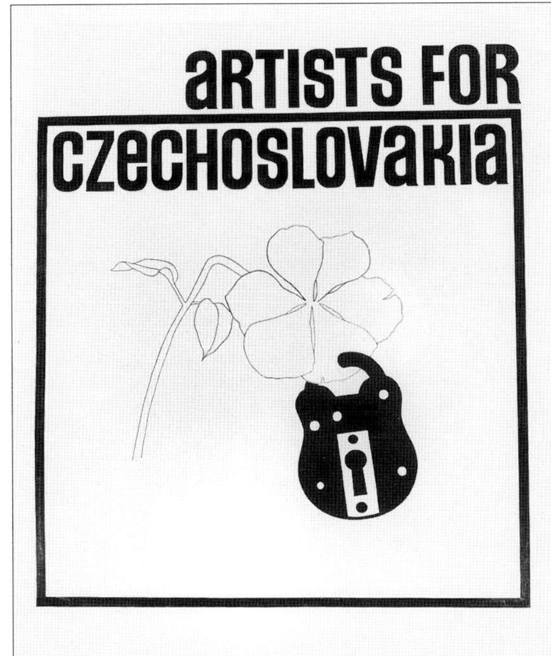

57 *Artists for Czechoslovakia*, c.1969
Screenprint
76 × 73.5cm (30 × 29in)

elements which thrust this most conventional of subjects into a more political
arena. In *Flower and Collage* (plate 56), harmony is disrupted through the inclusion
of a torn fragment of newspaper that bares the headline 'Americans bomb in error
another friendly village', and in another painting, *The Ultimate Absurdity* (plate 58),
Vietnam is alluded to with the inclusion of a pruning knife stabbing a flower
that bleeds. In 1969, he even exhibited a 13ft (4m) painting at the I.C.A. as a
commentary on the Russian invasion of Czechoslovakia and designed a poster
in protest, too (plate 57). More recently, the war in Iraq has led to a massive dark
painting, *War Triptych* (plate 137).

Despite different forms of direct action, Greaves recognised that social realism
had failed to attract a popular audience. As early as 1959 he looked back with
sadness at his work of the mid 1950s. He wrote of the deliberation behind it and
of his intention to communicate with his audience but concluded, despairingly,
'... feeling a desire to lessen the gap that exists between audience and painting,
I made attempts to form a pictorial language from nature which would be easily
accessible to all who cared to look. To do this in England at the present time ... is,
I have realised, aesthetic suicide'.[26]

The foregrounding of still-life motifs during these years would continue,
but increasingly Greaves would also turn his attention to the female nude and

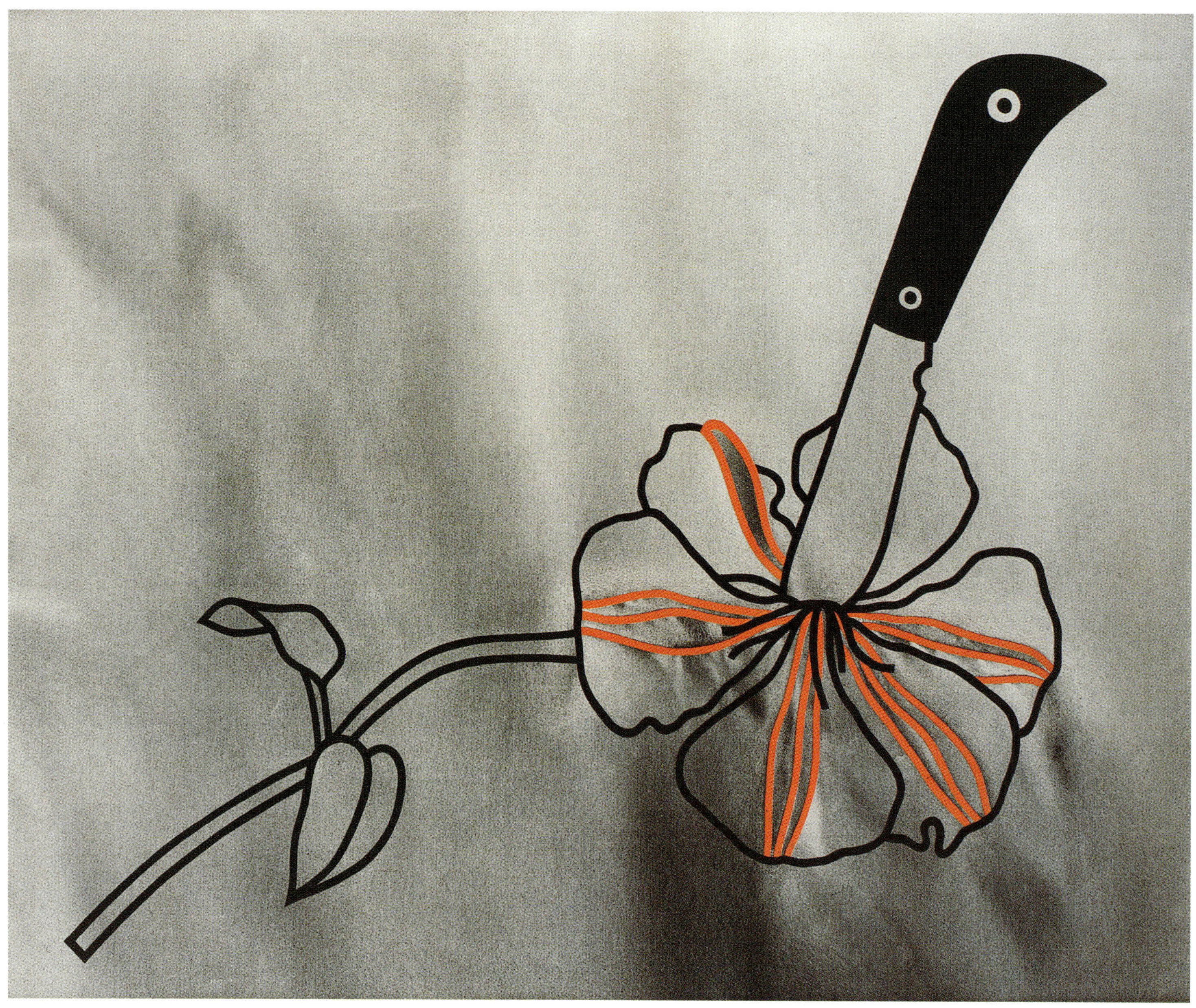

58 *The Ultimate Absurdity, c.*1968
Oil on canvas
144 × 127cm (56.7 × 50in)

to couples, developing new and bolder ways of bringing disparate elements together, and increasing the formal and iconographic complexity.

By the mid 1960s Greaves was painting more and more flatly, so that he could measure more precisely the relationships between forms and create a more harmonious surface. A shift from oil to acrylic paint would facilitate this. Once again, Greaves would destroy many of these paintings, but they illustrate the growing importance of Fernand Léger and Henri Matisse in the role now being given to flat colour and such changes would, by the late 1960s, lead to some of Greaves's greatest paintings. Increasingly, too, Greaves would explore the roles of proportion, measurement and even geometry, so that by the end of the 1960s his paintings would be of a scale and ambition that superseded all that had gone before.

Notes

1. Ray Watkinson, 'Derrick Greaves', *Art News and Review*, 8 November 1958. Artist's Archive.

2. John Bratby, 'A Painter's Credo', *Art News and Review*, 14 April 1956, vol.8, no.6, p.1 and p.9.

3. Derrick Greaves, letter to John Bratby, 12 November 1956, contained in Bratby's own scrapbook, held by Julian Hartnoll Gallery, London.

4. Ray Watkinson, op cit. Exhibited paintings included *Two Steelworkers*, *Children on a Red Ground*, *Lovers* and *Linford at Night*.

5. Information is from correspondence and a conversation with Derrick Greaves in June 1994.

6. Hitchens's 'mural' for the English Folk Dance and Song Society was not painted directly on the walls but comprised 11 strips of canvas, each of which was painted separately, totalling 69 × 21ft (21 × 6.4m). It provided a woodland setting for motifs inspired by various dance forms.

7. John Berger, 'Darkness is Zero', *New Statesman*, 29 November 1958, vol.56, no.1446, p.756.

8. Ibid.

9. John Berger, 'Exit and Credo?', *New Statesman*, 29 September 1956, vol.52, no.1333, p.372.

10. John Berger, 'Darkness is Zero', *New Statesman*, 29 November 1958, vol.56, no.1446, p.756.

11. John Berger, 'Greaves and Hogarth', *New Statesman*, 10 December 1955, vol.50, no.1292, p.792.

12. Derrick Greaves, conversation with James Hyman, June 2006.

13. John Berger, 'Art Shows', *New Statesman*, 8 November 1958, vol.56, no.1443, p.634.

14. Nevile Wallis, 'Sex and Symbolism', *Observer*, 1959. Artist's Archive.

15. Derrick Greaves, undated statement, circa 1960.

16. Jack Smith, 'A Painter's Development: an interview with Basil Taylor', *Ark*, Summer 1960, no.26.

17. Ibid.

18. Anonymous, 'Heraldic Touch in Flowerpieces. Mr Derrick Greaves Exhibition', *The Times*, 27 September 1960, p.13. Meanwhile, in the *Guardian*, Eric Newton also reflected on the monumentality such enlargement allowed and the fact that no two works were alike, suggesting that a process of simplification was 'at the root of their intensity'. Eric Newton, *Guardian*, 21 September 1960. Artist's Archive.

19. Nevile Wallis, 'The Pilgrim's Progress', *Observer*, 25 September 1960. Artist's Archive.

20. Derrick Greaves quoted in William Duck, 'The Explosion that began in Sheffield', *Sheffield Telegraph*, 7 February 1962, p.3.

21. Eric Newton, 'A Painter's Journey', *Guardian*, 26 January 1962. Artist's Archive.

22. Anonymous, 'Painter worth trying to understand', *The Times*, 26 January 1962. Artist's Archive.

23. Alan Bowness, 'A Generation on Parade', *Observer*, 28 January 1962. Artist's Archive.

24. Derrick Greaves quoted in Anonymous, 'An Artist on his own terms', *Morning Telegraph*, Sheffield, 17 September 1971. Artist's Archive.

25. The *A.I.A. Newsletter* of July 1959 (unnumbered) publicised this forthcoming vigil explaining that 'each three hours of this vigil will be manned by a different profession. The Campaign for Nuclear Disarmament has allotted 3–6 and 6–9 pm to artists'. It also referred to the support given to C.N.D. by Carel Weight, Derrick Greaves, Michael Ayrton, Peter Lanyon and Josef Herman.

26. Derrick Greaves, 'Painter's Purpose', *Studio*, March 1959, vol.157, no.792, p.82.

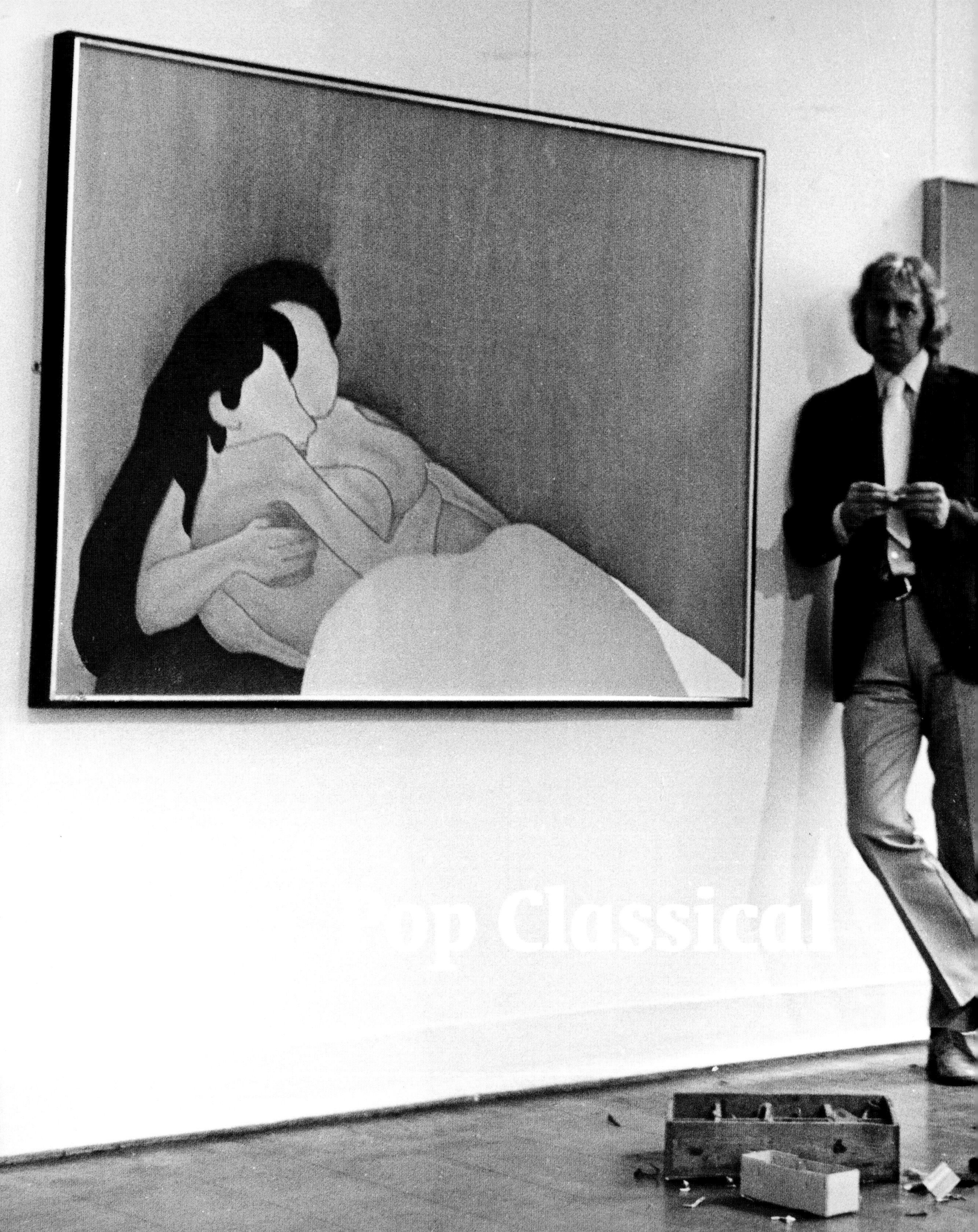
p Classical

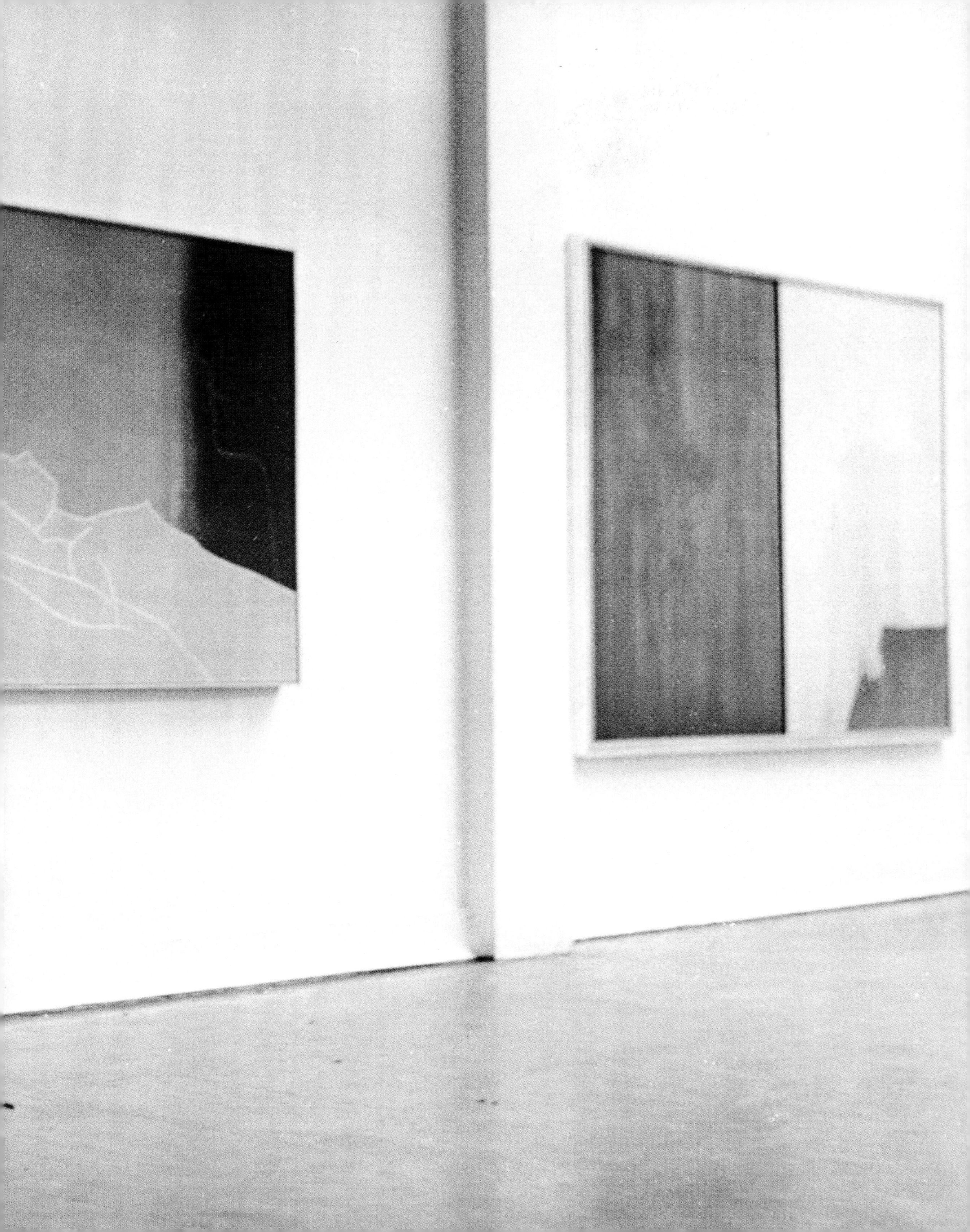

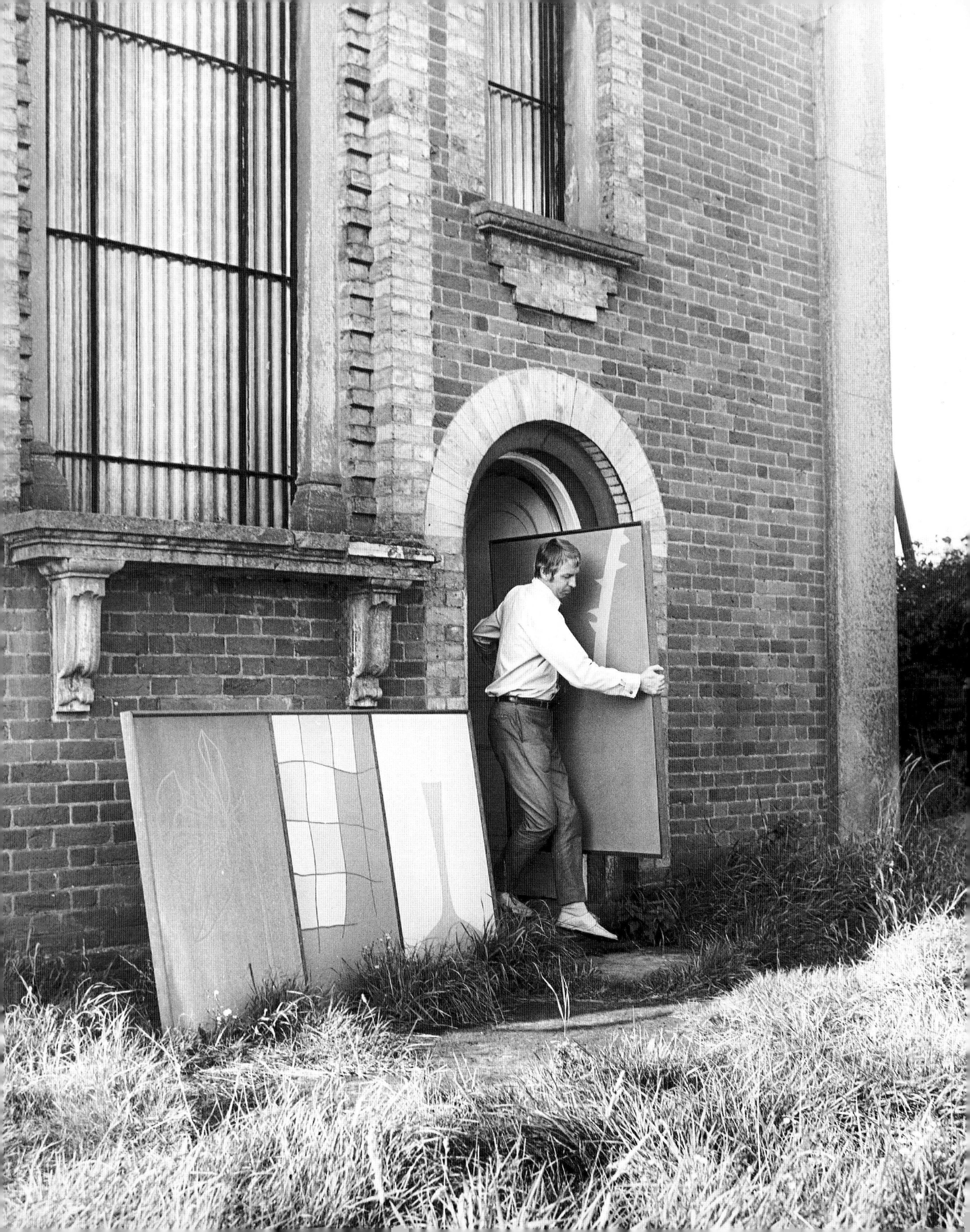

5. Pop Classical: Derrick Greaves and Pop Art

Since the 'fifties Greaves has become progressively more subtle in style, technique and use of imagery. His recent large, cool, delicately balanced canvases have come a long way from Peasant Interior *of 1953, or* Spaghetti Eaters, *a forthright image of two workmen self-evidently unlikely to enjoy tea at the Ritz. Greaves has transformed his art since then, both gradually and logically. His imagery now tends to reflect the more sophisticated hedonism that has pervaded a good deal of British and American art of the 'sixties. His sources are sometimes similar to Pop sources. But the important thing about his work generally … is that it is beautifully classical.*

Mark Glazebrook, 1967[1]

In 1967, the *London Magazine* published an essay by Mark Glazebrook (Director of the Whitechapel Art Gallery from 1969–72). Entitled 'Pop-Kinky/Pop-Classical', it addressed the work of four major artists – Patrick Caulfield, Derrick Greaves, Fernand Léger and Roy Lichtenstein – and was accompanied by illustrations of four works by Caulfield and five by Greaves, including *Triptych – Bedroom* (plate 61). Admitting their differences, Glazebrook nevertheless dwelt on their similarities:

They all avoid the handmade look, the expressive brushstroke. They all compose with thickish painted lines which both delineate forms and strike up a strong rhythm … In the too little known recent work of Derrick Greaves the line is often a pale one, dividing two darker areas like the swap of black for white on a photographic negative. Partly because of their clarifying use of line and partly because all four use strong doses of flat colour, their paintings have great impact as designs … A relevant point about subject matter is that if it is familiar, either from everyday life or from artistic tradition, it helps establish communication.[2]

Comparing the work of these four artists to that of Allen Jones, then gaining notoriety for his fetishistic images of women, Glazebrook concluded that:

Whereas Jones is mostly what might be called Pop-Kinky, Léger, Greaves, Lichtenstein and Caulfield are all what could be called Pop-Classical. The latter four all take popular themes in order to establish at least the possibility of being

Previous page:
59 Derrick Greaves hanging the Whitechapel Gallery. London, 1973

Facing page:
60 Derrick Greaves at his studio, Woburn, 1960s

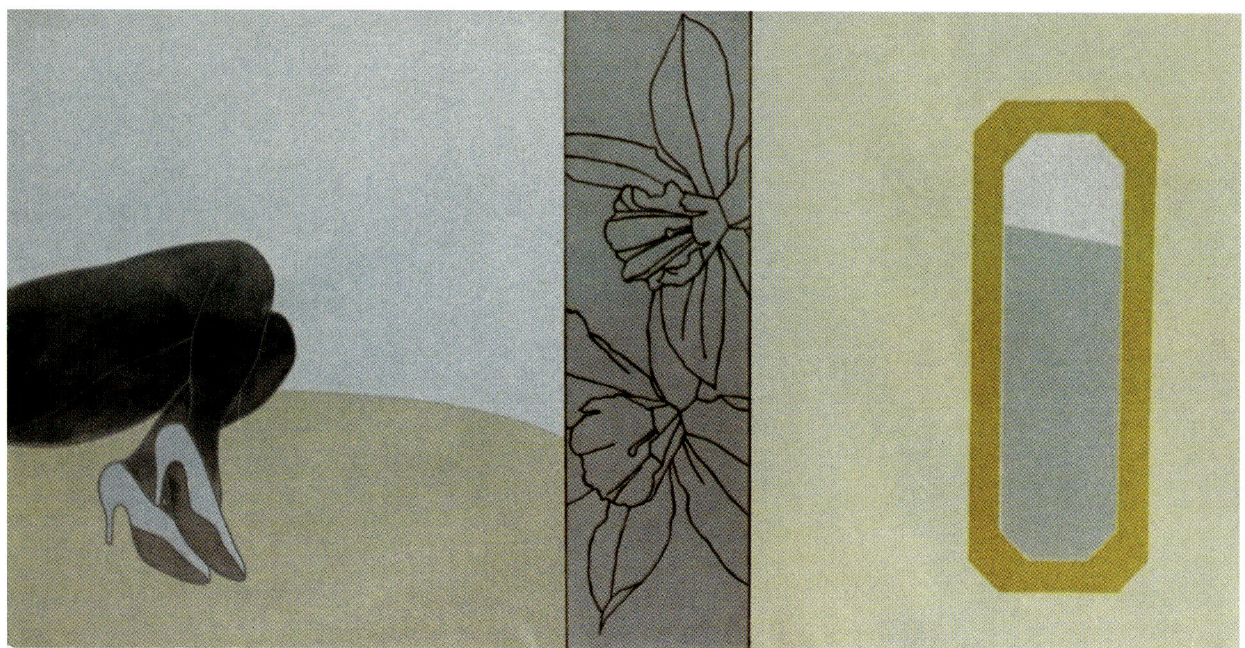

*understood. But very soon the picture takes over ... Greaves, though not above
the odd surrealist device such as seeing a woman's body in terms of the sky, pares
down the linear rhythm to achieve his own brand of more with less.*[3]

Finally, Glazebrook felt the necessity to extract Greaves from the milieu of
the 'angry young men', 'social realist group' or 'Kitchen-Sink' school. Glazebrook's
characterisations were prescient in recognising that Greaves had developed a
style that was spare yet subtle, that combined clear precise lines with flat areas
of colour. He was prescient, too, in his emphasis on Greaves's maturity and the
distance he had come from his youthful paintings of the mid 1950s and, not least,
prescient in suggesting an engagement with, but also a separation from, the
ideals of Pop Art.

An appreciation of the classicism of Greaves's work was pursued to different
ends just two years later in a review by his long-time champion, Pierre Rouve.
Writing of Greaves's simultaneous exhibitions at the I.C.A. and at Ewan Phillips
Gallery in 1969, Rouve perceived 'a controlled radiance that can best be described
as classical'.[4]

In contrast to his Zwemmer exhibitions at the beginning of the 1960s,
Greaves ended the decade with praise ringing in his ears.[5] One champion was
the most important museum director of the day, Bryan Robertson, who through

his exhibitions at the Whitechapel in the late 1950s and 1960s – among them
Jackson Pollock, Robert Rauschenberg, and Mark Rothko – did as much as anyone
to internationalise British art. Responding to Greaves's London shows in 1969, he
wrote of the need for a large exhibition of Greaves, prefiguring such an exhibition
at the Whitechapel Art Gallery in 1973. Implicitly illustrating how far Greaves
had moved from the 'cosmic unease' that Alan Bowness had previously identified
in his work of the early 1960s, Bryan Robertson now wrote of the 'absolute
command' of a confident painter in control of his idiom.[6]

Greaves had succeeded in rejuvenating his work, pulling it apart and
reconstructing its vocabulary and syntax, and the late 1960s and early 1970s
would witness some of his most powerful works. Flatness was a key, as Greaves
himself recognised:

*At a certain time in my life – and I remember it well – the world as I saw it flattened
for me. Things, objects became flat. That is, they had a certain controlled depth.
It was not Cézanne's flatness, neither was it Cubism, 'hermetic' or 'synthetic'. It
was mine – I hadn't looked for it – how could you? – but it was mine. It did concern
the identity of the object but the 'interval' – the intervening space, invaded, and
to a certain extent, annexed the objects. Similarly the object pressurised its
environment. Edges became crucial. Outline became crucial, ambiguous and
then an end in itself. Line emerged as form.[7]*

He had also continued to paint big, continued to present his imagery in an
accessible way and continued his long-standing desire to communicate with an
audience. To this Greaves added a new, more economical approach to colour
derived from his appreciation of Léger, as he explained in an undated note on
the artist:

*Whatever is there is positive and extreme. A red is a red – black is black. An area
is proportionately calculated. A line is a line. Even background is background
(realised as positive support). All the ingredients can be plainly seen and each
judged as the painter has agonizingly judged them, adjusted them, sometimes
eradicated them, then put them back again in a new-found way etc. And yet,
from all this classical listing the 'message' – the overall feeling and spirit of the
picture – the thing that is not shown – indeed that can only be shown by such
calculation and careful adjustment – is the invisible ingredient which rules all
the decisions made.[8]*

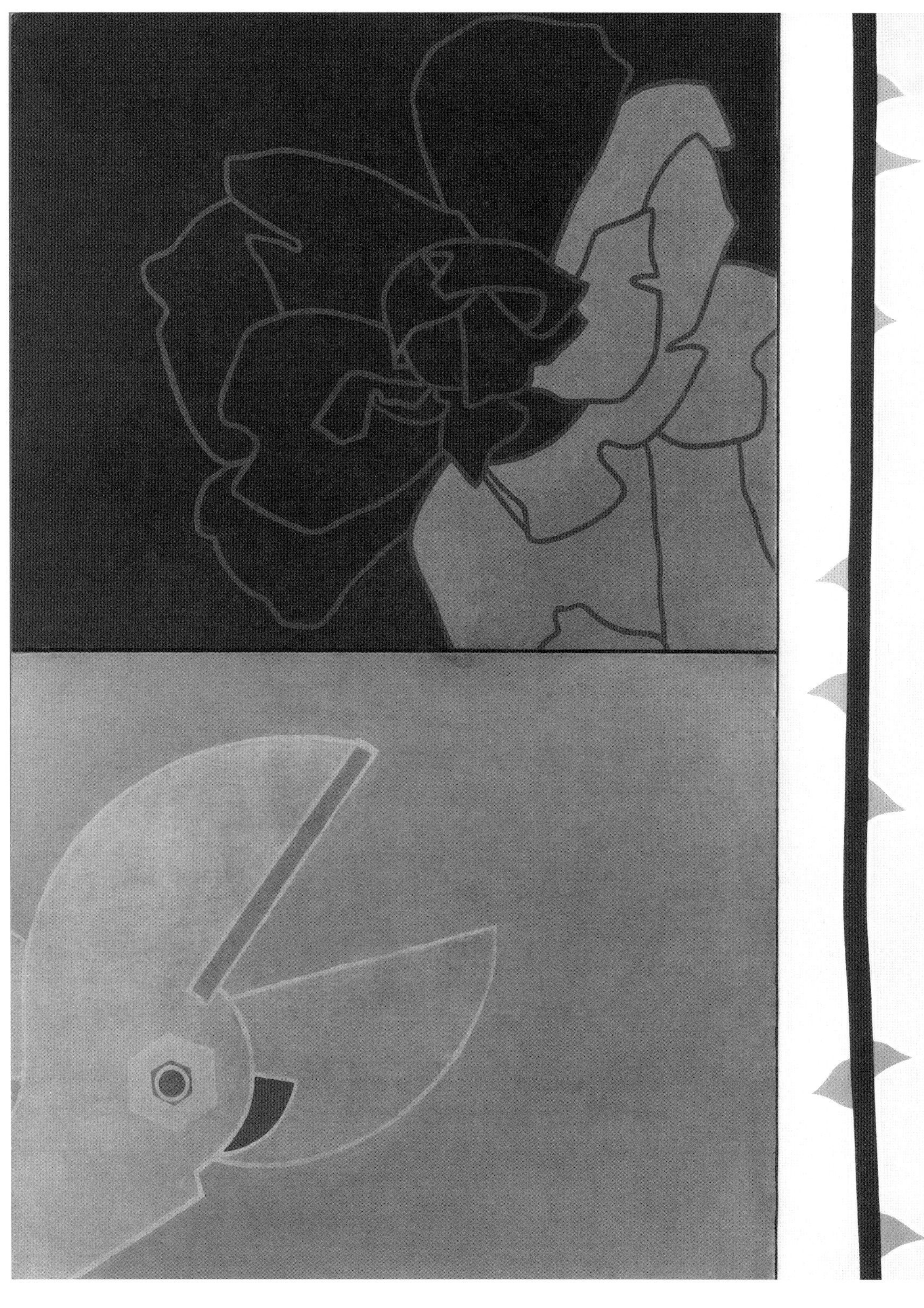

62 *Triptych – Rose with Secateurs*, 1967
Acrylic and oil on canvas
152.5 × 122cm (60 × 48in)
Private Collection

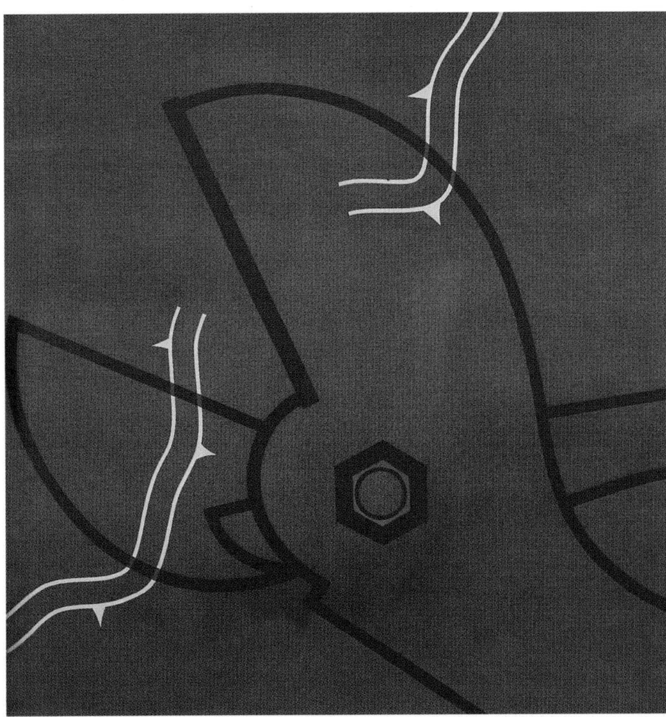

63 *Secateurs and Briar*, 1967–9
Acrylic and oil on canvas
120.5 × 120.5cm (47.4 × 47.4in)
Private Collection, Norfolk

The heraldic quality that critics had already identified in paintings of the early 1960s now came to the fore, as in a number of paintings of a rose and secateurs such as *Triptych – Rose with Secateurs* (plate 62) and *Secateurs and Briar* (plate 63). Greaves's skill as a sign writer and his desire to communicate were well suited to Pop Art's demand for immediacy. Furthermore, the graphic style of Greaves's paintings of the later 1960s and early 1970s paralleled the presentation of many Pop artists and possessed particular affinities with contemporaneous paintings by Patrick Caulfield. Indeed, the apparent confidence of these works suggest that had Greaves not established his reputation at such a young age he might have emerged just a few years later as a powerful contributor to Pop Art.[9] Certainly such a fate was enjoyed by Joe Tilson, a matière painter in the 1950s who, without such deep branding, did succeed in freeing himself from that decade to re-emerge as a major figure in British Pop Art of the mid 1960s. In contrast, such was the fame that Greaves gained in the mid 1950s through his promotion as a 'Kitchen-Sink' painter that it would be hard to shake off.

Greaves's work, like that of Patrick Caulfield, was always highly individual and highly sophisticated, making any characterisation as a Pop Artist as misleading as it is revealing. But there are striking affinities. Greaves went from

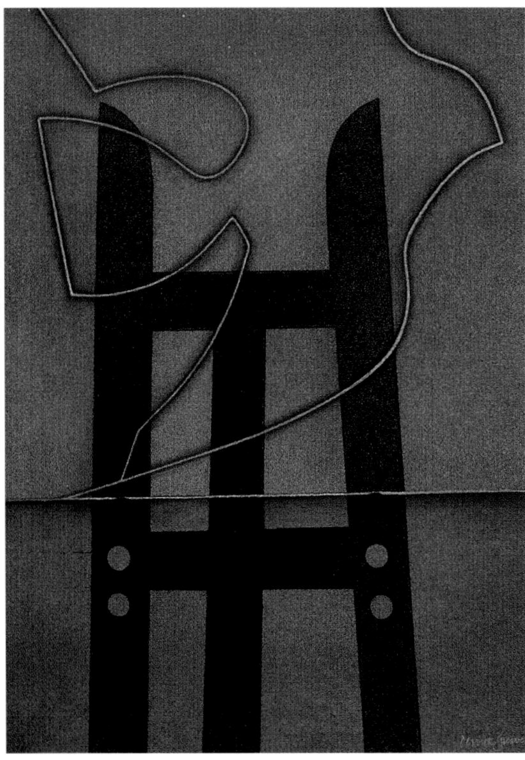

64 *The Pleasures of Drawing*,
1969
Charcoal and conté crayon on
paper
64 × 47.5cm (25.2 × 18.7in)
Private Collection, Norfolk

sign writing to painting and Caulfield from graphic design to painting, while both
spent the mid and late 1950s producing thickly worked social realist paintings
before developing signature styles in which a graphic boldness was married to
an heraldic quality. Both conceived of painting as a sign and the object as an
emblem. Both individualised their objects and drew from the lessons of Synthetic
Cubism, Caulfield from Juan Gris and Greaves from Georges Braque, and at times
both drew from the semiotic playfulness of René Magritte.

Individualism, playfulness and semiotic complexity are all to the fore in a
highly finished drawing of 1969 that encapsulates the way that Greaves had
reformulated his visual language. A manifesto picture, *The Pleasures of Drawing*
(plate 64) is the most finished of a series of works showing an easel with a picture
on it and can be read as a surrogate self portrait. The easel stands in for the
artist and a bird in flight represents painting as an act of liberation.

The Pleasures of Drawing also plays games. It plays formal games with the
parameters of the picture and the transparency of forms, but also games with
what is real and what is imagined. Is what is represented a bird that flies past
or is it a picture of a bird? The conceit is shared with Magritte's paintings of a

canvas before a window and Braque's atelier paintings, with their interpenetrating forms and leitmotif of a bird in flight. Yet in its linear emphasis the work
also exemplifies the concerns of Derrick Greaves. For, whether drawing or
painting, Greaves places a strong emphasis on the animation of line, pictorial
flatness and visual wit.

As Greaves restructured his compositions, he wrestled with how to include
the subject without being too illustrational and how to pare it down without
becoming completely abstract. He considered how a painting might be attention-
grabbing like the boldest sign, yet still keep one engaged like the most sophisticated painting – offering enough, but not too much.

It was not just drawing that changed, so too did the colour. Although there
are works in which subtle silvers and greys set off the form, there was also a
heightening of the colour and a new boldness that suggests another influence:
Vincent van Gogh. In 1967 Greaves went to Provence in southern France with
the photographer, Dave Mindline: 'as a result of my suggestion that every decade

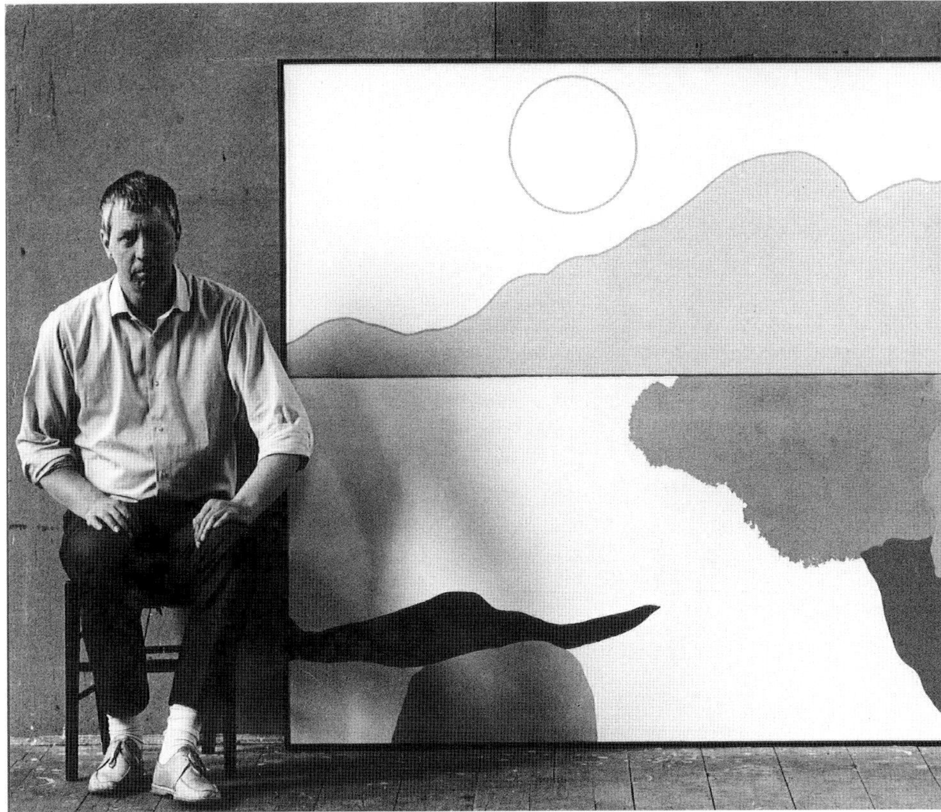

65 Derrick Greaves with
Provence-inspired diptych,
c.1968

or so, I felt I re-understood van Gogh … It was very odd coming to it through
my own work'.[10] The result was a series of large drawings such as *The Sower* (plate
66), some ambitiously composed paintings such as *Diptych – A Window in Arles*
(plate 67) and a portfolio of big screenprints:

> *Along with the celebratory character of van Gogh's Provence work, which was*
> *more highly chromatic than before, I saw him as a kind of self victim … van*
> *Gogh's work was about high chroma but also hysteria, and my own work was*
> *somewhat critical of that. The suffering that he went through was something*
> *that I didn't share, that self martyrdom. I'm more detached and intellectually*
> *removed than that. But I did a lot of drawings around that theme so it must*
> *have had a significance that was heavy enough for me to go on doing it.*[11]

A cluster of exhibitions in the early 1970s – at La Citta Gallery in Italy and, in
London, at Basil Jacobs and the Whitechapel Art Gallery – showcased Greaves's
latest achievements. Praising him as 'a formidably gifted artist who is modern,

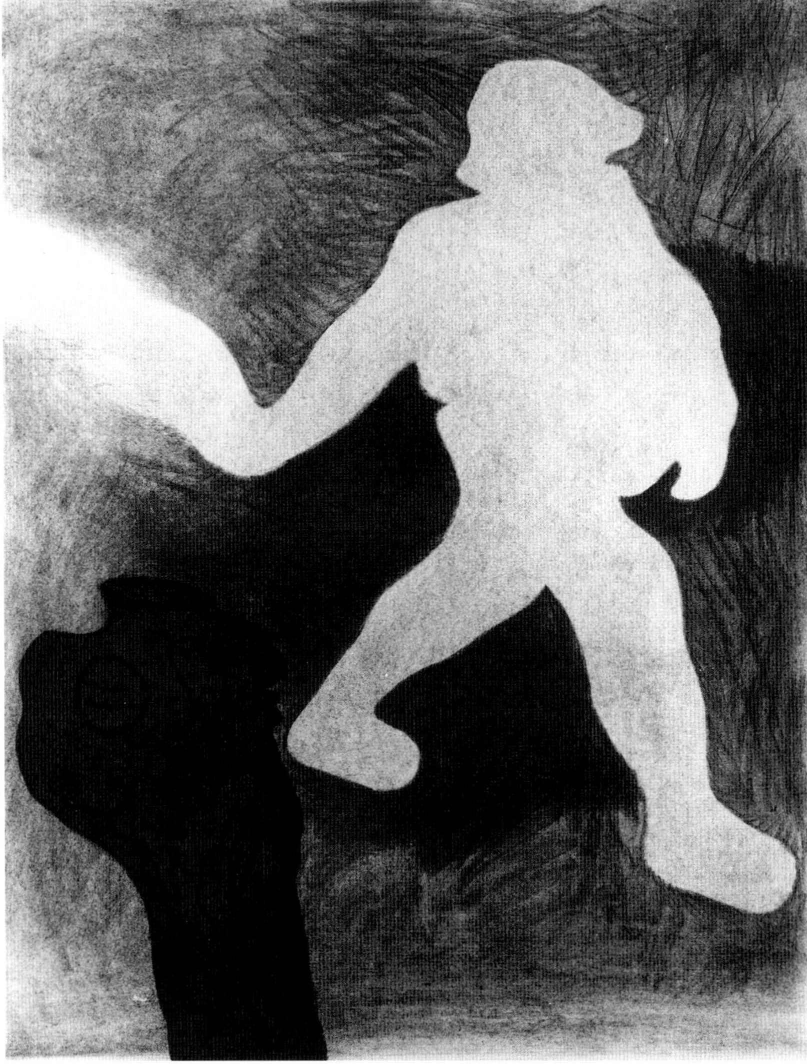

66 *The Sower*, 1967
Charcoal
89 × 76cm (35 × 30in)

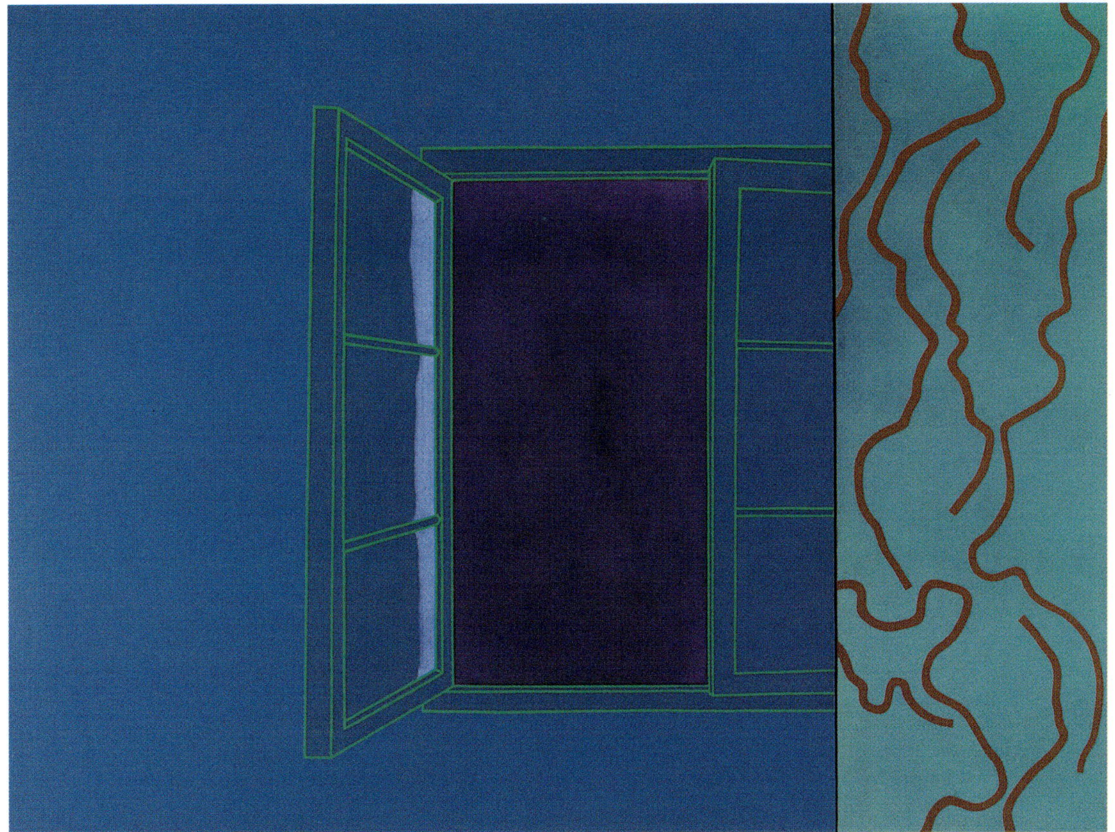

contemporary, strikingly individual ... a master of line and colour', Marina Vaizey
recognised that:

> *for all Greaves's apparent austerity – his economy, his discipline, his precision –
> the effect is rich and resonant, a Western rendering of the virtues of Oriental art ...
> He abstracts from the particular, a single vase, a flower, the outline of the human
> form, the line of the horizon, to produce images which stand for all flowers, all
> peoples, all horizons ... He is obviously one of the most interesting artists at work
> in Britain, and his work is memorable, distinctive and movingly beautiful.*[12]

The following year this success was confirmed by a solo show that was
presented in Belfast and then Dublin, attracting superlative reviews. The *Irish
Herald* declared the exhibition to be 'one of the most important exhibitions by a
modern painter seen in Dublin for some time'[13] and the *Irish Times* wrote of
'someone you simply can not walk away from. He changes your consciousness,
becomes a part of one's private mythology'.[14]

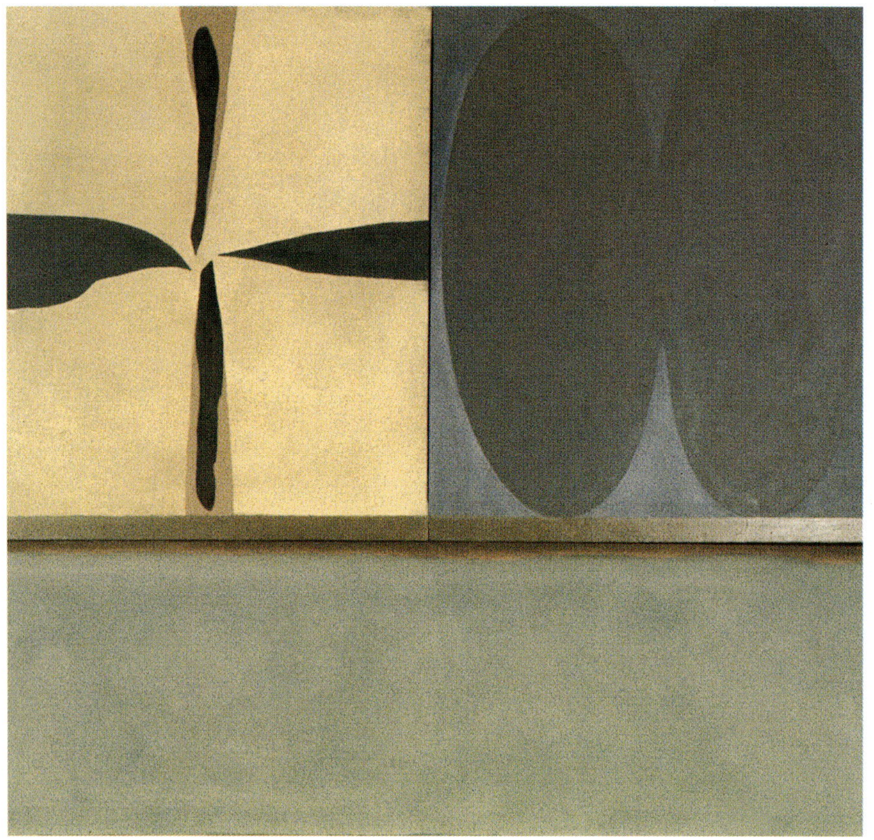

68 *Triptych – Large Grey Still Life,*
*c.*1965
Acrylic on canvas
183 × 183cm (72 × 72in)

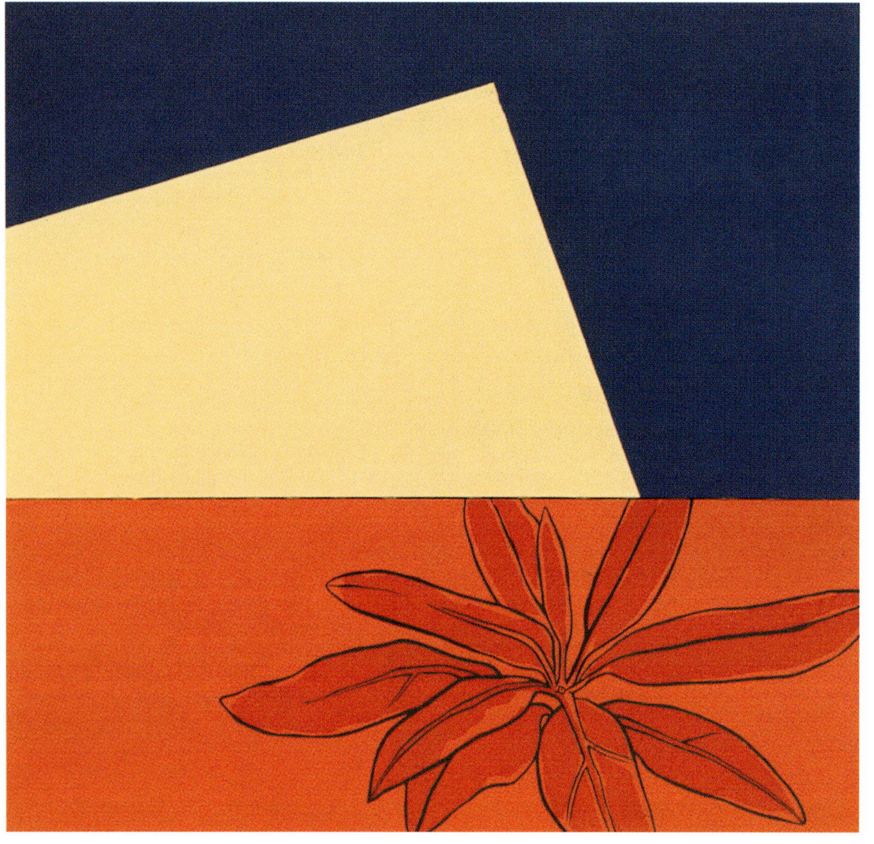

69 *Diptych – Red Leaves, c.*1965
Oil on canvas
139.7 × 144.8cm (55 × 57in)

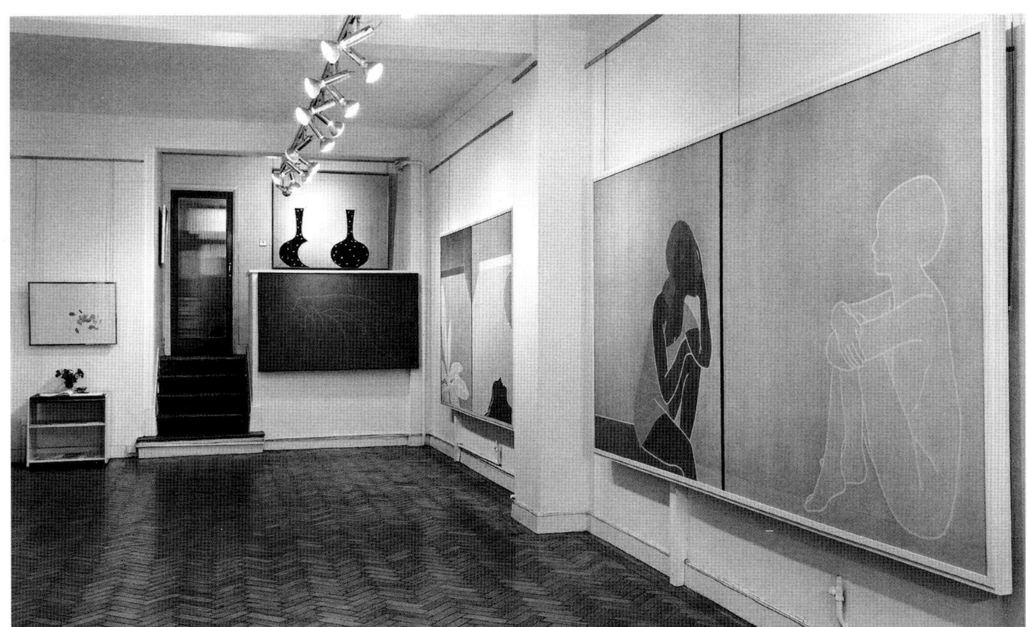

70 Installation, Basil Jacobs, London, 1971

The use of diptychs and triptychs in paintings of the later 1960s and early 1970s allowed Greaves to suggest the passage of time between one image and the next, or to combine incidents in different places brought together for contemplation. In paintings such as *Triptych – Large Grey Still Life* (plate 68), *Diptych – Red Leaves* (plate 69) and *Diptych – Veranda* (plate 71), the effect of this attempt to address a subject from different angles, literally and metaphorically, added a more complex literary or narrative element to the static medium of painting.

However, this was a solution that would ultimately prove dissatisfying for the artist and, although many paintings did employ this format, he later rejected the approach to narrative that had been their *raison d'être*, and he destroyed several of these works. Others he reduced to a single canvas or severely cropped. Their success certainly varied. Sometimes a painting was stronger as a single canvas, rather than a diptych, and the lessons learnt led to a restructuring of these single canvases.

In Praise of the Right Angle (plate 72), for example, was originally a single, large horizontal painting that was effectively a diptych in conception. On the right was a vase with the overlapping form of a flower on a stalk, coming in at a right angle. On the left was the same vase, and filling it was the same flower, no longer attached to a stalk. However, Greaves subsequently felt that this two-part painting was too obvious, cutting it in half and keeping the left-hand section as an independent painting. This radical process of cropping individual canvases and splitting up diptychs and triptychs lessened the literary quality of these paintings, and returned them to the realm of pictorial imagination. Despite their clarity of form, the cropping of these works reinforced their allusiveness. Greaves recently wrote:

> *Editing for me is always there as a decisive part of the process in the studio. The omnipresent anxiety or discontent that I feel as I work is often quickly focused by a casual glance towards canvases that have been set aside for whatever reason. Urgent surgery suggests that by compositional change or cutting the canvas size pictorial life could perhaps be saved by such previously unpremeditated action. Sometimes it works – at least to keep the discontent at a distance. In the end one knows that a bonfire can always 'draw the final line'.*[15]

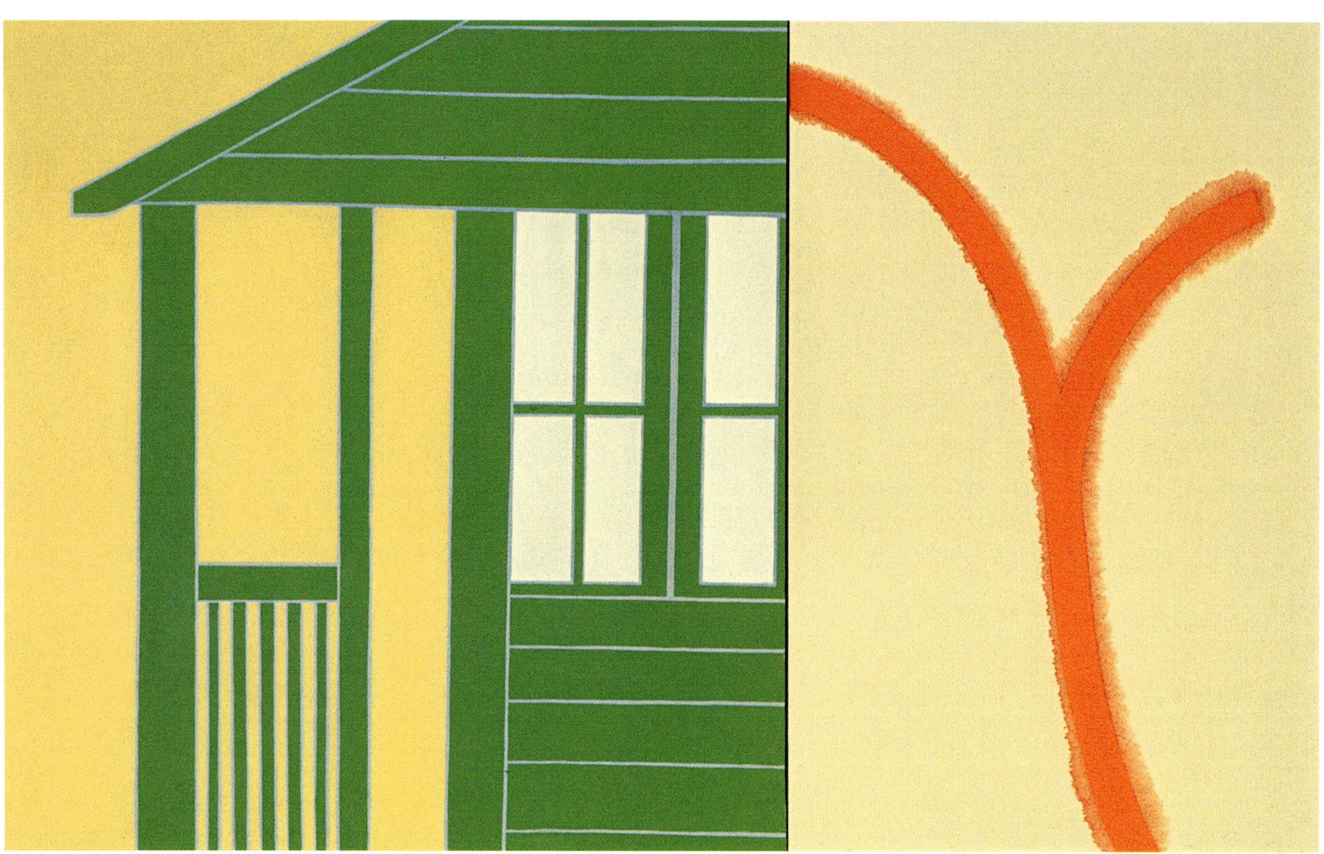

71 *Diptych – Veranda*, 1964–6
Acrylic on poplin
76 × 127cm (30 × 50in)

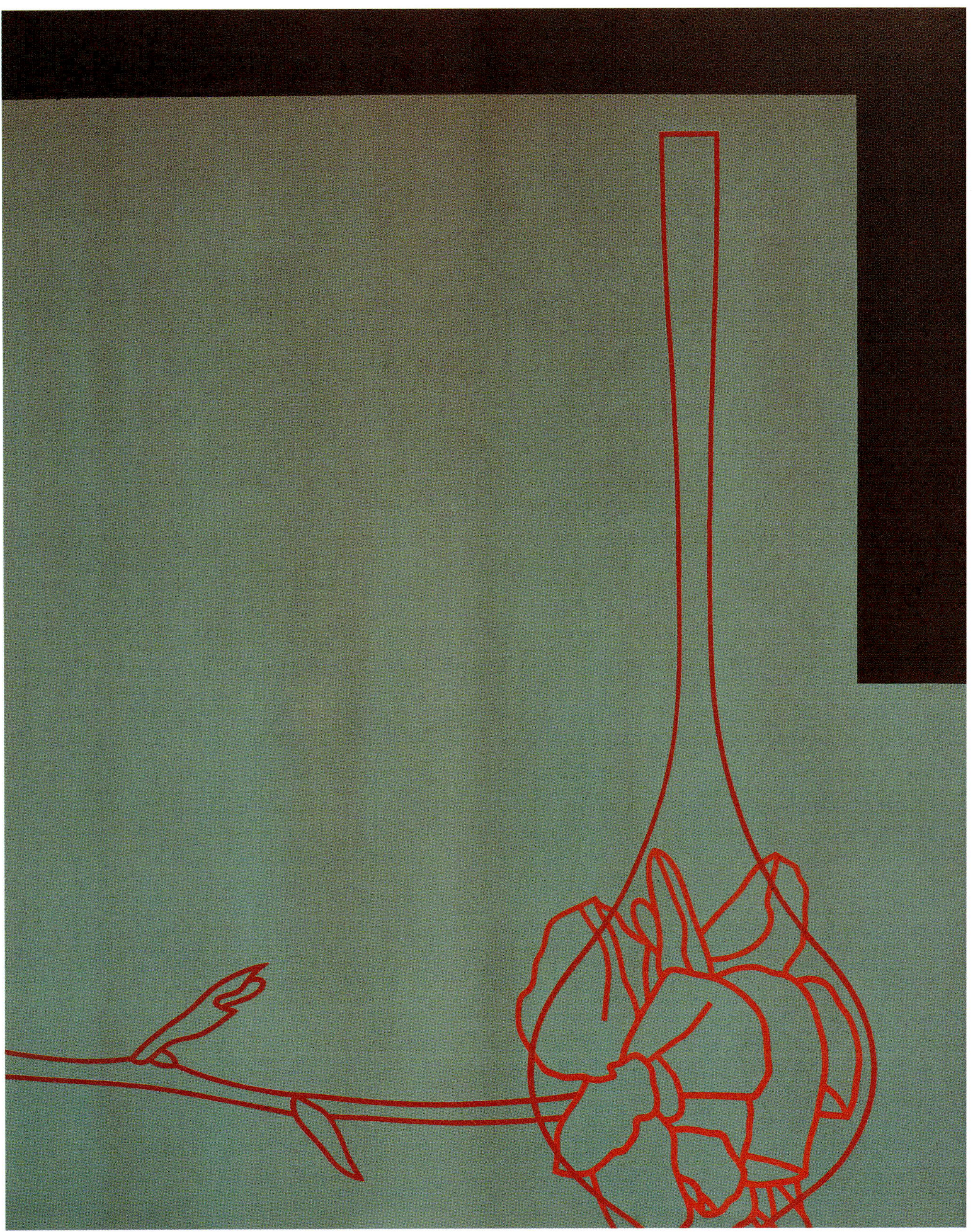

72 *In Praise of the Right Angle*, 1973
Acrylic on canvas
134 × 108cm (52.8 × 42.5in)
Private Collection, London

73 *Shadow of a Bird on a Road*, 1971
Acrylic on canvas
159.5 × 123cm (62.8 × 48.4in)
Private Collection, London

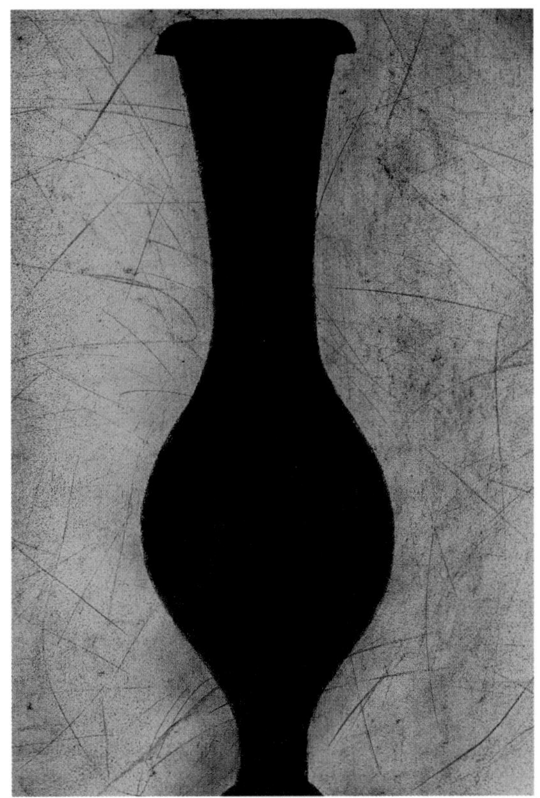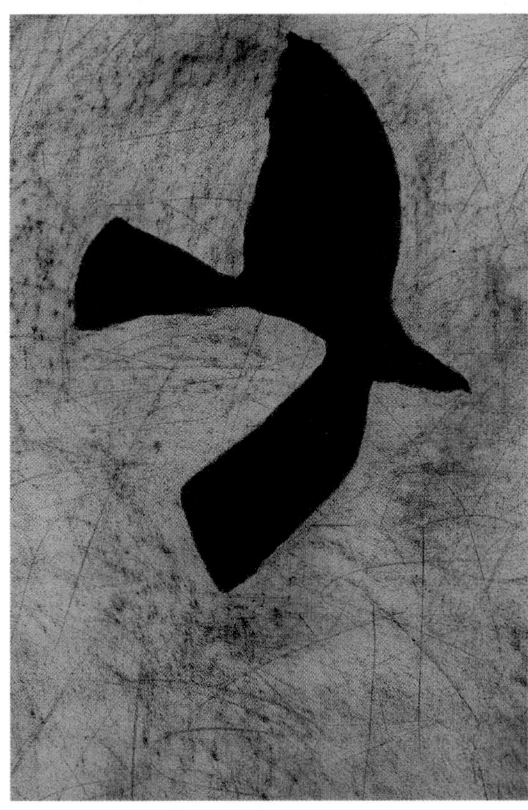

74 *Bird and Vase Diptych*,
1971
Charcoal on paper
92.5 × 59cm (36.4 × 23.2in)

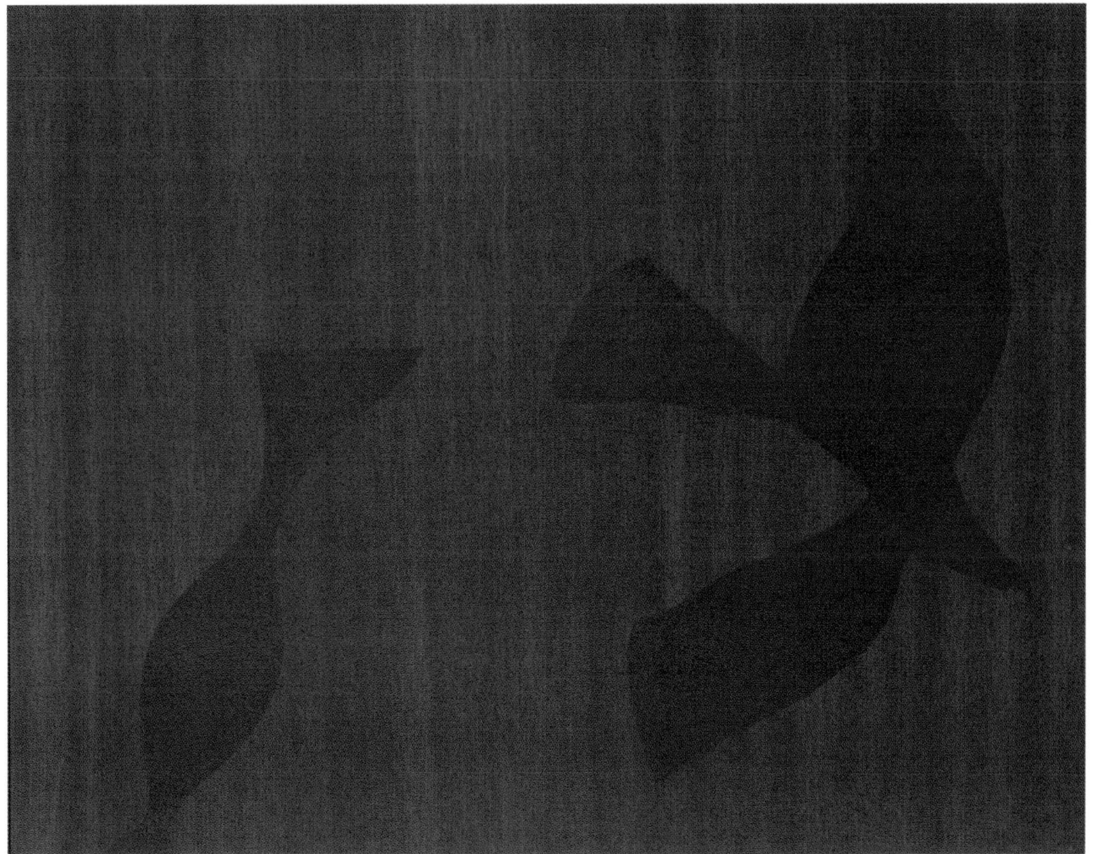

75 *Shadows*, 1971
Acrylic on canvas
74 × 94.5cm (29.1 × 37.2in)
Private Collection, London

Greaves's assault on his own work led to regrettable losses, as well as undoubted improvements. One of the greatest losses is the large painting *Triptych – Bedroom* (plate 61), which was clearly one of his most significant pictures of the 1960s and was illustrated along with work by Patrick Caulfield in *London Magazine* in 1967. It shows three elements – a woman's legs and stilettos, two flowers and a bedside mirror – presented side by side to provide a clear, well-structured composite view of a bedroom.

Meanwhile, *Shadow of a Bird on a Road* (plate 73) was originally a diptych that consisted of one canvas showing the shadow of a bird and a second, almost empty, canvas that created an enlarged sense of space. However, Greaves rejected this emptier canvas. The resulting single canvas is one of Greaves's most beautiful paintings of the period, one whose origins as a diptych perhaps explains the daring composition in which the bird is displaced to one side, a device that gives the painting its great strength.

The limpid fluency of *Shadow of a Bird on a Road* was facilitated by the wateriness of thinned down acrylic, which allowed Greaves to paint 'watercolours' of huge magnitude, perhaps inspired not just by English landscape watercolours but also by the paintings of Helen Frankenthaler, which he admired. Despite the echoes of Braque's birds, the subject was observed on a journey by car from Italy and Switzerland, travelling through the Valle d'Aosta. The sun was high and Greaves noted in a sketchbook: 'everything crystal, what strange luminosities the mountains'.

Related works share these qualities. The drawings of *Bird and Vase Diptych* (plate 74) are concerned with movement and stasis and also with presence and absence. Are we shown a vase and a bird as the title suggests, or merely their shadows? For all the monumentality, what is depicted is a shadow rather than the bird itself and this encourages us to read the lipped vase as similarly lacking in substance. Complicating this is the relative substantiality of the charcoal ground, which has been so worked and scratched into that it has a greater materiality than the things depicted. Braque's bird had been let loose from the confining atelier, its flattened form well illustrating Greaves's rejection of modelling and the illusionistic creation of volume and weight. This would pave the way for the linearity and lightness of his later work with its interpenetration of forms and use of transparency.

Meanwhile, the nocturnal painting *Shadows* (plate 75) combines these two motifs on a single canvas, in which the vase is as flattened and as animate as the

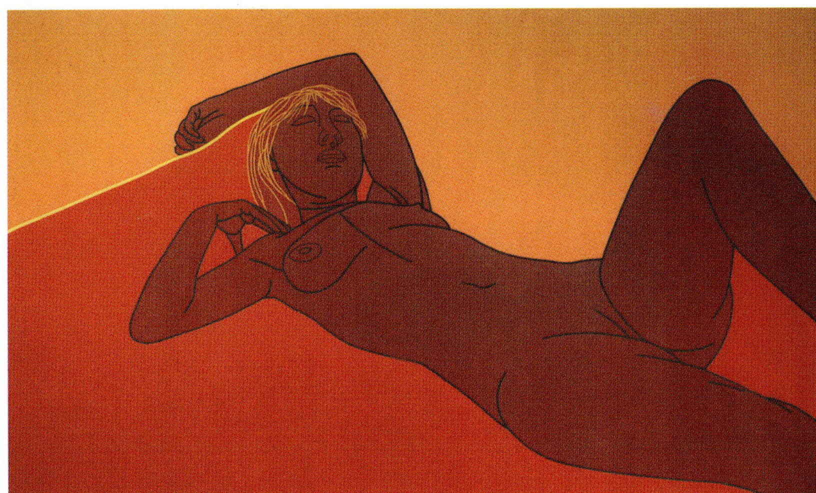

76 *Red Odalisque*, 1972
Acrylic on canvas
122 × 213cm (48 × 84in)
Private Collection, France

bird and tilts drunkenly, perhaps the result of Greaves's use of an epidiascope, which he had begun to use in the late 1960s to project the source drawing at an angle. Here, as in many other works, a shadow has the substantiality of an object.

As Caroline Tisdall recognised in her review of his Whitechapel show of 1973:

There's a predilection for the moment when things in nature change from one state to another; the gust of wind, the shadow of a bird cast on a road, a petal falling. Then there's the range of subjects where the ambiguity is more overt: woman with spider, Pandora, a nervous girl, touches of lesbianism and sleeping figures. All this and Greaves's carefully graphic lines give his work a hint of nostalgia for classicism.[16]

The Whitechapel exhibition also demonstrated a new complexity to Greaves's compositions in which the interstices took on a new prominence. Experimenting with combining canvases, either placed directly together or using the structuring formats of triptych or diptych, allowed Greaves to combine motifs, upset the chromatic scale and draw new attention to the space between figures, objects and settings.

The diptych *In the Garden* (plate 77) is one of Greaves's most successful paintings. If there is a narrative then it is implied, not stated, alluded to rather than explained. But there is no obfuscation, just clarity. On the left an apple tree sapling spikily extends from bottom to top in contrast to the curvaceous figure in the right-hand panel. The subject is reduced to essentials – a twig, a single figure – yet despite the economy, the effect is rich.

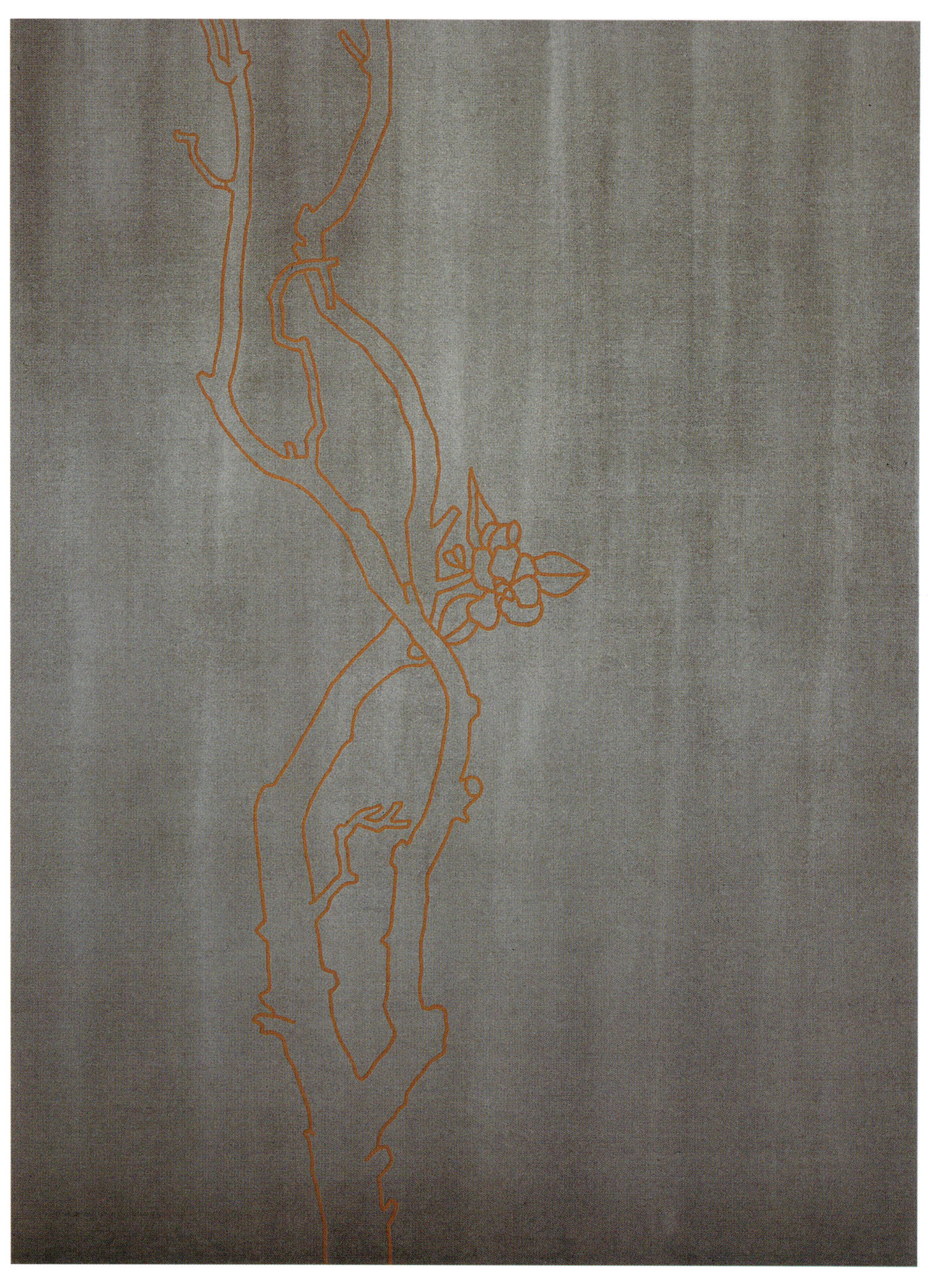

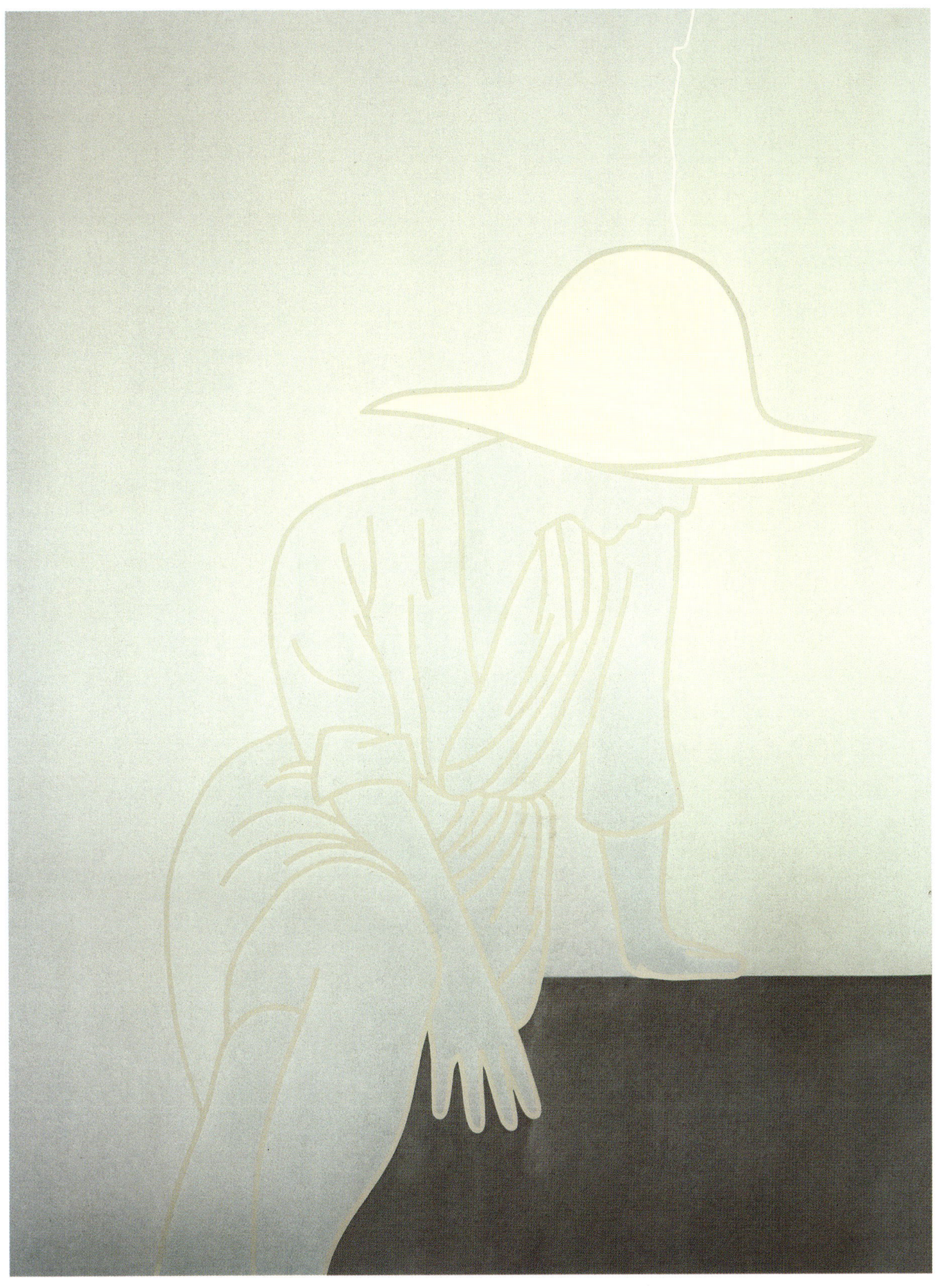

77 *In the Garden*, 1971
Acrylic on canvas
159 × 239cm (62.6 × 94.1in)
Private Collection, London

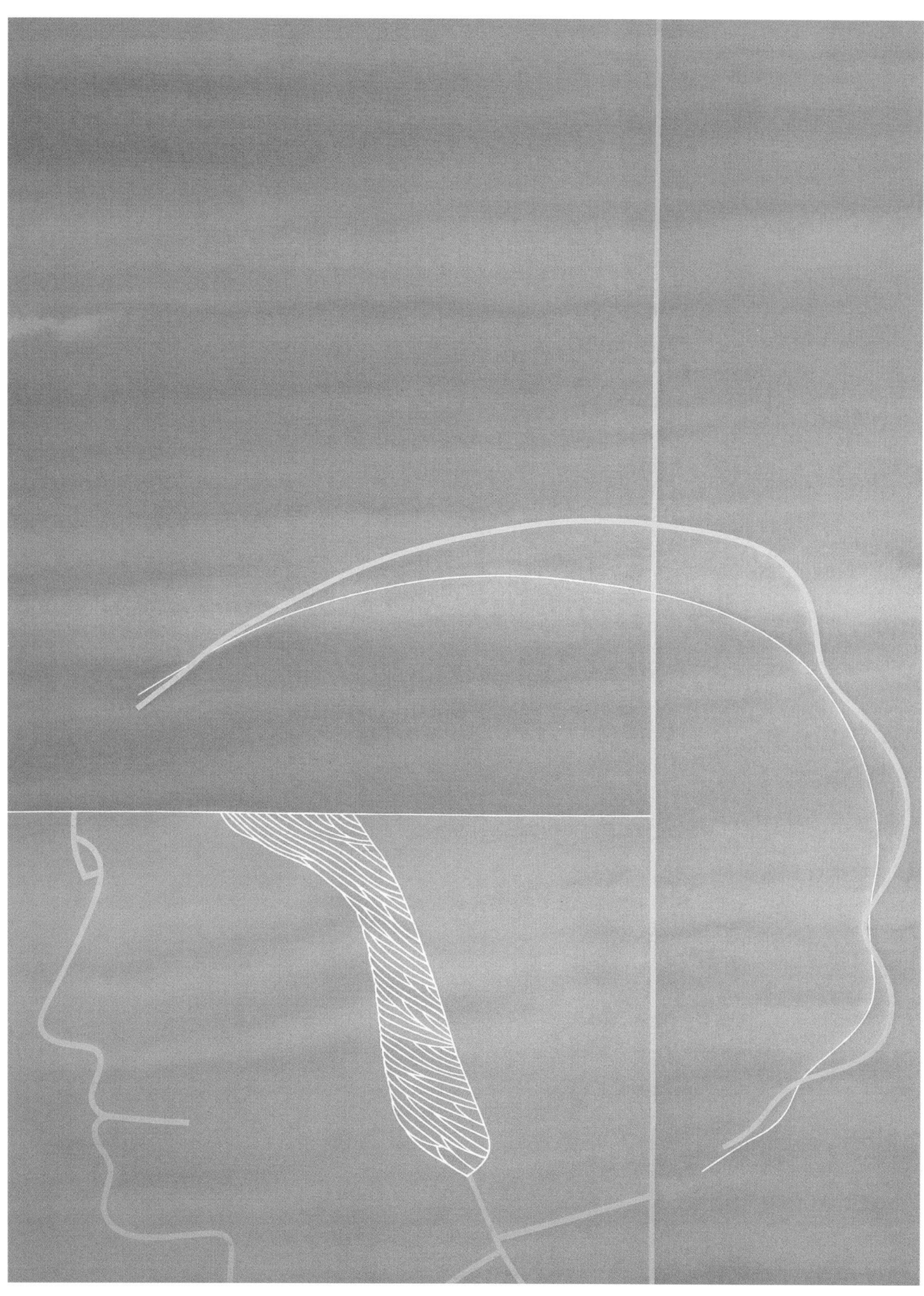

78 *By the Sea (Portrait of Prunella Clough)*, 1972
Acrylic on canvas
159.5 × 118cm (62.8 × 46.5in)
Private Collection, London

Greaves also revealed a new clarity to his portraiture that is especially
evident in a painting of his friend Prunella Clough.[17] *By the Sea (Portrait of Prunella
Clough)* (plate 78) is a large-scale portrait of the artist inspired by the car journeys
that she would take to watch storms over the sea and suggests both the enclosure
of a car and the horizonless expanse of sea blurring into sky.

Meanwhile, *The Jungle* (plate 79) is a triptych in conception if not actuality. One
of Greaves's most powerful large-scale paintings and one that anticipates his later
development, *The Jungle* combines three separate elements into an harmonious
whole. In place of overlapping forms Greaves now separates them out, allowing
each its own autonomy rather than literally imposing a setting onto the figures.
This clarity and the distinctiveness of each form would become leitmotifs of
the paintings that followed. In them Greaves would objectify his subjects, more
and more, to democratically suggest an equivalent importance to each element.

In developing his imagery in this way, Greaves also gives grandeur to his
exploration of sexual dynamics. This had recently found expression in his book

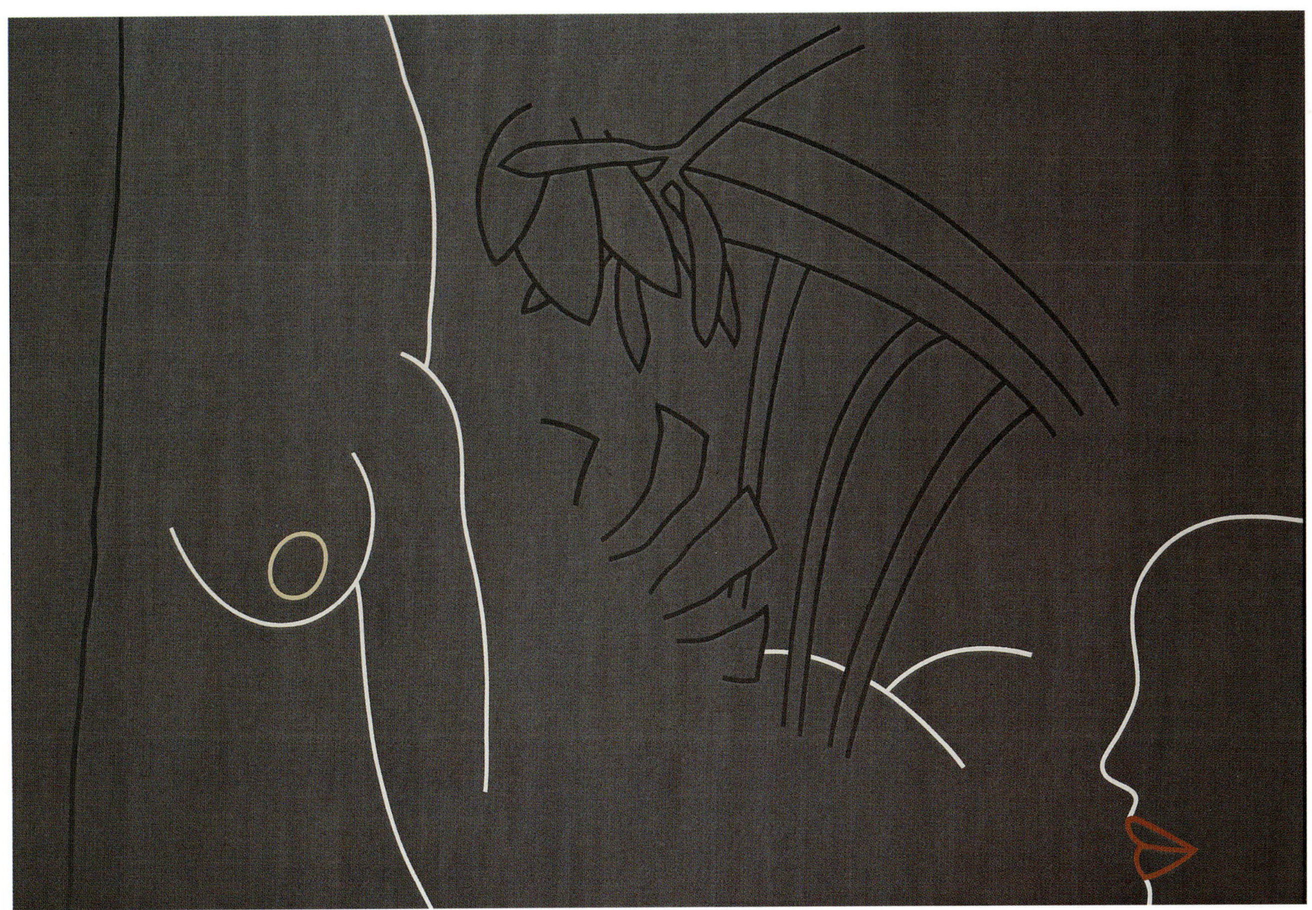

79 *The Jungle*, 1970
Acrylic on canvas
149 × 213cm (58.7 × 83.9in)
Private Collection, London

designs, such as the dust jacket designs for Paul Theroux's novel *Girls at Play* (plate 80) and Rosemary Tonks's *Businessmen as Lovers* (plate 81), in which a married businessman places his hand on the leg of a mini-skirted woman. This is taken further still in the post-coital painting *A Woman and a Man* (plate 83), in which a woman lies back with a cigarette between her fingers as a man walks away from her. Greaves, too, was moving in new directions. New stimuli would lead to another reformulation of his language.

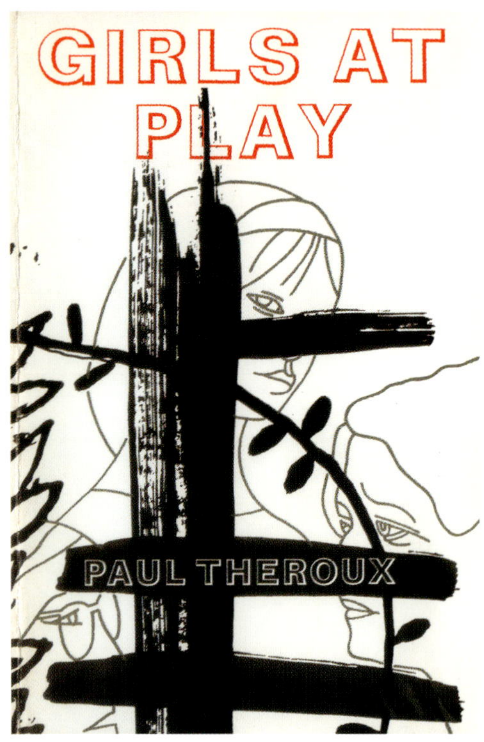

80 Book jacket design
for Paul Theroux, *Girls at
Play,* 1969

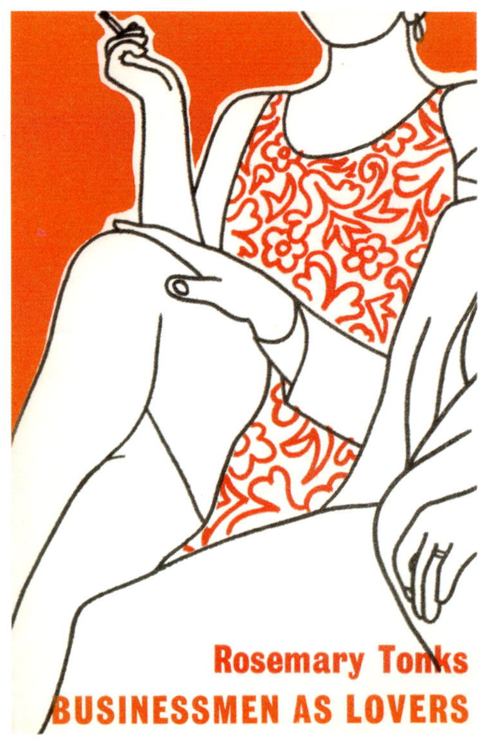

81 Book jacket design
for Rosemary Tonks,
Businessmen as Lovers,
1969

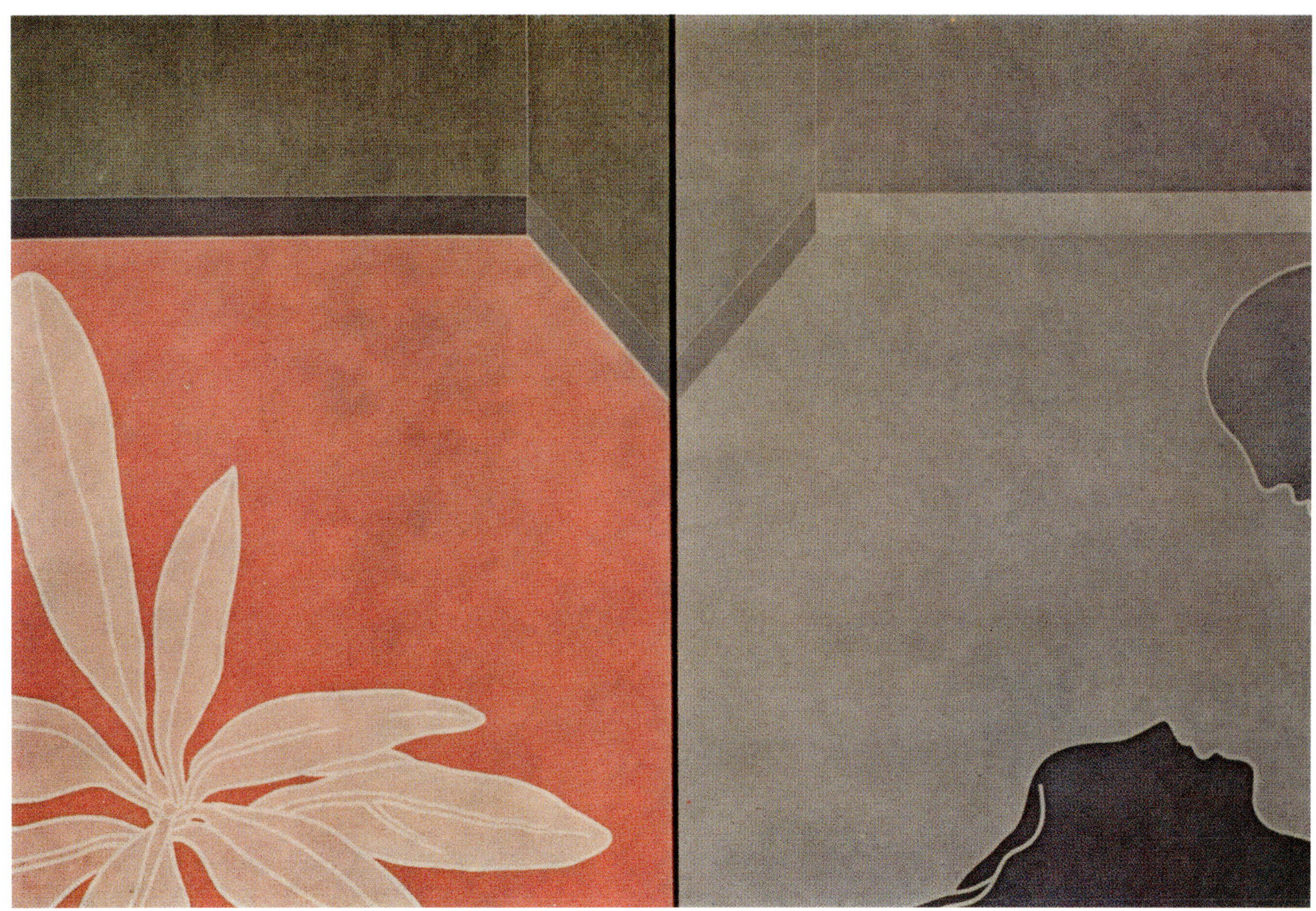

82 *Two Rooms*, 1971
Acrylic and oil on canvas
160 × 233.7cm (63 × 92in)
Private Collection

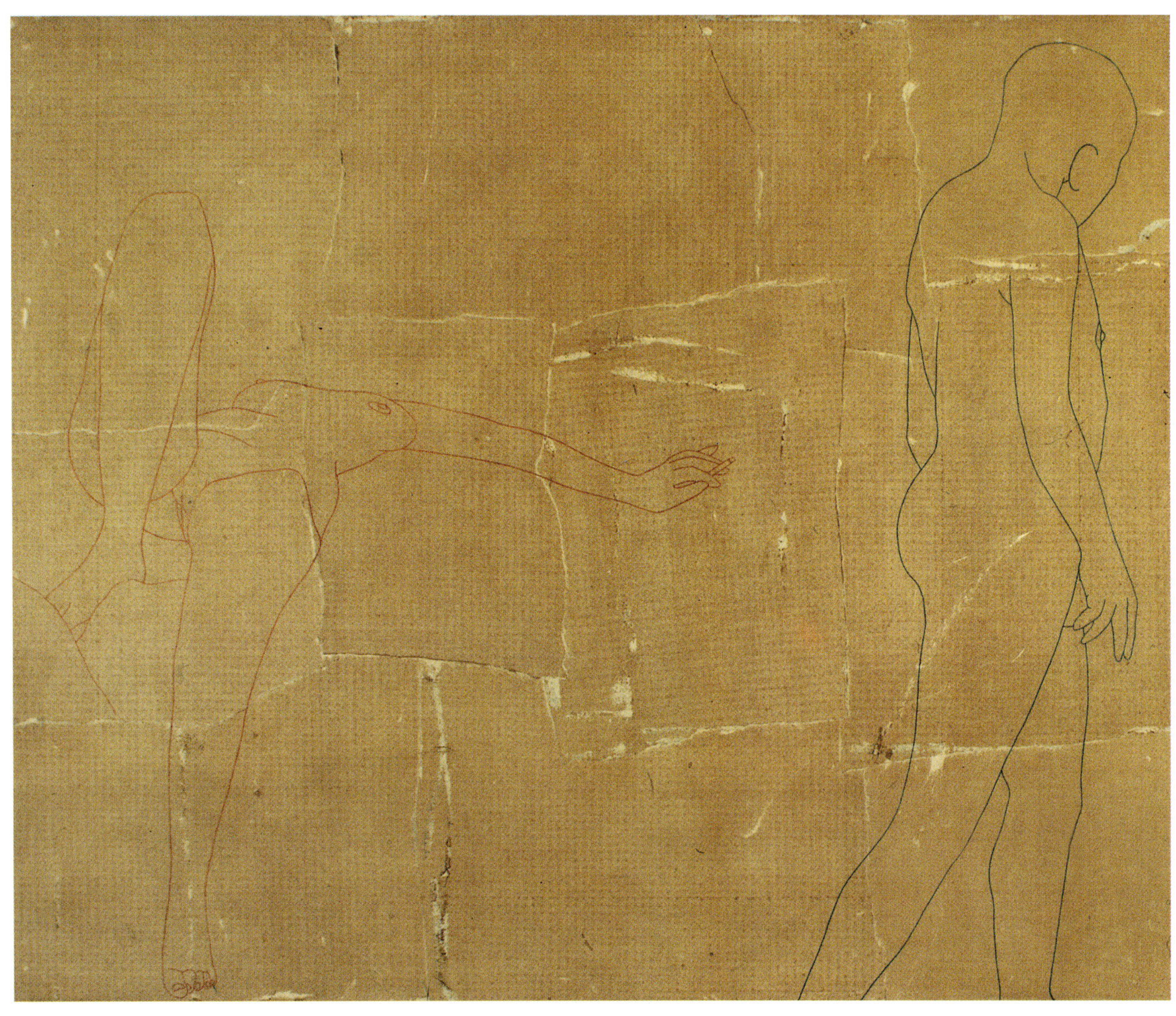

83 *A Woman and a Man*, 1979
Acrylic and collage on canvas
156.2 × 190.5cm (61.5 × 75in)

Notes

1. Mark Glazebrook, 'Pop-Kinky/ Pop-Classical', *London Magazine*, September 1967, vol.7, no.6, pp 62–7.

2. Glazebrook. Op. cit.

3. Glazebrook. Op. cit.

4. Pierre Rouve, 'Derrick Greaves', *Arts Review*, 25 October 1969. Artist's Archive. Rouve argued that 'this is a display of reconciled tensions and practical oppositions: an evidence of inner balance which is in turn a proof of artistic maturity … for once there is an artist who composes his work and whose work helps us compose ourselves … Derrick Greaves makes a brave stand against the devaluation of standards. He does it without any ostentatious din: his aims are stated, not proclaimed … But the truth remains: today, the plea for order is a revolutionary roar.'

5. John Russell (*Sunday Times*, 19 October 1969, Artist's Archive) wrote that 'Greaves is what he always was: a beautiful draughtsman. Added to this is, now, a feeling for the grand slow eye-music of colour-areas left unadorned and most precisely and elegantly set off by fragmented images – a thorn, the shoulder of a pot, a girl's profile. Greaves disdains to push and shout for our attention, but it would be a defective survey of the period that left him out of account.'

6. Bryan Robertson, 'Upstream', *Spectator,* 25 October 1969. Artist's Archive. Robertson wrote that 'the artist has explored for years the idea of a dialogue between occupied and vacant space, between an image and its reflection, or an image reduced to an emblem balanced or disrupted by a complementary form. The paintings have absolute command over their selected terms of reference: the colour is weightless and strong, the use of line increasingly sharp and telling … Greaves is an abstract-symbolist'.

7. Derrick Greaves, unpublished journal entry, undated.

8. Derrick Greaves, unpublished journal entry, undated.

9. Greaves recalls seeing Caulfield's paintings of the early 1960s such as *Ring* and *Portrait of Juan Gris* in the *Young Contemporaries* and *New Generation* exhibitions. He so admired the painting of a ring that he tried to buy it, but by the time he had the money together it had been bought by another artist. Derrick Greaves, conversation with James Hyman, 23 December 2002.

10. Derrick Greaves, interview with James Hyman, 14 April 2006.

11. Derrick Greaves, interview with James Hyman, 14 April 2006.

12. Marina Vaizey, 'Derrick Greaves', *Art International*, 1971. Artist's Archive.

13. P.F. Byrne, 'Outstanding works by a modern painter', *Irish Herald*, 13 October 1972. Artist's Archive.

14. Harriet Cooke, 'Derrick Greaves paintings', *Irish Times*, 28 September 1972. Artist's Archive. This was a review of the show in Belfast prior to its staging in Dublin.

15. Derrick Greaves, undated text, June 2006.

16. Caroline Tisdall, review, 1973. Artist's Archive.

17. Greaves and Clough first met in the 1950s, but Greaves already knew of her work before going to study at the Royal College, probably through reproductions in *Picture Post* or *Penguin New Writing*. Greaves recalls she was reticent about expressing her views but decisive on committees: 'She had very precise opinions … The kindest possible person with people in hospital, bereaved, very, very supportive in the quietest possible way … But also possessing a very sharp, very critical edge.'

6. Precise Ambiguity

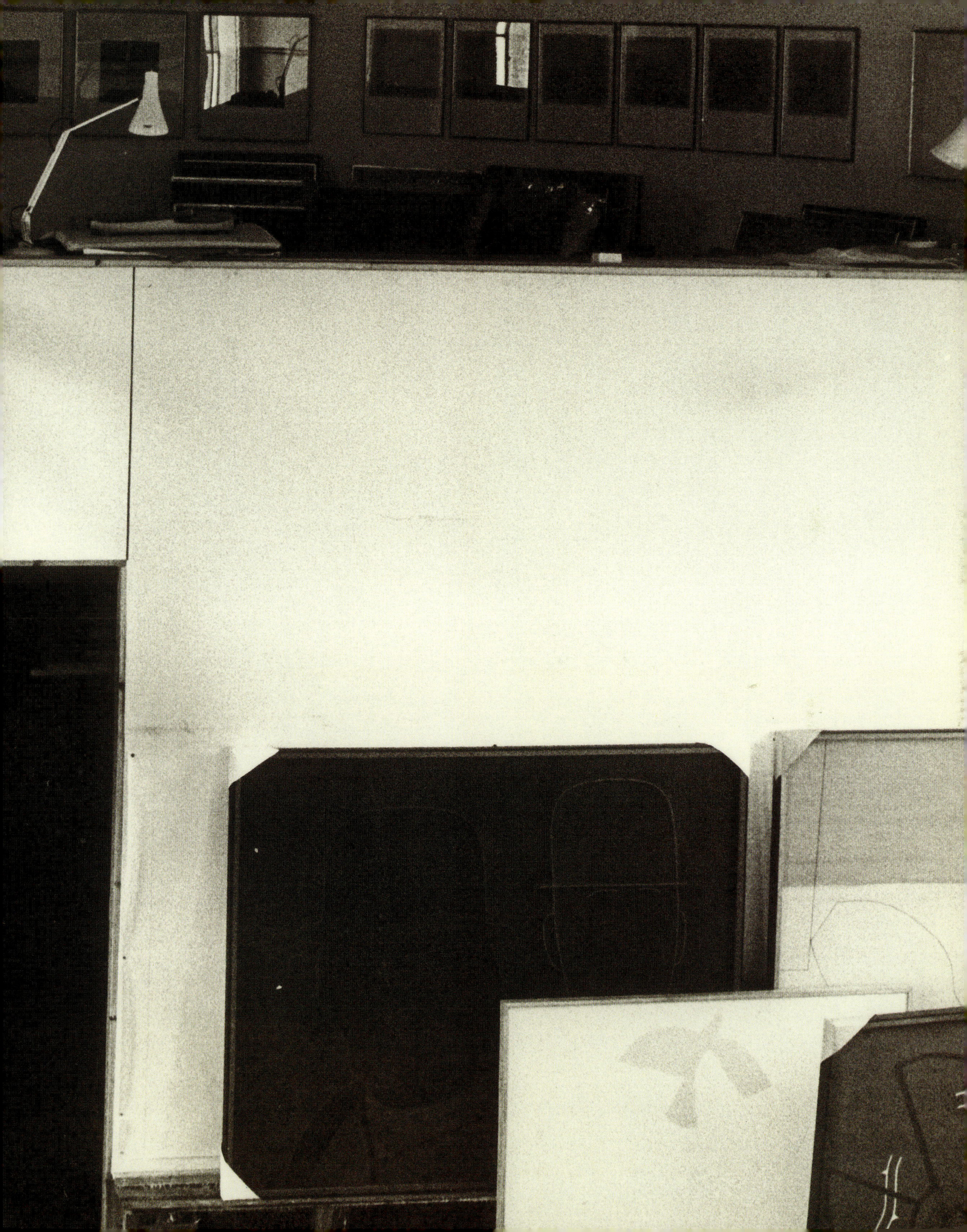

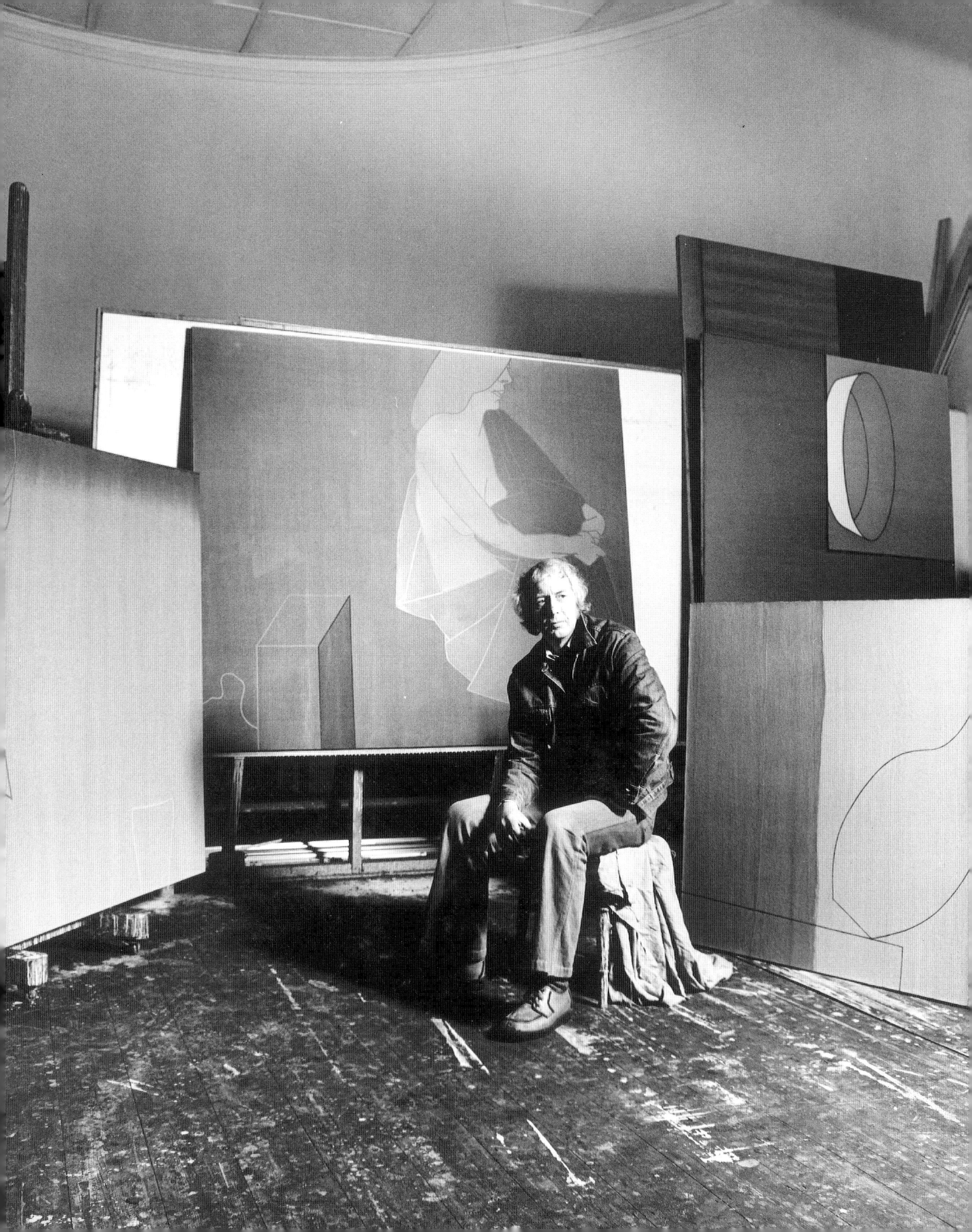

6. Precise Ambiguity: The 1970s and 1980s

Each painting has a particular logic or lyricism which declares itself during the process of painting only gradually. It is so easy to damage and thus lose the life or heart of the image by misunderstanding this slowly unmasking and uncompromising logic – which may be / is peculiar and particular to the image.

Derrick Greaves, undated[1]

Having pared down his vocabulary, Greaves set about enriching his imagery. The iconographic complexity increased in two new ways: first, through the inclusion of words and then through the fortuitous adoption of collage, not just in works on paper, but in large-scale canvases.

Restructuring his language allowed Greaves to incorporate words in order to introduce a narrative element into strongly formal compositions. At a time when even figurative artists adopted a Modernist rhetoric which rejected narrative or storytelling – most famously and articulately in the interviews given by Francis Bacon – Greaves's sardonic response was to introduce actual words and narratives to accompany highly pared-down images. Greaves had already written narratives in his notebooks and in several paintings of the 1970s and 1980s he incorporated pre-existing words, phrases, sentences and even stories.

One of the first of these word paintings is *Ladder* of 1976 (plate 86), in which a ladder in the centre of the picture is accompanied by the words 'sudden fierce rain silences the birds'. The disrupted image is made even more disjointed by the staccato words. Just as collaborating with Edward Middleditch on *The Four Seasons* mural (plate 48) had taken Greaves in new directions, so too did the chance to work creatively with the poet Roy Fisher. The 'concrete poets' were not part of Greaves's social circle, but this was a fruitful collaboration. The two men were introduced by Ian Tyson of the Tetrad Press and initially Fisher suggested a dialogue by post in which the poet would send a line and Greaves an image to produce a series of works. Fisher's first missive was: 'We are settling in among

Previous page:
84 Derrick Greaves in his Woburn studio, late1970s

Facing page:
85 Derrick Greaves in his Woburn studio, 1970s

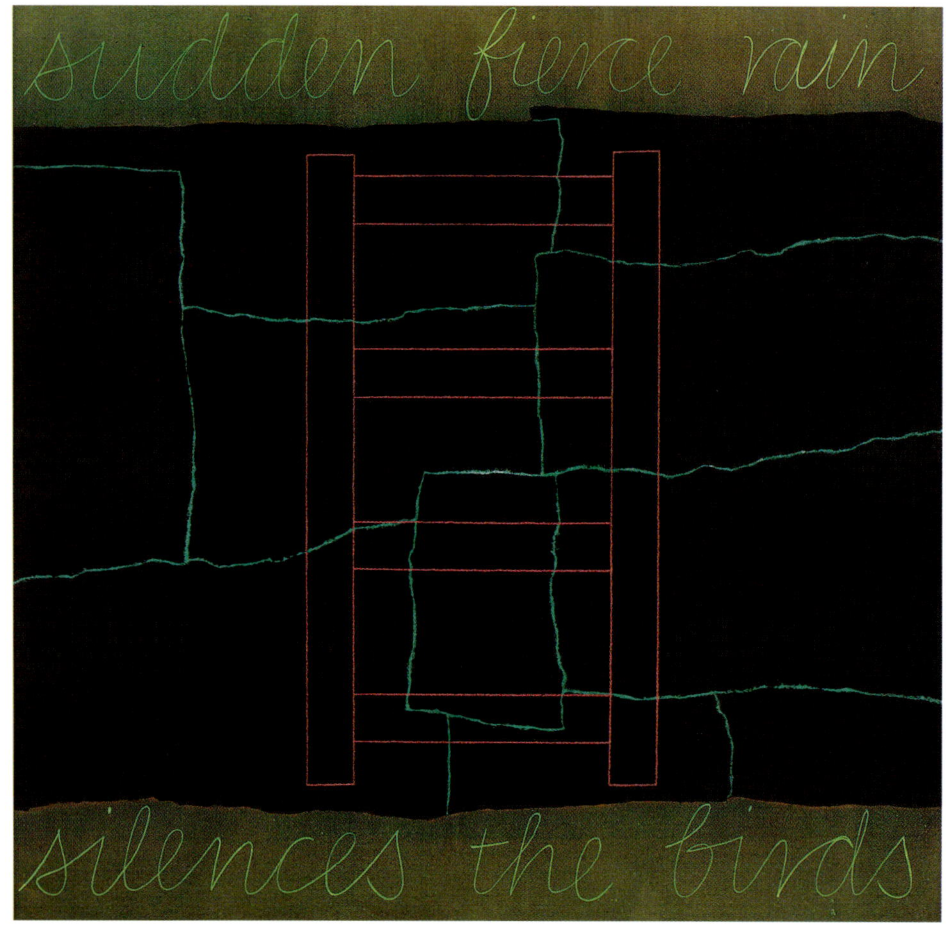

86 *Ladder*, 1976
Acrylic and collage on canvas
119.4 × 124.5cm (47 × 49in)
Private Collection

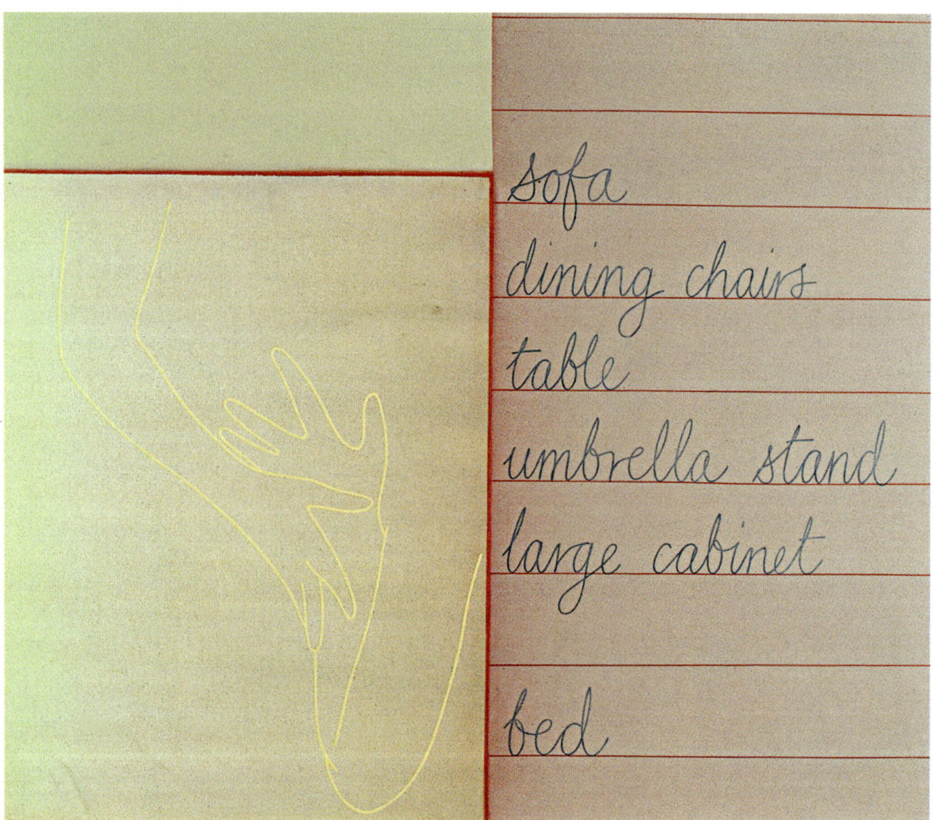

87 *Word Painting II*, 1976
Acrylic on canvas
101.6 × 142.2cm (40 × 56in)

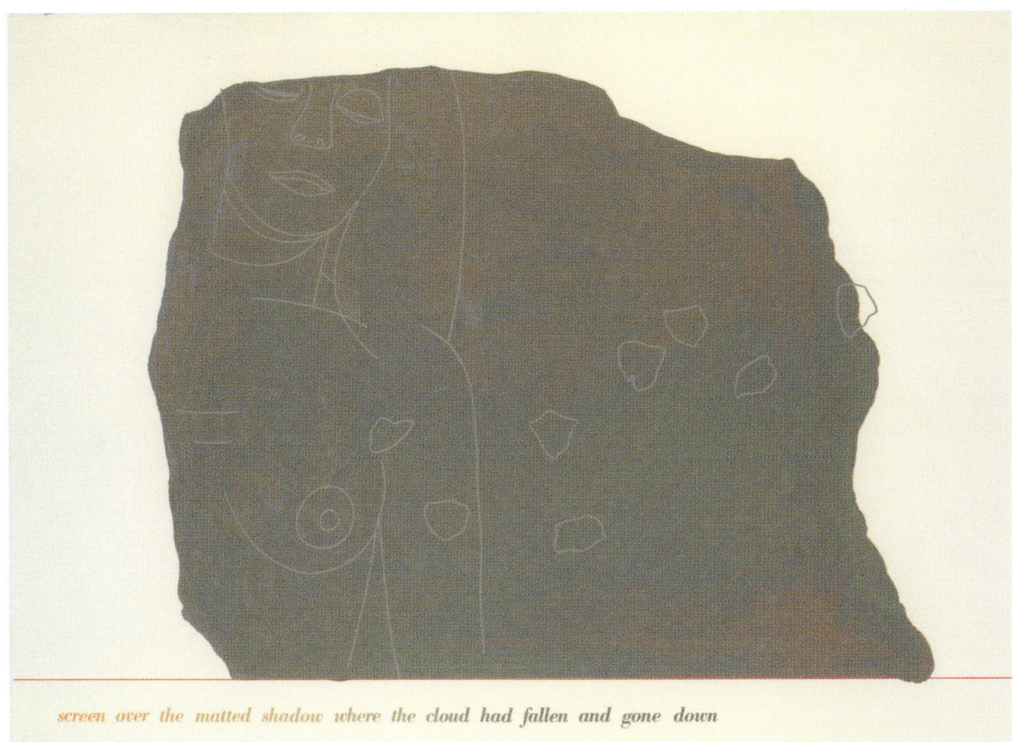

88 *Also* (from a set of seven
screenprints), 1977
Screenprint on paper
47 × 65cm (18.5 × 25.6in)

the stacks'. However, the correspondence foundered and a new way of working
was devised. The idea was for a series of prints with an accompanying poem,
entitled *Also* (plate 88), which when exhibited in a line around a small room would
be intimate and decoratively continuous, in that the poem would go round and
round, seemingly eating its own tail.

As with the earlier mural, Greaves again improvised as part of the creative
process. Sharing with Fisher a love of piano-jazz – Fisher is also a pianist –
Greaves worked with the printer Chris Prater to make jazz-like improvisations,
moving from colour to colour in a spontaneous way. The prints marked a significant re-engagement with the medium, anticipating the centrality it would later
assume, and led to the creation of several paintings that prominently include
lines of text.

Words act in different ways in these paintings. One such painting, *Word
Painting I* (1976), contrasts an idyllic holiday view of sailing boats with the
mundane realities of a shopping list: 'onions, wine, sausage, coffee, cheese'.
Another, *Word Painting II* (plate 87), shows crossed arms and inventorises house-
hold furniture: 'sofa, dining chairs, table, umbrella stand, large cabinet, bed'.

89 *Narrative Painting I*, 1978
Acrylic on canvas
156 × 191cm (61.5 × 75in)

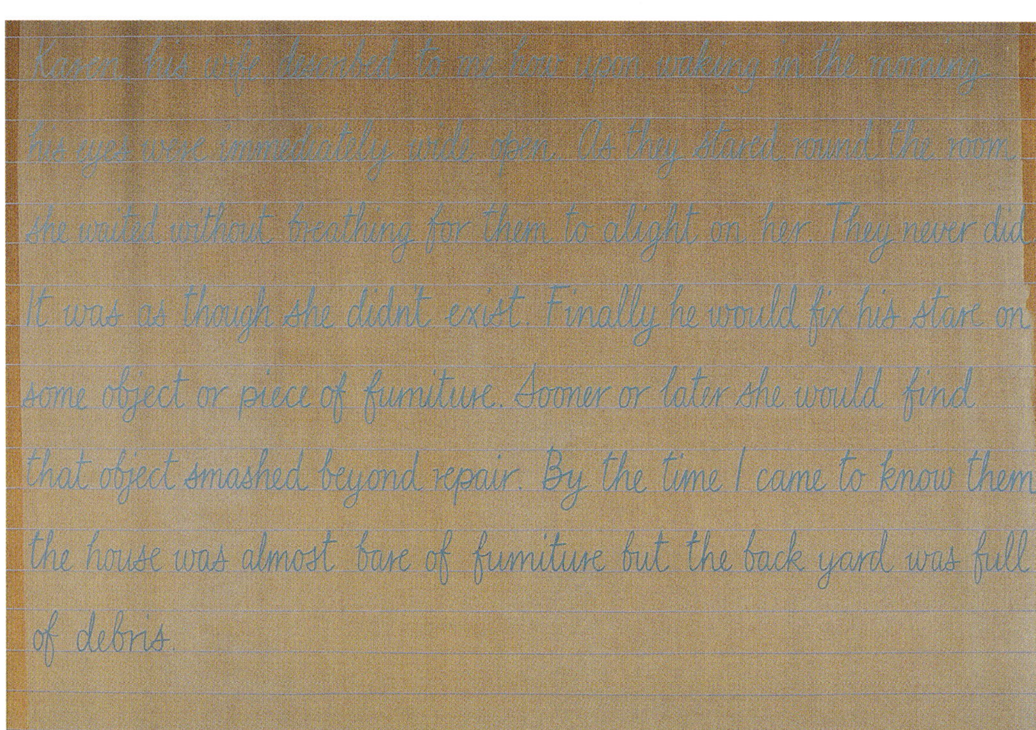

90 *Narrative Painting II*
(Karen his wife), 1978
Acrylic on canvas
121.92 × 182.88cm (48 × 72in)

Other paintings are entirely word based, a witty riposte to a conversation in which the artist Jo Tilson had argued that it was no longer possible to do narrative painting. In *Narrative Painting I* (plate 89) and *Narrative Painting II (Karen his wife)* (plate 90) lines of words fill the entire picture surface with a short story.

Collage was the other major development. In 1975, there was a flood at Greaves's studio in a converted chapel in Woburn. Water pipes burst and for four days, while the artist was away, water poured down the walls. The mezzanine was flooded, destroying five years of prints (which the artist had been holding back for a show), as well as drawings and watercolours by friends, and much of his library, although the paintings on the floor below were largely unscathed. When Greaves returned, the wallpaper was peeling from the walls. After the shock of the devastation, he realised that the lining paper might be salvageable. Covering some old paintings in fragments of this paper, Greaves embarked on a series of drawings on a scale he had never previously attempted.

The informality of the collage and its apparent randomness set up a fruitful tension with the formality of the drawn line. The result would have implications not only for Greaves's practice as a draughtsman but also as a painter: 'I would draw whole figures life size – always an ambition. By drawing across the torn areas I became aware of the inner formal dialogues emerging between the accidentally informal ground and the imposed more formal drawing. Because of this stimulating and surprising inner life the drawing was able to be firmer, far less figuratively descriptive.'[2]

Greaves developed a new diagrammatic way of drawing that was informal and chancy. The ground allowed a new schematic way of working that set up a dialogue between this ground and the figure. This is especially evident in the way that this took Greaves's still-life paintings in a new direction. The image of a flower and a vase is a recurring motif in Greaves's work, from prints to drawings to vast canvases. Through such images one can trace Greaves's preoccupations from the Braque-ian concerns of the early 1960s and the Matissean refinement of the mid 1960s, through to the increasingly heraldic imagery of later years, which at times has the emblematic quality of a florist's sign. Indeed, by the mid 1970s these flower paintings were often extremely decorative, something Greaves tempered in two ways: iconographically through the introduction of a political dimension and the incorporation of more violent ingredients such as a knife, and formally through the creation of collage grounds whose active presence provided a new tension.

The tension, created by the coexistence of different languages, is even more overt in large figurative works of the later 1970s, such as *Entering a Room with Difficulty* (plate 91), *Confidences or The Introduction of Geometry* (plate 92) and *The Actress Entertained* (plate 94). The combining of different types of line also prefigures the way in which recent works have allowed for the coexistence of different visual languages with individual elements rendered in distinct and separate styles.

The results of this new direction were presented in a powerful exhibition at Fischer Fine Art in 1980. Including 25 'collage drawings', all of which had minimum dimensions of around 3ft (1m) and rose to as much as 8ft (2.5m), these were 'drawings' on an epic scale that used a canvas rather than paper ground. With respect to the role given to line, the classification as 'collage drawings' was wholly appropriate, but given that they are on canvas the term 'collage paintings' perhaps better reflects the forceful presence and scale of works such as *An Eclipse of Childhood* (plate 93).

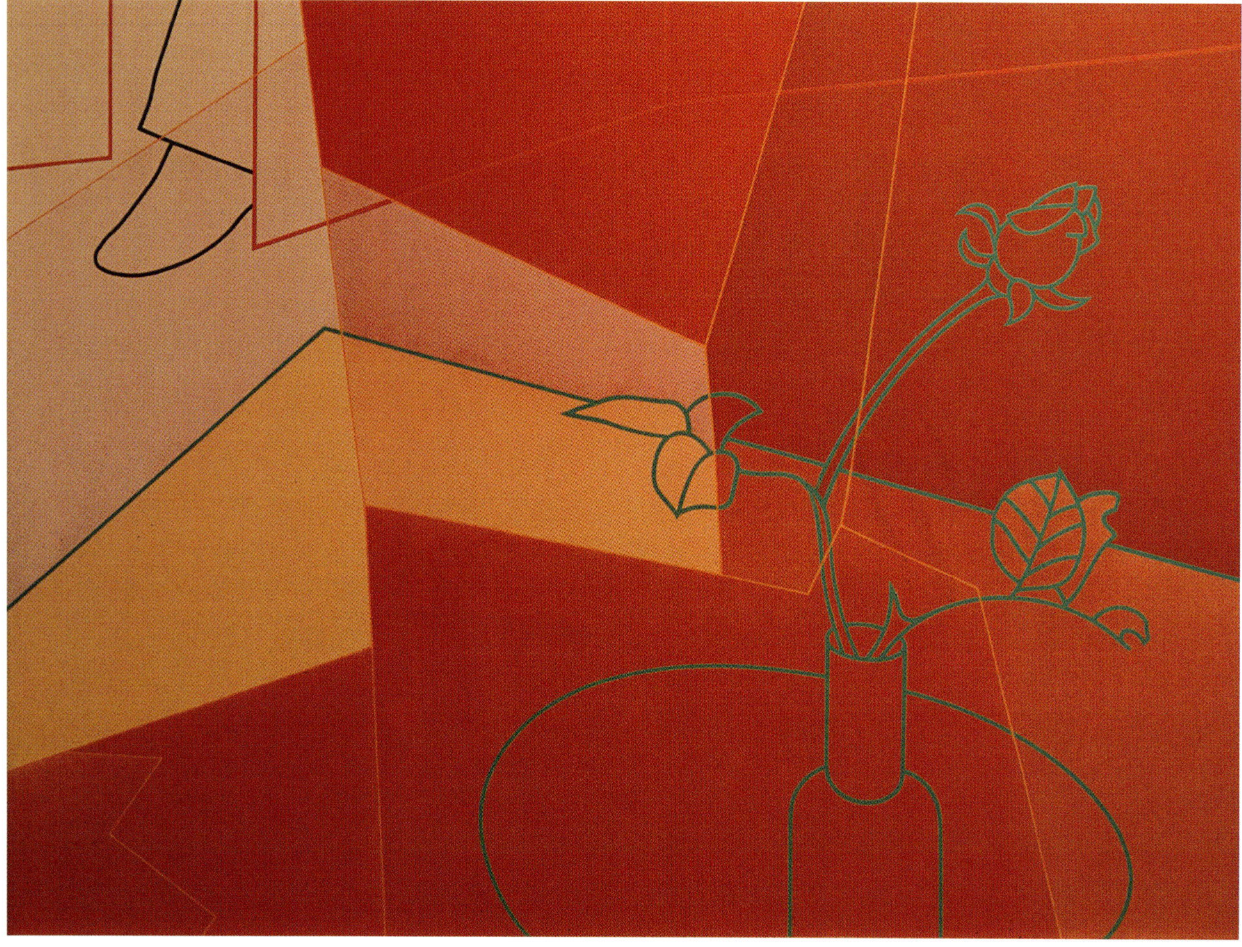

91 *Entering a Room with Difficulty*, 1979
Acrylic on canvas
137.2 × 181.2cm (54 × 71.3in)
Norfolk Museums Services (Norwich Castle Museum)

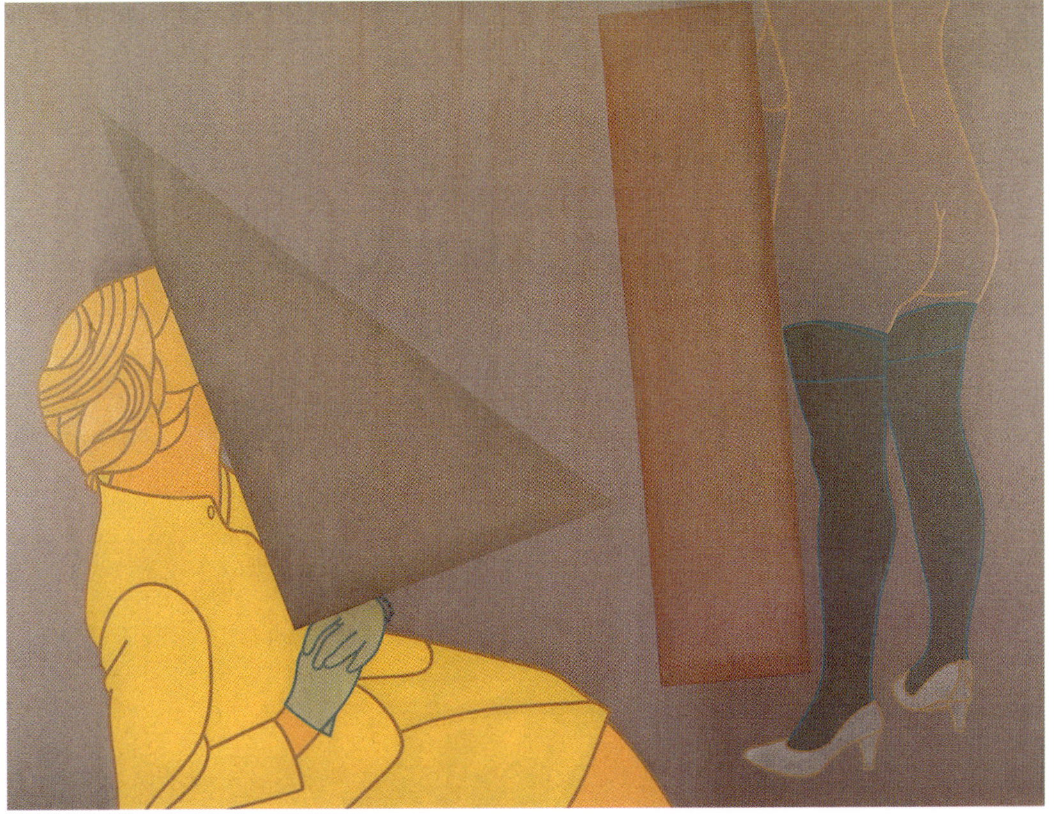

92 *Confidences or The Introduction of Geometry*, 1979
Acrylic and collage on canvas
158.8 × 213.4cm (62.5 × 84in)

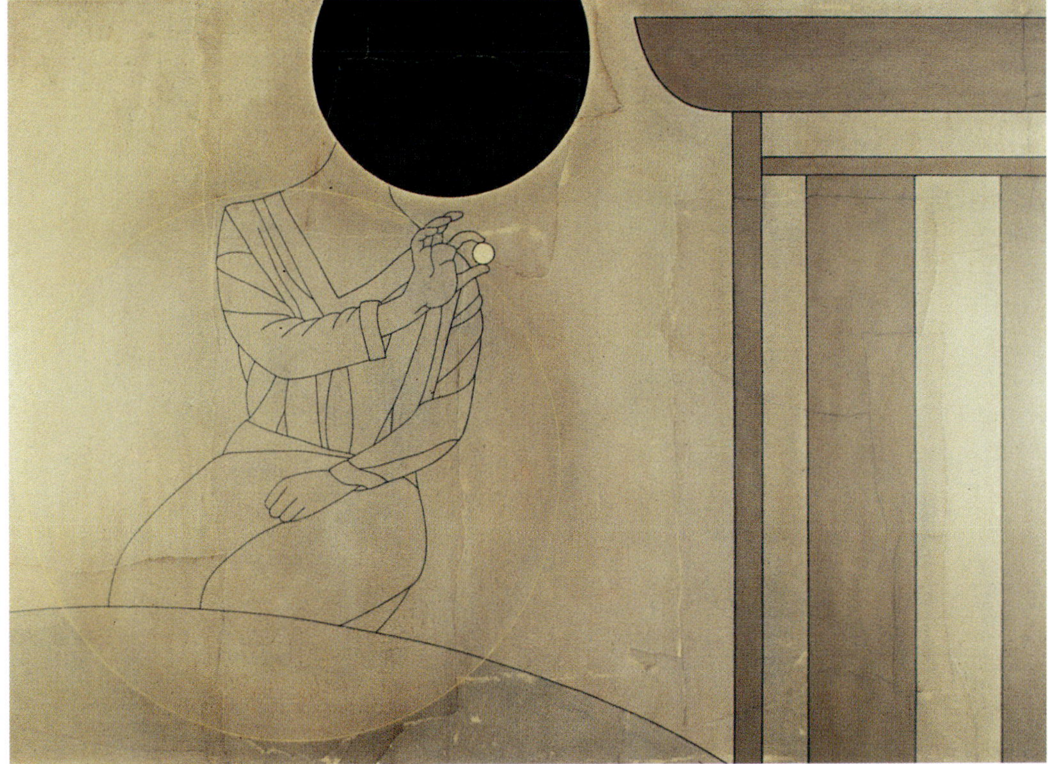

93 *An Eclipse of Childhood*, 1979
Acrylic and collage on canvas
158.8 × 241.3cm (62.5 × 95.8in)
Private Collection

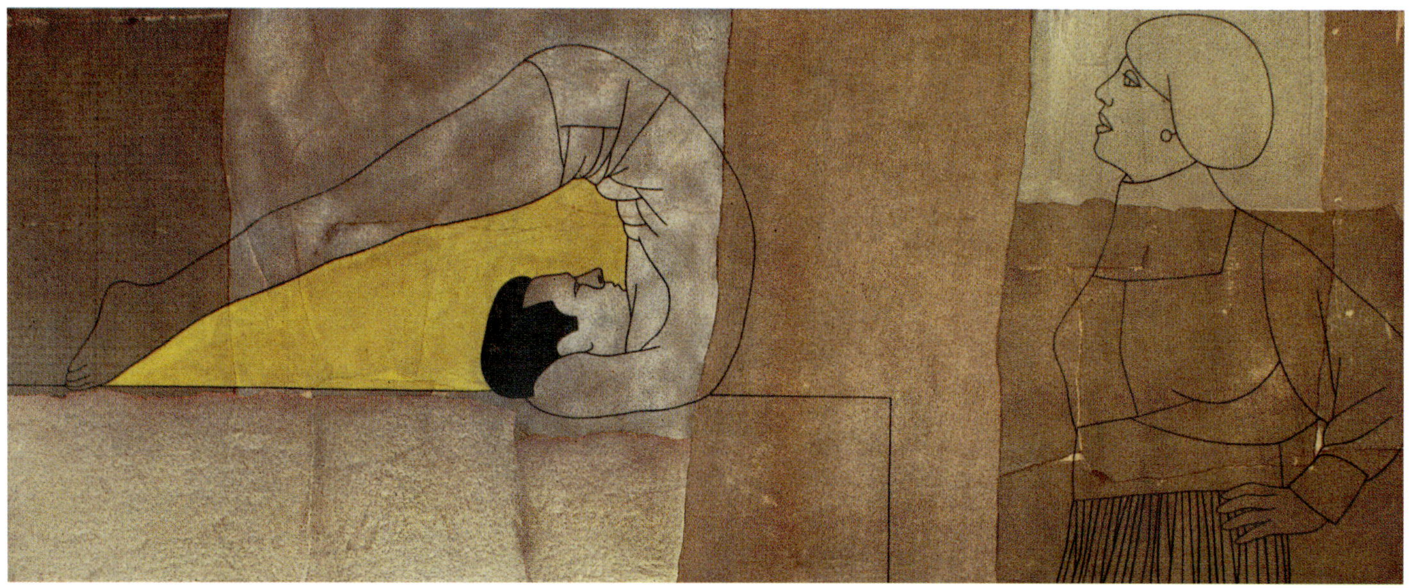

94 *The Actress Entertained*, 1979
Acrylic and collage on canvas
93 × 227cm (36.6 × 89.4in)

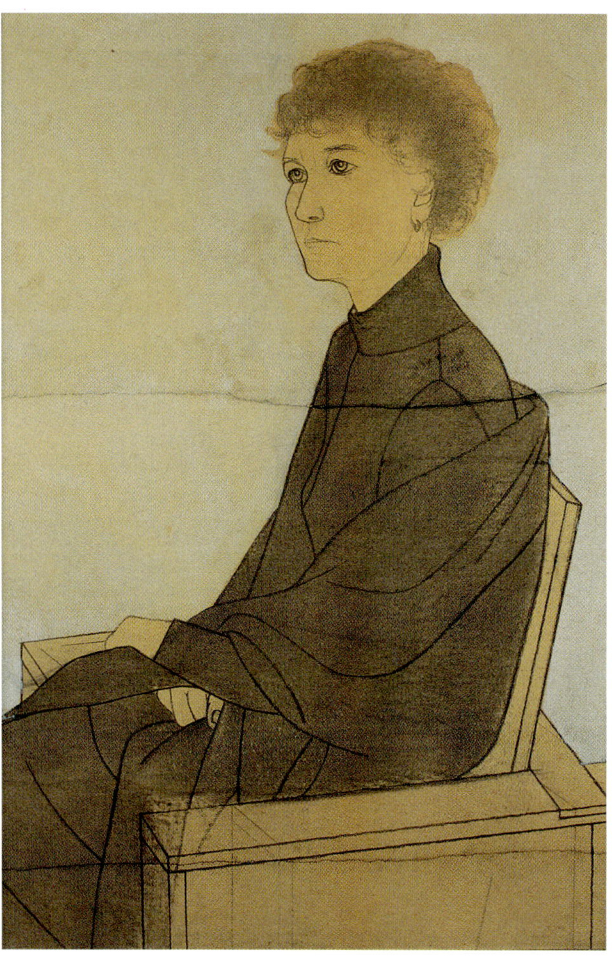

95 *Margaret Greaves*, 1977
Charcoal, pastel and collage
on canvas
101.5 × 70cm (40 × 27.6in)
Private Collection

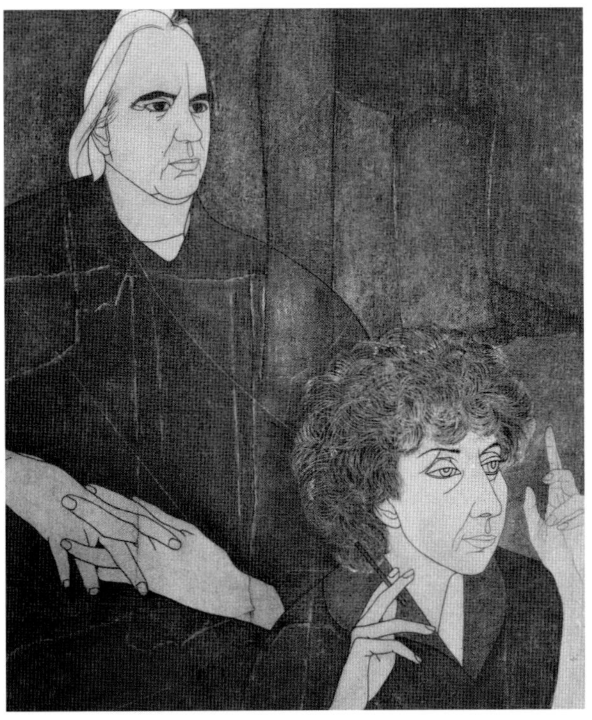

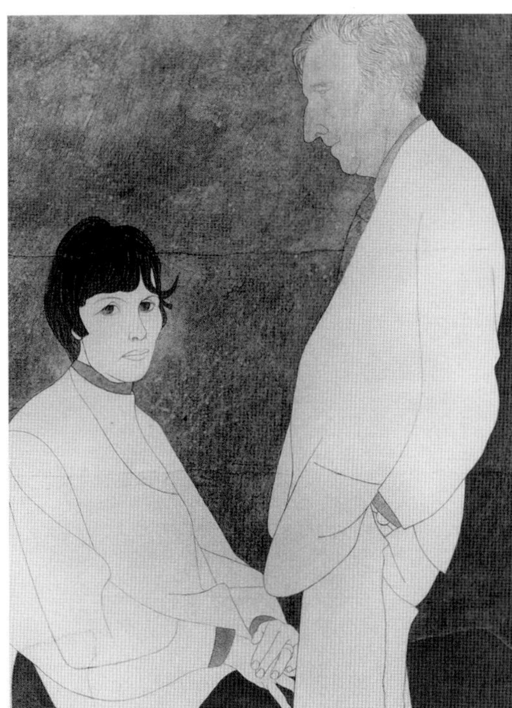

The exhibition revealed that as Greaves's first marriage came to an end, the subject of relationships had found its way to the foreground of his work. A series of double portraits (plates 95 and 96), among them a strong depiction of Victor Musgrave and Monika Kinley, are some of the most charged pictures of his career. Just as his still-lifes often pared down forms and explored the interstices between them, so these portraits used formal elements such as separate and overlapping forms to convey a psychological charge. In exploring the complexities of marriage, corroboration was provided by Greaves's appreciation of D.H. Lawrence, who had originally wanted to give *Lady Chatterley's Lover* the title 'Tenderness'. For Greaves, his own portraits were about 'tenderness or frustrated tenderness', which also fuelled his prints on the theme of the lesbian poems, *Les Chansons de Bilitis*.

Greaves's double portraits are of relatives or close friends and deploy a stripped-down graphic language to express the varied and complex character of each subject. Yet there is also a psychological frisson to many of the more allusive works of this period, works in which Greaves sets up a dialectic between elements, whether they are objects or people. This period also coincided with some of the most acutely psychological portraits of Greaves's career, including a series of pictures of the art dealer Edna Reed that have a highly sprung tension, and a powerful portrait of his first wife (plate 95).

Greaves's use of collage was also put to good effect in his response to a visit to Israel. In 1979, he was invited to visit Israel to produce work for an exhibition to be staged both in Tel Aviv and back in England.[3] Keen to go to the Negev, he stayed at Sde Boker, a kibbutz specialising in alternative technology to make the desert more productive. Greaves would walk in the desert alone, overwhelmed by the lonely, silent, beautiful place. At a loss as to how to respond to its past, present and future, Greaves found the country disturbing on many levels. He visited the tomb of David Ben-Gurion, the former Israeli Prime Minister, and, as the fighter planes roared overhead, he did some rubbings of the stones on the grave. In the early hours of the morning, unable to sleep, he started drawing on these rubbings, creating his own Negev landscapes (plates 99 and 100). Back in England these became the basis for large-scale paintings over collage grounds. The diagrammatic, schematic drawing contrasts with the accidental, organic nature of the grounds, an overlaid mapping that is equivalent to the imposing of borders on the desert. Some of the most elaborate Negev collage-canvases included foot-wide frames that incorporated further collages. *Negev 2: Night and Day in the Desert* (1979–80) had a map-like border and declared its location, Negev,

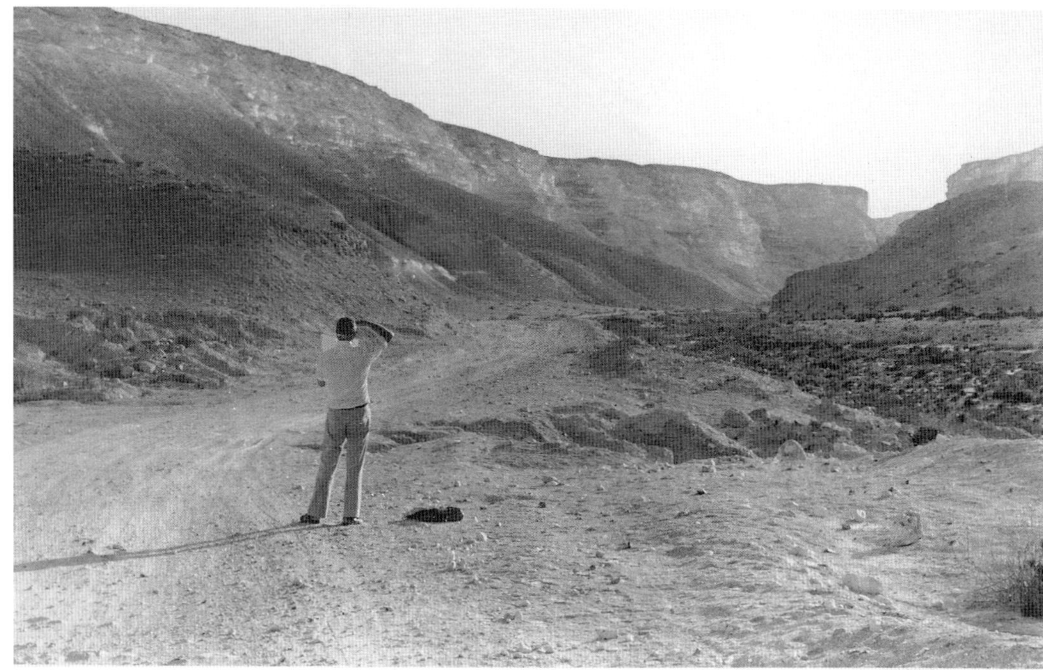

98 Derrick Greaves in the Negev desert, 1979

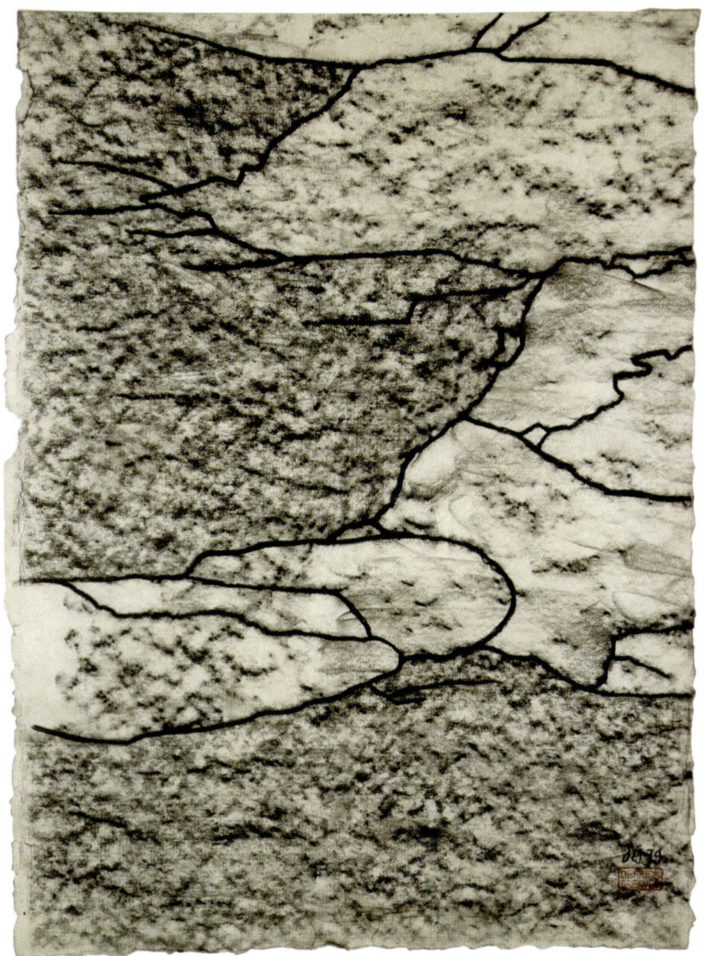

99 *Negev 1*, 1979
Conté crayon on paper
32.7 x 23.5cm (12.87 x 9.25in)
Private Collection, London

100 *Negev 2*, 1979
Conté crayon on paper
32.4 x 24cm (12.75 x 9.5in)
Private Collection, London

in bold Hebrew lettering. In another work, *The Spirit of the Negev* (1979–80), a shadow is given the substantiality of an object.

Amongst the most successful responses were the most pared-down works. A small series showing parched plants gain much of their power from their large size and possess a grandeur that belies their delicate forms and economic, though precise, drawing. In contrast, another powerful Negev painting, *The Greening of the Desert* (1981–5) is an altogether richer experience. Plants are no longer leafless but bud, and the stripped down colour of the desert is replaced with rich colours, not an equivalence of the experience so much as an idealised view of a Utopian

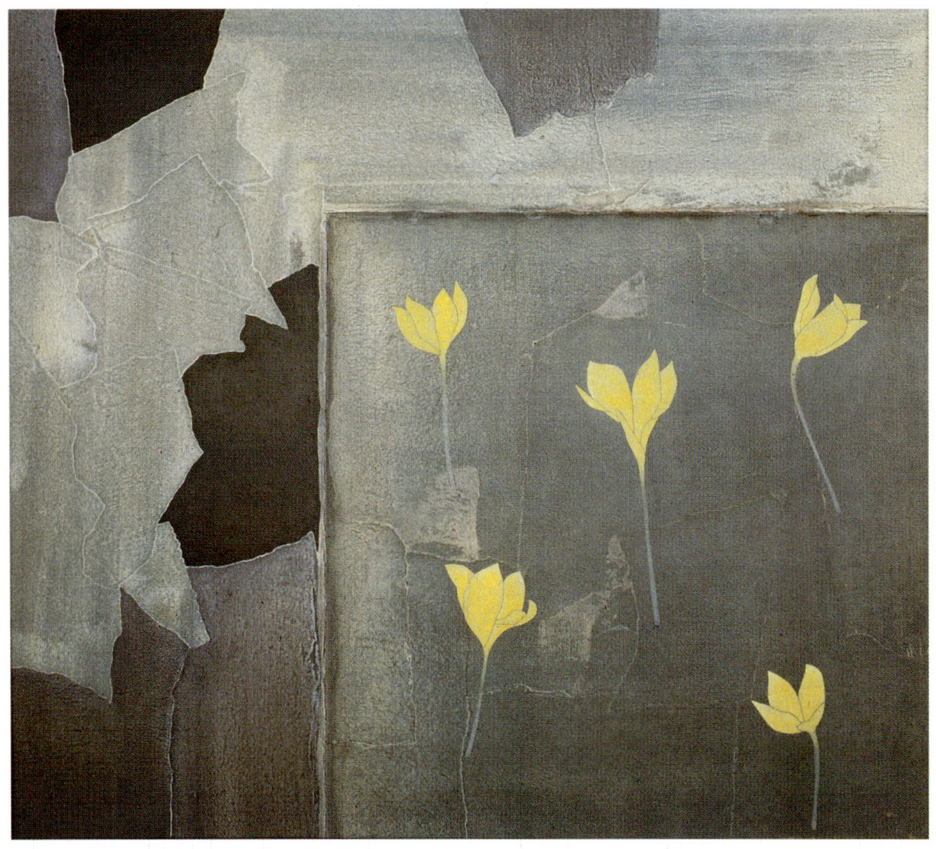

101 *It was almost dark when we found flowers in the desert, I,* 1979
Collage and acrylic on canvas
132 × 140cm (52 × 55.1in)
Private Collection

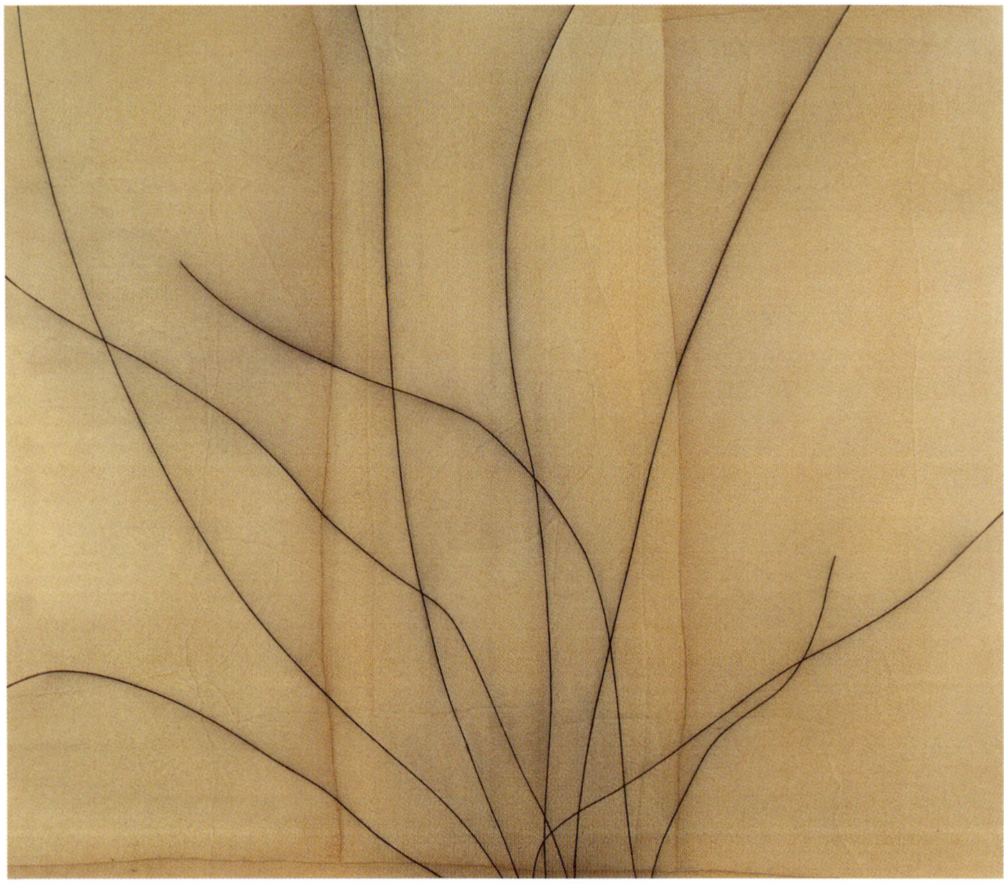

102 *Negev: Leafless Bush II*, 1979–80
Acrylic on paper collage on canvas
128 × 151cm (50 x 60.4in)

future in which the desert blooms. The surprising blue alludes to the desert dweller's life-and-death obsession with water.

In another collage painting, *Asleep in the Desert* (plate 103), Greaves alludes to the pervasive sense of history: the Adonis-like figure has the quality of classical sculpture and the pose of a forever sleeping Pompeian. A related painting shows another male figure, this time identifiable as a rare, all be it veiled, depiction of the artist, but now the keynote is not calm but anxiety, not comfortable repose in an untroubled environment, but with hands up in defence, mouth open in anguish and a sense of threat provided by the fighter planes. The work is entitled *Self Portrait of the Artist as Madman (King Kong)* (plate 105) and the traces of a building could be a skyscraper, but the state of anxiety is surely rooted in the artist's disturbing experience of the Negev.

Self Portrait of the Artist as Madman (King Kong) also contains echoes of an occasional leitmotif in Greaves's paintings, the fall of Icarus. As a student he won a prize for a lithograph on the subject. At a difficult time in the late 1950s he again depicted Icarus in pastel and around the time of *Self Portrait of the Artist*

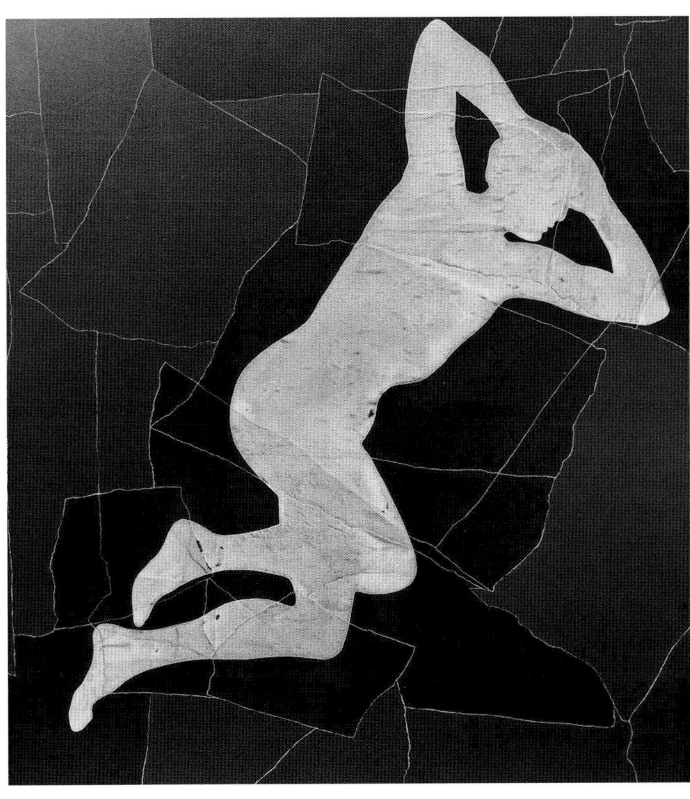

103 *Asleep in the Desert*, 1981–5
Acrylic and collage on canvas
166 × 151cm (65.4 × 59.4in)
Private Collection, Switzerland

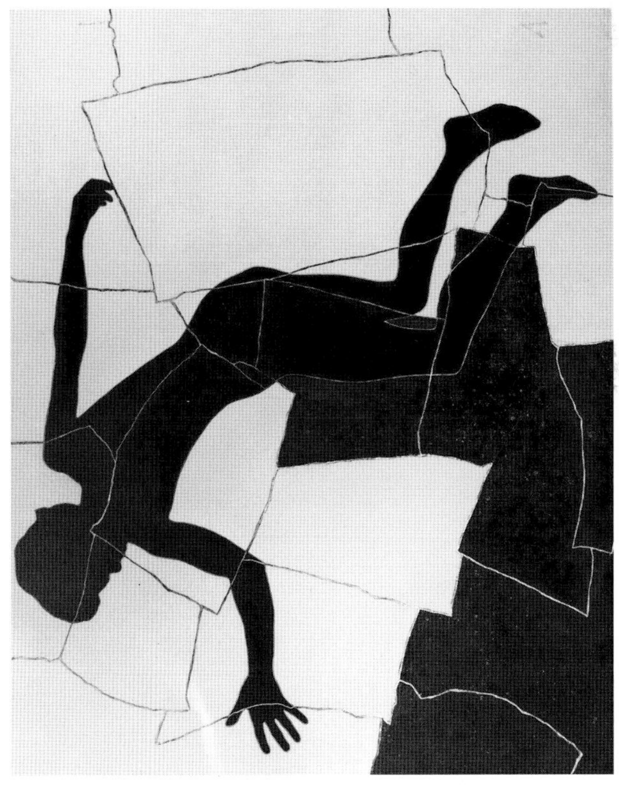

104 *Falling II (Icarus)*, 1985–6
Acrylic and collage on canvas
191 × 156cm (75.2 × 61.4in)

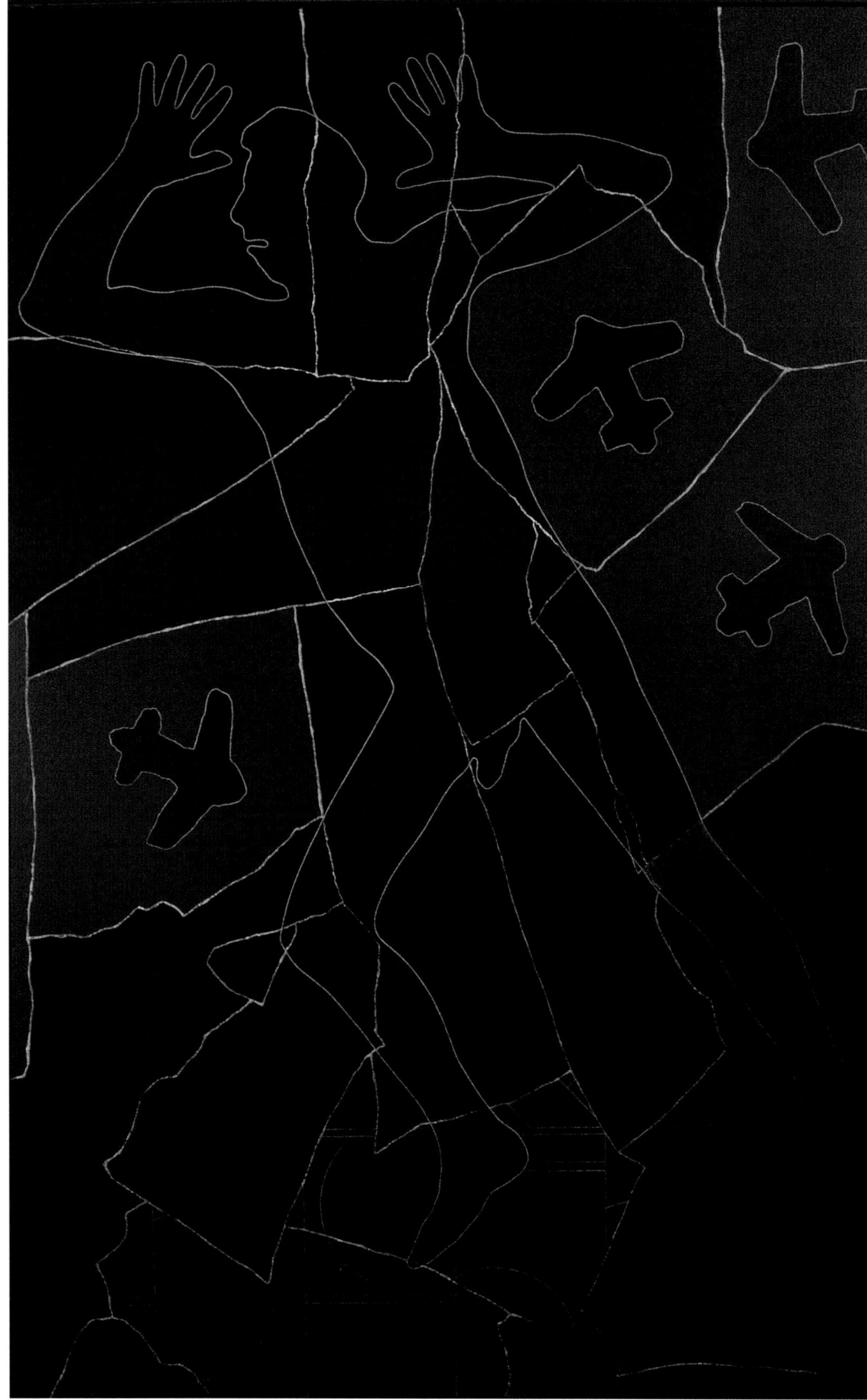

105 *Self Portrait of the Artist as Madman (King Kong)*, 1986
Acrylic and collage on canvas
213 × 145cm (83.9 × 57.1in)

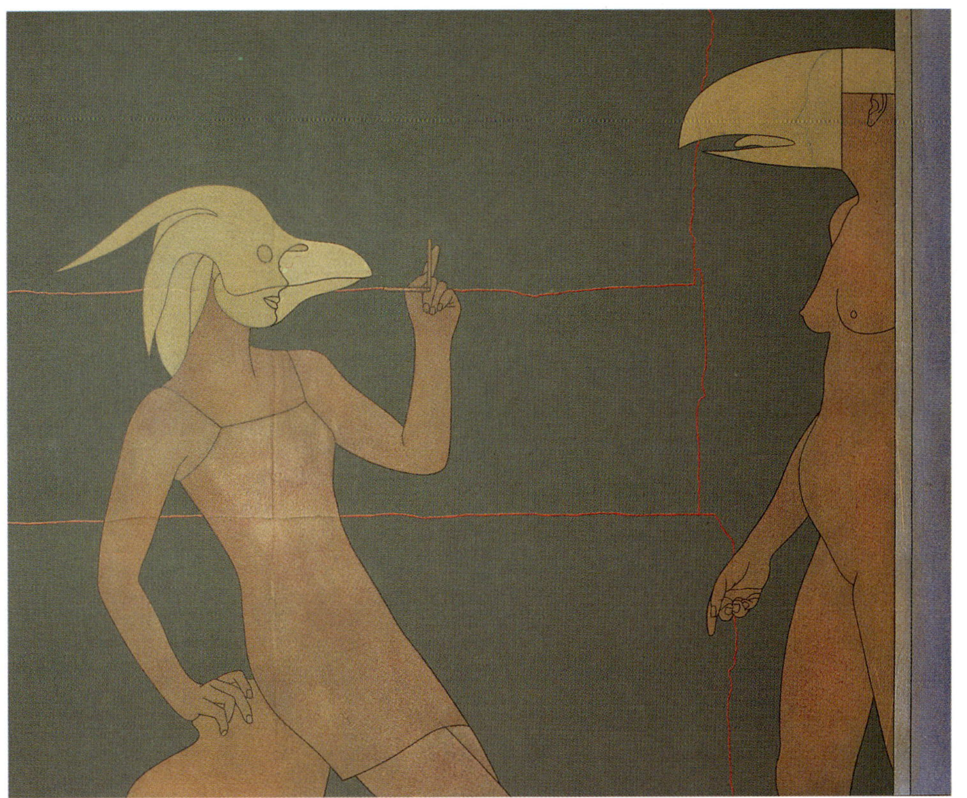

106 *The Green Room*, 1982–4
Acrylic and collage on canvas
159 × 244cm (62.6 × 96.1in)
Private Collection, Norfolk

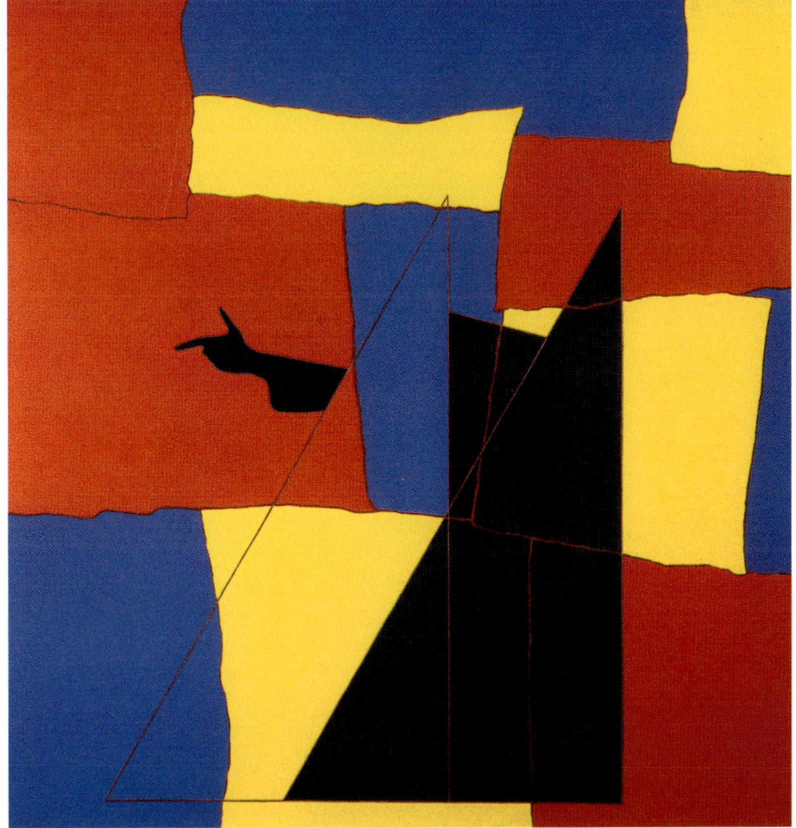

107 *The Little Pedagogue*
(Self-Portrait as Teacher), 1985
Acrylic and collage on canvas
142 × 142cm (55.9 × 55.9in)

as Madman (King Kong), he produced two large collage paintings on the subject
(plate 105). Each serves as a surrogate self portrait in its expression of the artist's
anxieties. Given such a reading and the rarity of such autobiographical elements
elsewhere in Greaves's work, it is hard not to consider *The Little Pedagogue (Self-
Portrait as Teacher)* (plate 107) as a foil to *Self Portrait of the Artist as Madman (King
Kong)*. The former is a self portrait of the artist as a teacher, in which all that is
discernible is the artist's hand and pointing fingers against the ironic certitude
of triangles and primary colours. But instead of a loss of equilibrium or fall from
grace, there is a sense of control, of composure and authority.

The reconstruction of experiences with a strong emotional and psychological
dimension remains present in later work, however schematic the drawing. In
The Green Room (plate 106) the line is firm and the structure tight, emphasised
by the Euclidian right angle created by a woman's compact. Ambiguity adds
another dimension. The title suggests that we are backstage, as do the masks
which partially or completely cover the women's faces, but perhaps the clue is
the compact that one holds, suggesting that what we see may be the image
of the woman reflected in her mirror. The masks serve to reflect the difference
between how we see ourselves and how others see us, while the backstage
setting further emphasises this theme of artifice and disguise, suggesting the
ways in which we may mask our true selves.

The painting also alludes to the overt eroticism of many of Greaves's paintings, drawings and prints, especially during the 1970s and 1980s. In addition
to the major print series, *The Songs of Bilitis* (1977), Greaves also made explicit
watercolours (many of them still unexhibited) and large-scale paintings with a
sexual dynamic. Above all, the nude took on a new importance in drawings and
paintings of new models, among them Joanna Field and Sally Butler (later the
artist's second wife). Taking them as a starting point, Greaves transformed them
into fantastic creations of an altogether different type. Seeking to combine 'the
vulgar and quotidian' with 'the erotic and the humorous',[4] there is at times a
glorious absurdity to these large-scale paintings. Admiring the erotic distortions
of Ingres's late paintings such as *Les Bains Turcs*, Greaves eroticised existing
motifs as in *Spanish Rococo* (1990), *Lamp* (plate 109) and a series of related
paintings. In contrast to their fleshy heat, *Demanding and Reluctant Love* (plate 108),
despite the title, is relatively restrained, attracting comparison with Matisse
when it was shown at the Royal Academy Summer Exhibition in 1998.[5] What
followed burst with new energy, singing colour and brilliant dynamism.

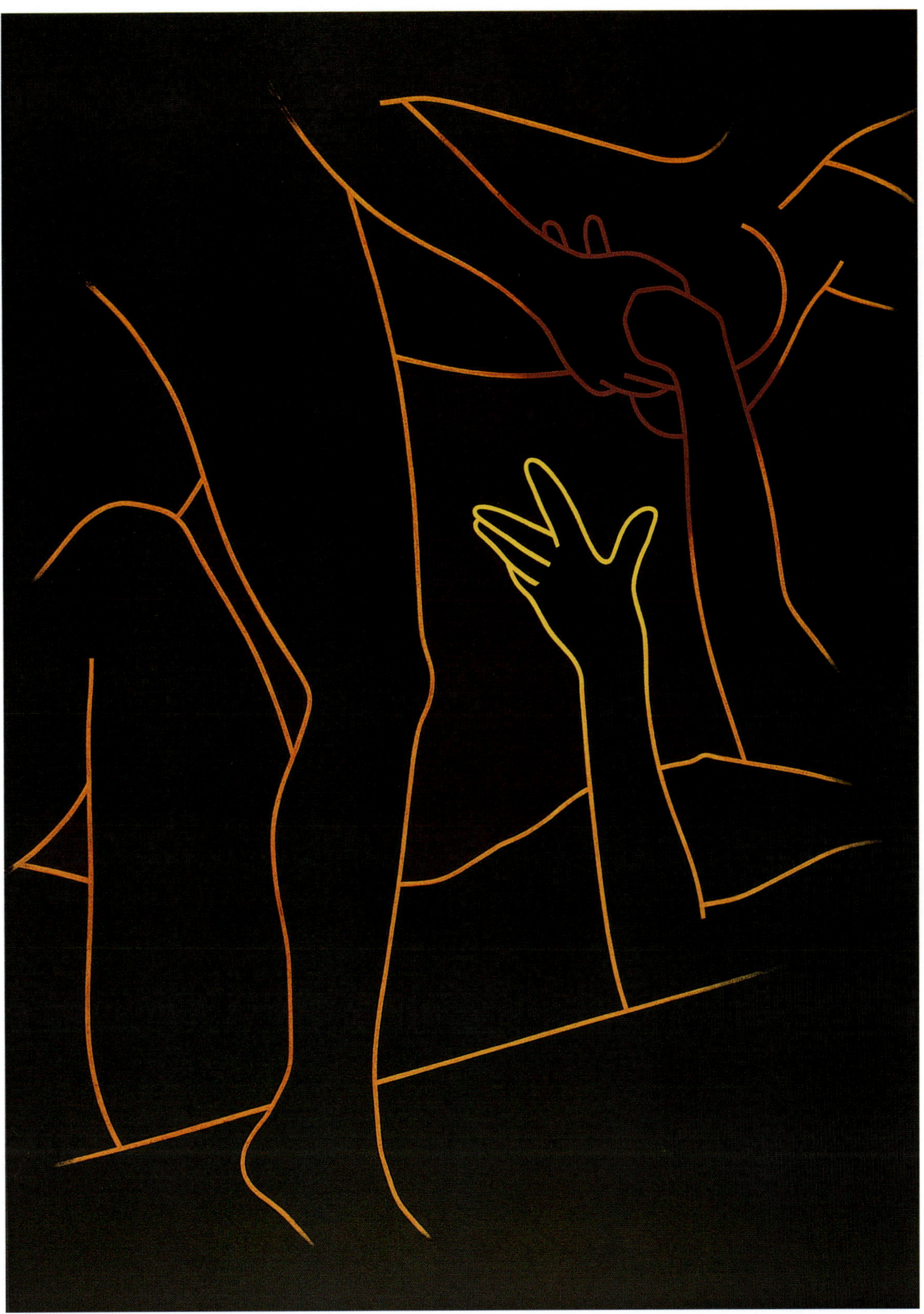

108 *Demanding and Reluctant Love*, 1994
Acrylic on canvas
147.5 × 95.5cm (58.1 × 37.6in)

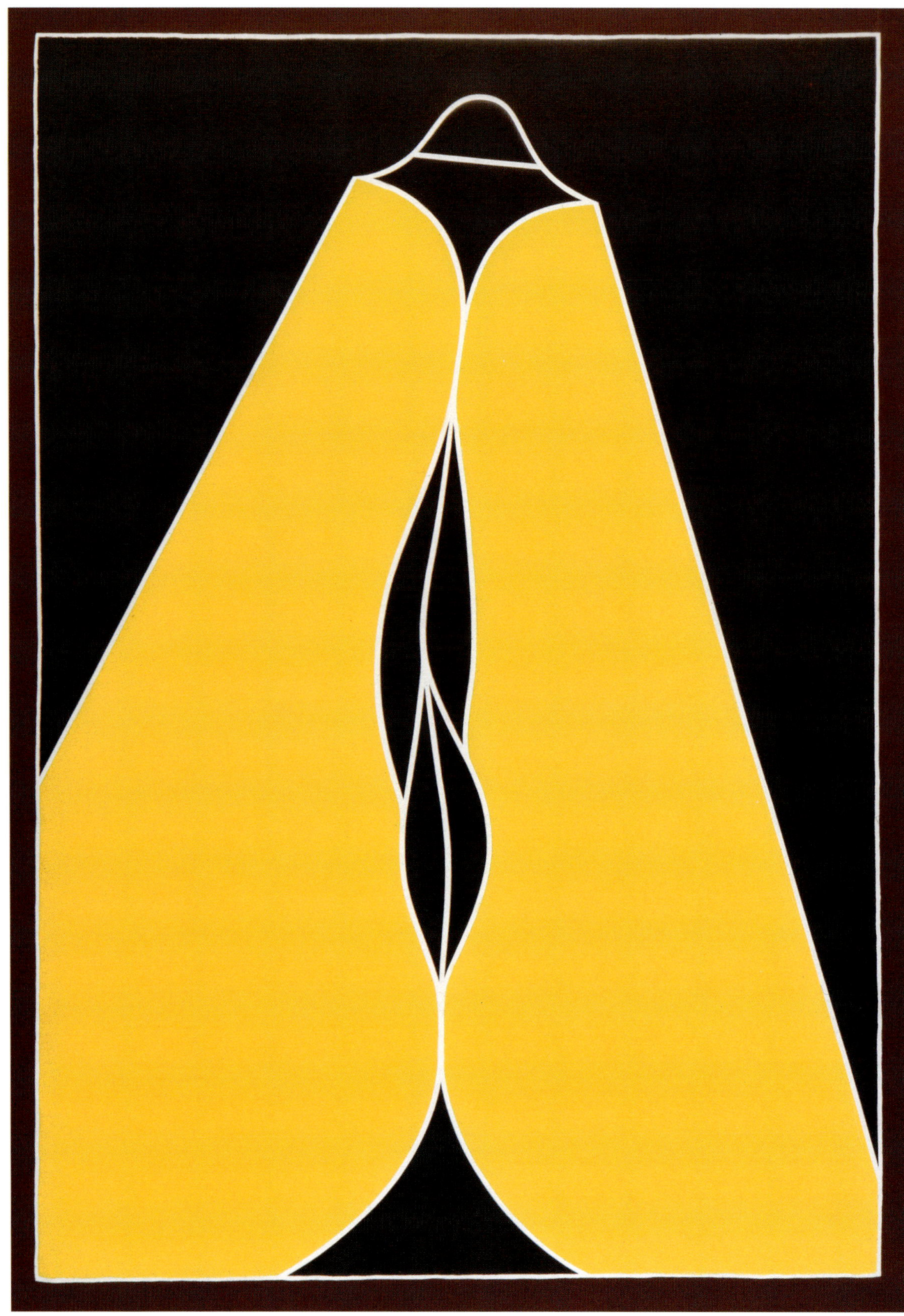

109 *Lamp*, 1995
Acrylic on canvas
167.5 × 120.5cm (65.9 × 47.4in)

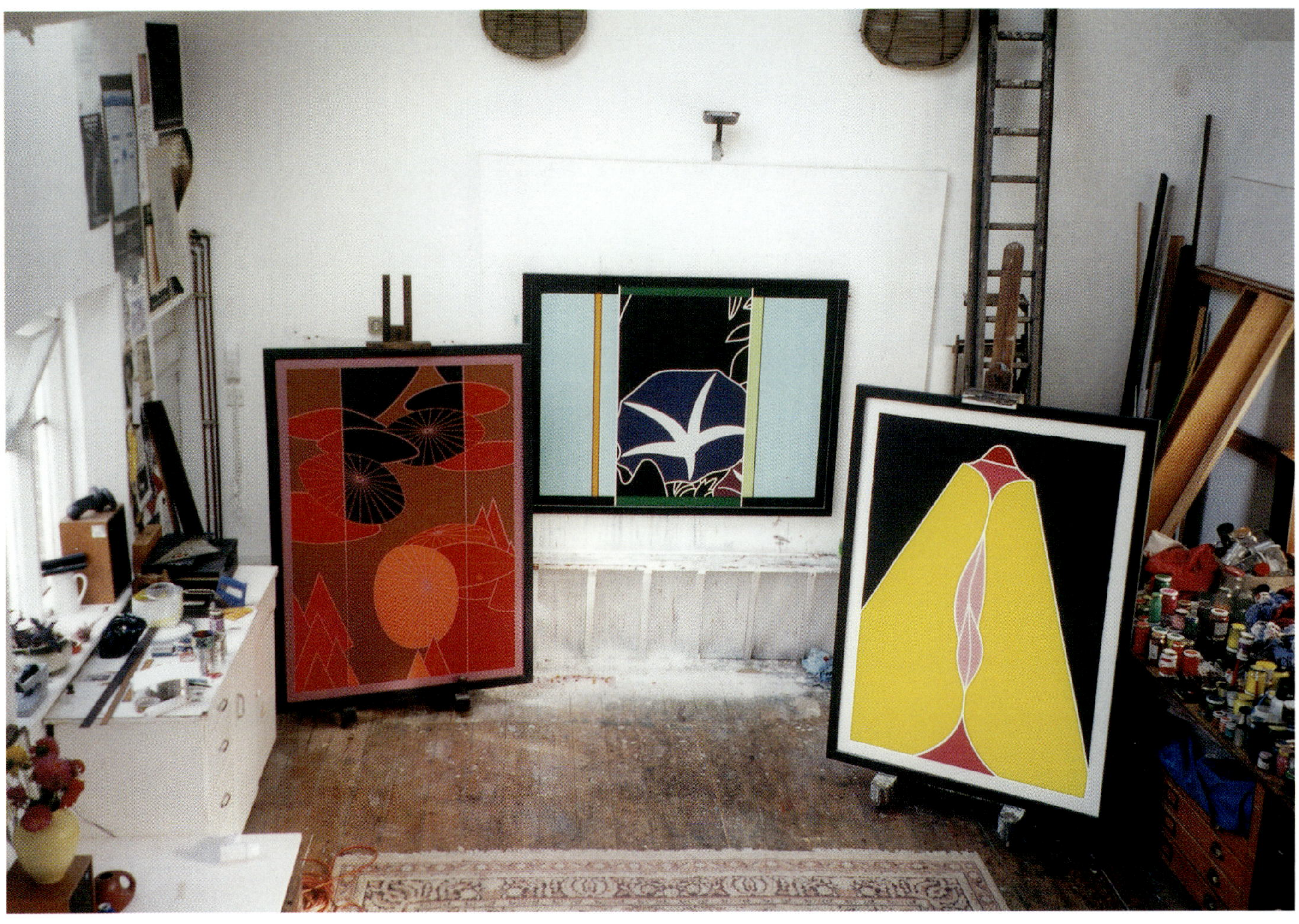

110 Studio with *Hokusai,*
Hiroshige and *Lamp,* before their reworking, 1995

Notes

1. Derrick Greaves, unpublished
journal entry, undated.
2. Derrick Greaves, unpublished
journal entry, undated.
3. He was one of a group of artists
that included Adrian Berg, Anthony
Eyton, Donald Hamilton Fraser,
Anita Ford, Philip Hicks, Lawrence
Preece, David Smith, Philip Sutton
and Brian Yale.

4. Derrick Greaves, conversation with
James Hyman, October 2002.
5. 'I liked the cool linear perfection
of Derrick Greaves's *Demanding and
Reluctant Love,* which reminded me a
little of Matisse.' Richard Dorment,
'At Last the RA gets it right', *Telegraph,*
29 May 1998, p.25.

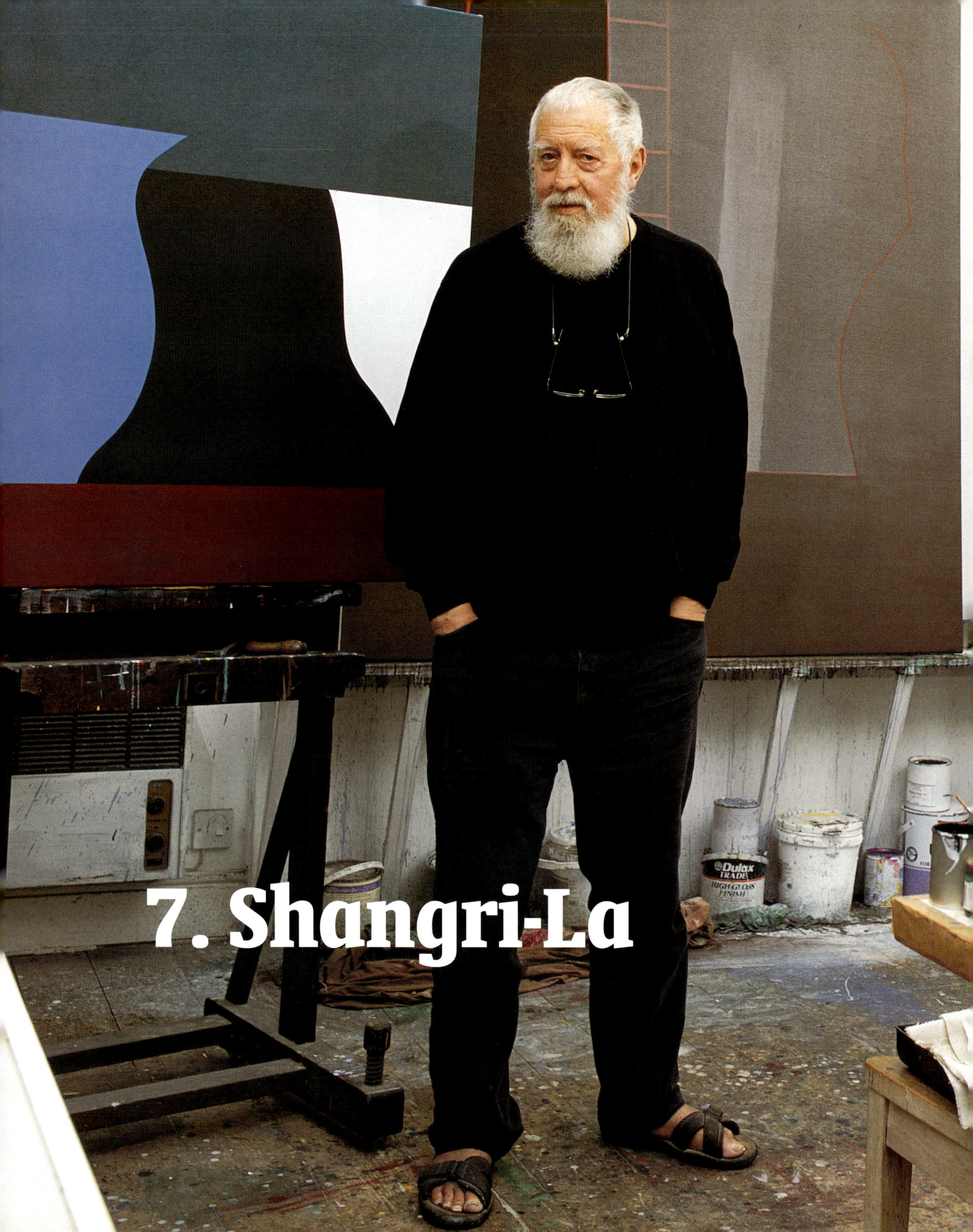
7. Shangri-La

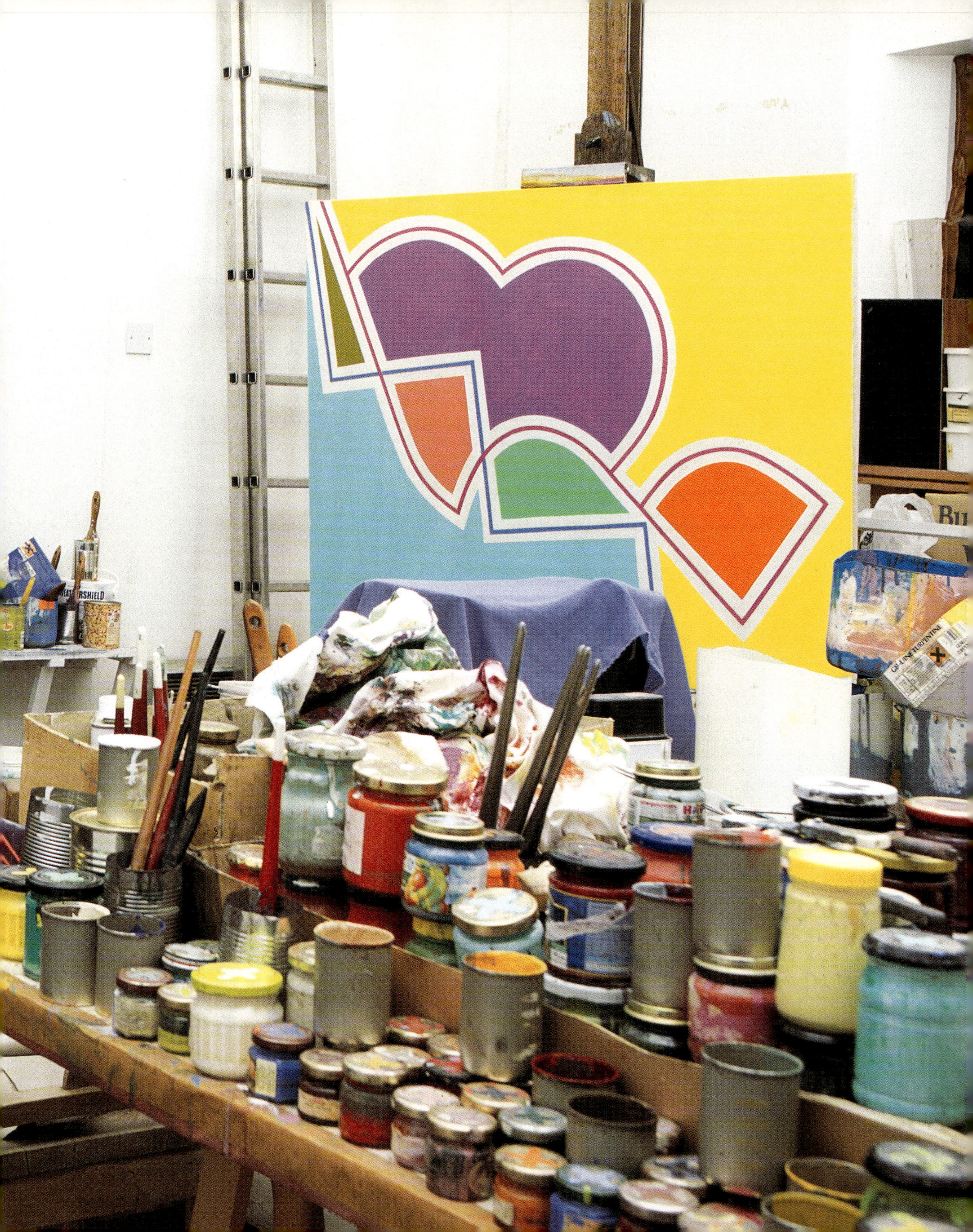

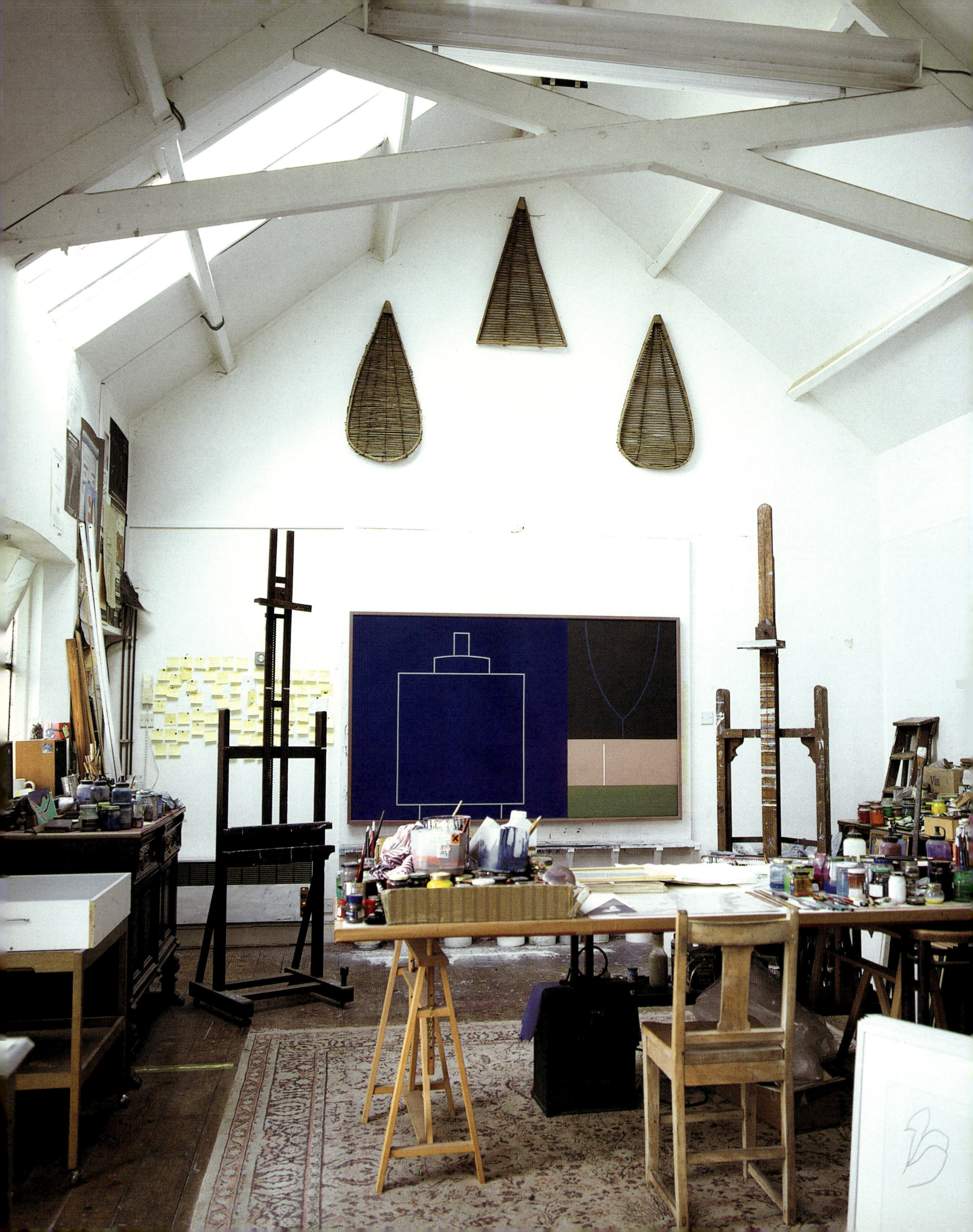

7. Shangri-La: The Recent Paintings of Derrick Greaves

In my work there has been a development towards a linear clarity. It's not deliberate but I now feel able to leave more and more out. Consistency is one thing but I deplore the formulaic … Things come out of the rough and tumble of the studio. Ideas flit in and out of mind. After working for over 50 years these things are hard-won. I'm still working towards greater freedom! It's about trying to retain the liveliness of real life as well as synthesising forms to reconstruct them. The challenge is to transcend the transient reality which has moved you to something that is apposite in terms of painting.

Derrick Greaves, 2004[1]

For an extraordinary number of years – almost 25 – Greaves did not hold a show in London's West End. Between 1980, when he had his last show at Fischer Fine Art, and 2003, when he had his first show at James Hyman Fine Art, Greaves had been shown sporadically by the Royal Academy in its Summer Exhibition, leading Tim Hilton to write: 'Two fine paintings by Derrick Greaves remind us that it is high time that this dedicated artist came out of his Norfolk retirement and gave us a solo show in London.'[2]

Greaves had not stopped actively painting or regularly exhibiting, but his major exhibitions had taken place outside London. Notable among them were *Derrick Greaves: Retrospective of Paintings 1953–1980* at the Graves Art Gallery in Sheffield in 1980 and the travelling exhibition, *Derrick Greaves – Forty from Ten*, which in 1986 showcased his large-scale collage-drawings of the previous ten years. Both were highly acclaimed by critics and artists, old and young. The eminent painter and teacher, Robert Medley, for example, wrote of being 'thrilled' by the 'extraordinary work' and 'filled with admiration'.[3] These shows were complemented by smaller group exhibitions including an Arts Council tour, *Books and Folios – Screenprints by Derrick Greaves, Robert Medley and Edward Middleditch*[4] in 1981 and *New Norfolk Drawings: Derrick Greaves, Roger Ackling, Anthony Benjamin* in 1993. His painting was reaching new heights but long exile from London meant it remained too little known.

In pursuing new challenges, the marvellous *Goldfish* (plate 113) points the way forward, economically conveying the darting forms of the fish. The search is for a

Previous page:
111 Derrick Greaves's studio, with *Falling Downstream* (2005)

Facing page:
112 Derrick Greaves's studio, Norfolk, 2002, with *Studio at Night with Garden* (2002)

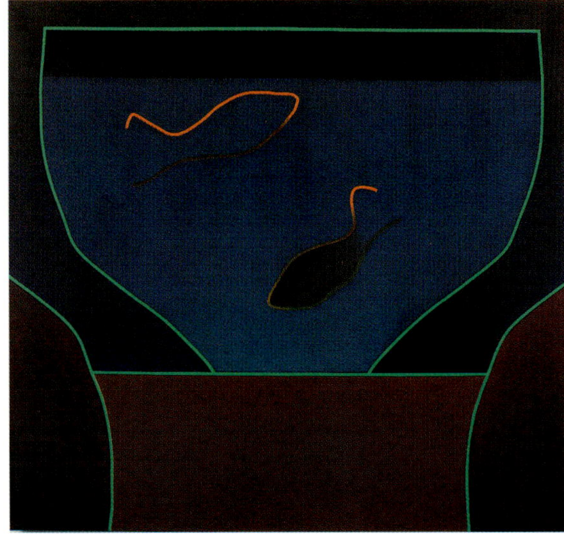

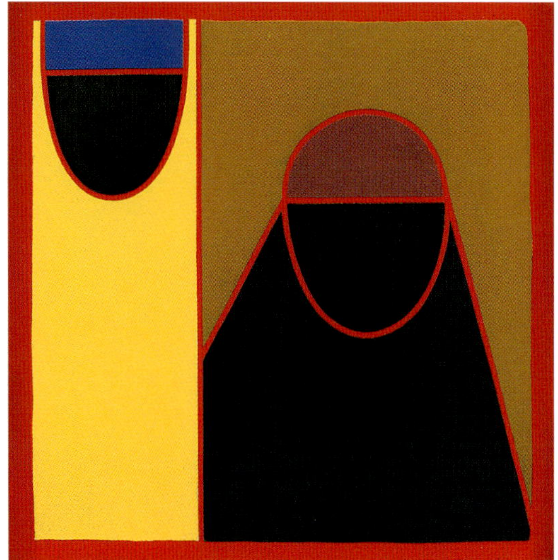

113 *Goldfish*, 1979
Acrylic on canvas
116 × 127cm (45.7 × 50in)
Private Collection, Scotland

114 *Two Moroccan Women*,
1992–5
Acrylic on canvas
53.5 × 52.5cm (21.1 × 20.7in)
Private Collection

bold economy; a use of paint that is plain-speaking, not confected; a composition
that is seemingly inevitable, not laboured; a subject that is 'plainly there at one
glance', yet also 'has resonances that play back at you the longer you look at
the picture'.[5] His search, then, is not for mere 'simplicity', but for the altogether
grander ambitions of 'economy' and of 'clarity'.[6] *Goldfish* is a painting that makes
explicit the artist's admiration for Matisse's famous fish bowls, yet in it Greaves
finds a language that is all his own. A vocabulary that is at once precise and
evocative eloquently conveys the movement of the fish and gives a hint at the
distorting effects of water in a bowl. For Greaves, then, what matters is 'putting
trust in the language of painting';[7] trust in the ability of painting to encapsulate
the artist's response and to convey it clearly to an audience.

Greaves's imagery received a boost with his move to Norfolk in 1983 to
set up and run the Printmaking Department at the Norwich School of Art. He
inherited marvellous technicians with impeccable skills, who had previously
had little status due to there being no formal printmaking department.

Previously he had taught part-time at various London art schools and at
Maidstone College of Art. Now, for the first time, he taught full-time, doing so
for a period of eight years. The art school also brought in a wide circle of full-
and part-time teachers. Middleditch was Head of Painting, and visitors included
John Lessore, John Wonnacott and even occasionally Lucian Freud. This was a
stimulating time, a fresh start, and Greaves's painting and printmaking burst
with a new vitality that pushed still further his ideas of colour, form and line.

The job was time-consuming but led to powerful prints, many of which are
now in the extensive holdings of Greaves's printmaking at University of Wales,
Aberystwyth. During this period Greaves never stopped painting, and throughout
it he produced strong works. Nevertheless, after finishing his teaching at the
Norwich School of Art in 1991, his painting assumed a new imaginative freedom;
a sense of liberation and boldness. Henceforth Greaves no longer just made
drawings from external objects and then translated them into painting: now the
unconscious started to play a part. In one recent dream image, Greaves paints a
modern *Martyr* (2002) in which Saint Sebastian has become a mere trace, a bodily
stain pierced with arrows. In another, *Empty Rooms* (plate 115), Greaves combines
the structure of a Japanese print with a dream image, using flatness to suggest
the denial of access. Despite the title, these rooms cannot be entered and,
although spacious, our feeling of freedom is frustrated. We are shut out. The
space is impossible to enter.

Such paintings retain their basis in drawing although the stimuli has become

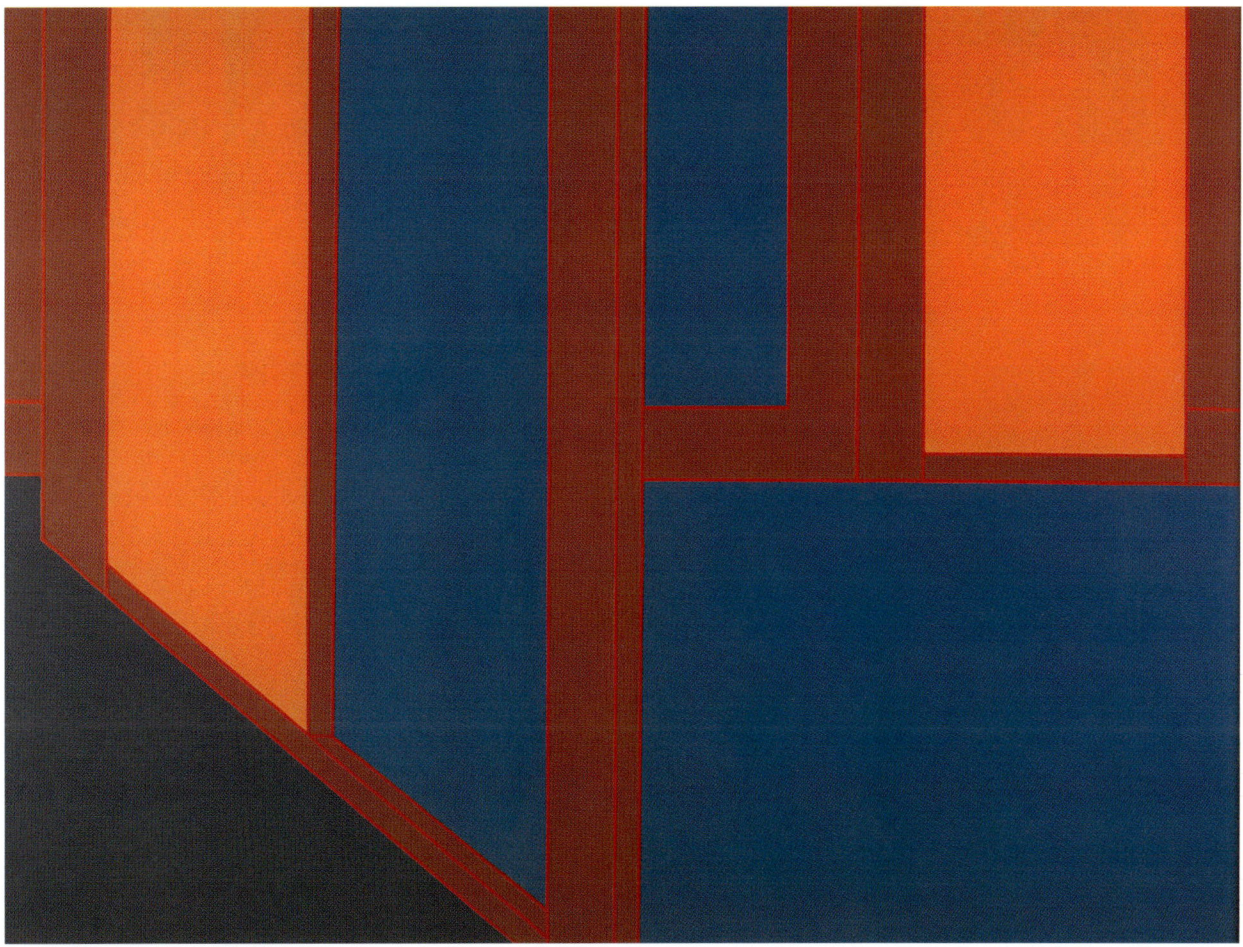

115 *Empty Rooms*, 1999–2000
Oil on canvas
137 × 183cm (53.9 × 72in)
Private Collection, London

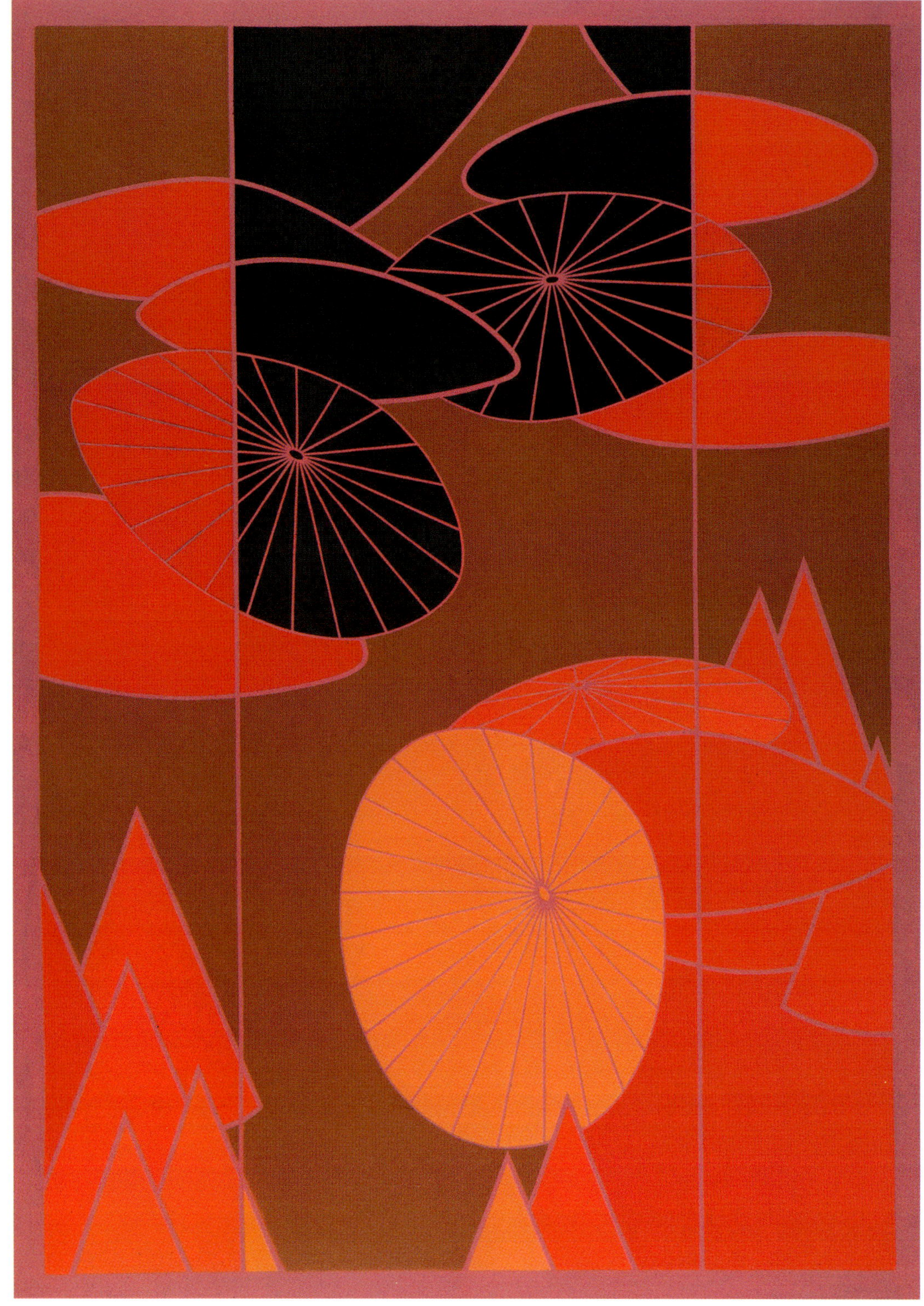

116 *Hokusai*, 1994
Acrylic on canvas
167 × 121cm (65.7 × 47.6in)

more studio-bound and investigative, but despite their formal imperatives, what concerns Greaves is not abstraction, but the way that he can give equal weight to the representational and abstract components of his work. In *Two Moroccan Women* (plate 114), the singing colour is comparable to Frank Stella's powerful square paintings of the early 1960s, yet the subject matter is indispensable. Similarly, in *Hokusai* (plate 116) Greaves's concern is as much with colour as it is with the formal properties of a Japanese woodcut. Greaves says:

> *I would throw a spanner in the works by adding a figurative element to stop it being merely an exercise in colour structure. I wanted my paintings to have a figurative factor as their impurity but to have the firmness of abstract painting. I wanted to be able to feed-in informal elements of my life in a symbolic rather than descriptive way, which I couldn't do if it was purely abstract. These impurities are like life. There are unforeseen circumstances, quirkiness, humour. Paintings have to reflect that.*[8]

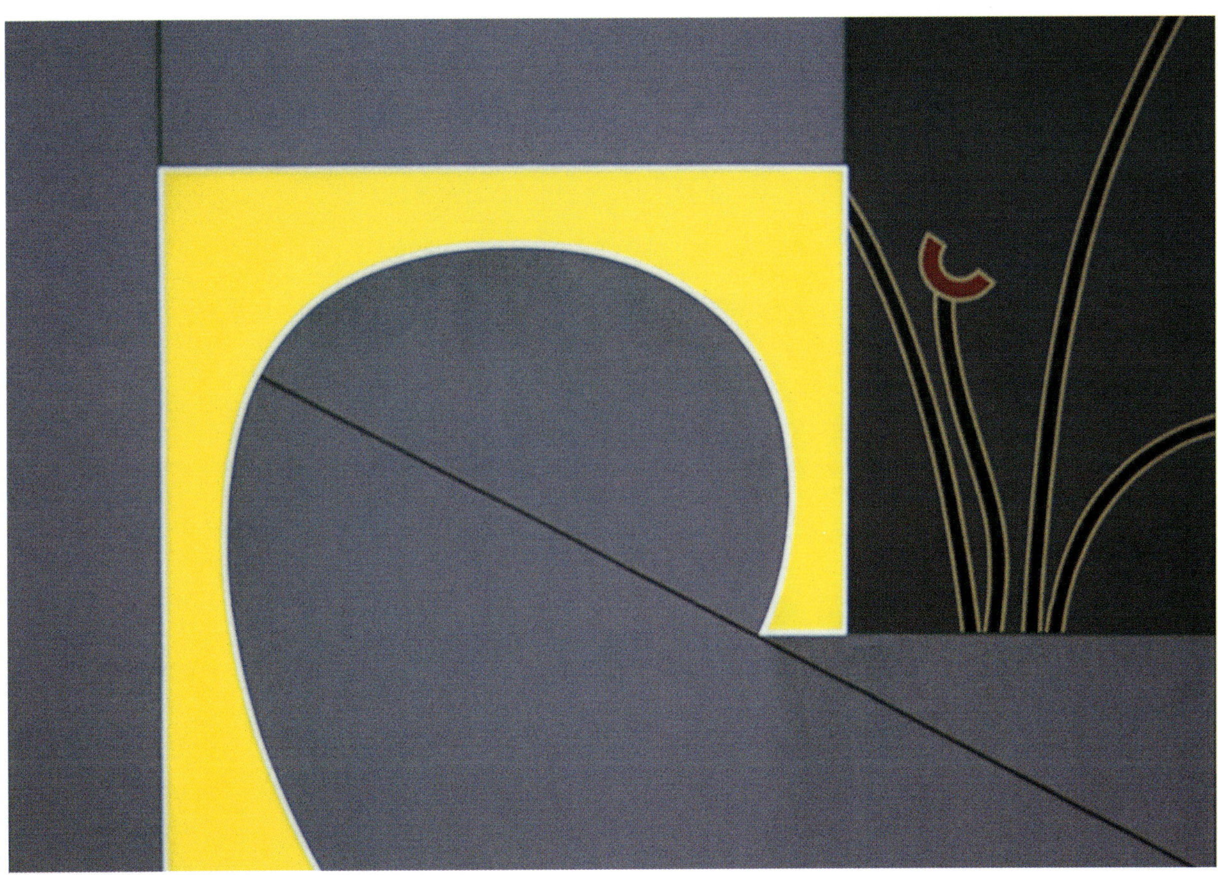

117 *Canal*, 1997
Acrylic on canvas
121.9 × 173cm (48 × 68.1in)
Tate Gallery

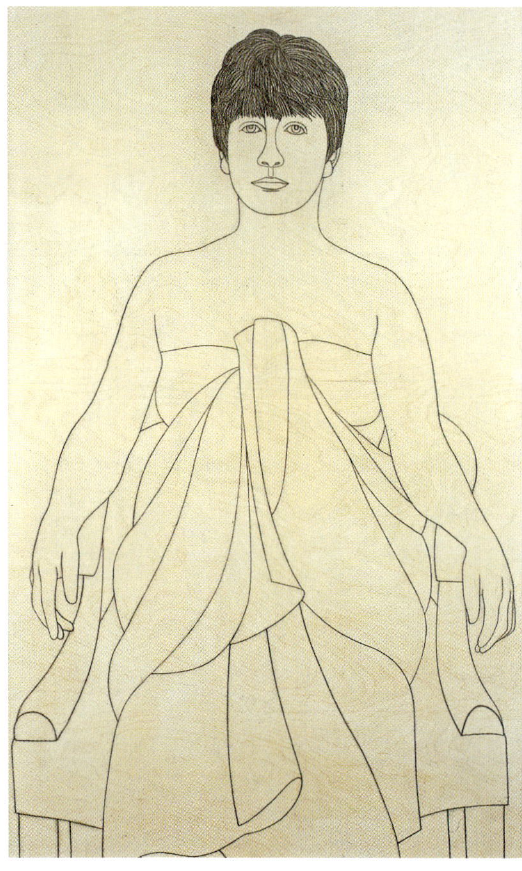

118 *Sally Butler in a Sarong*, 1995
Charcoal, conté crayon and acrylic on
wood panel
145 × 95cm (57.1 × 37.4in)
Private Collection, London

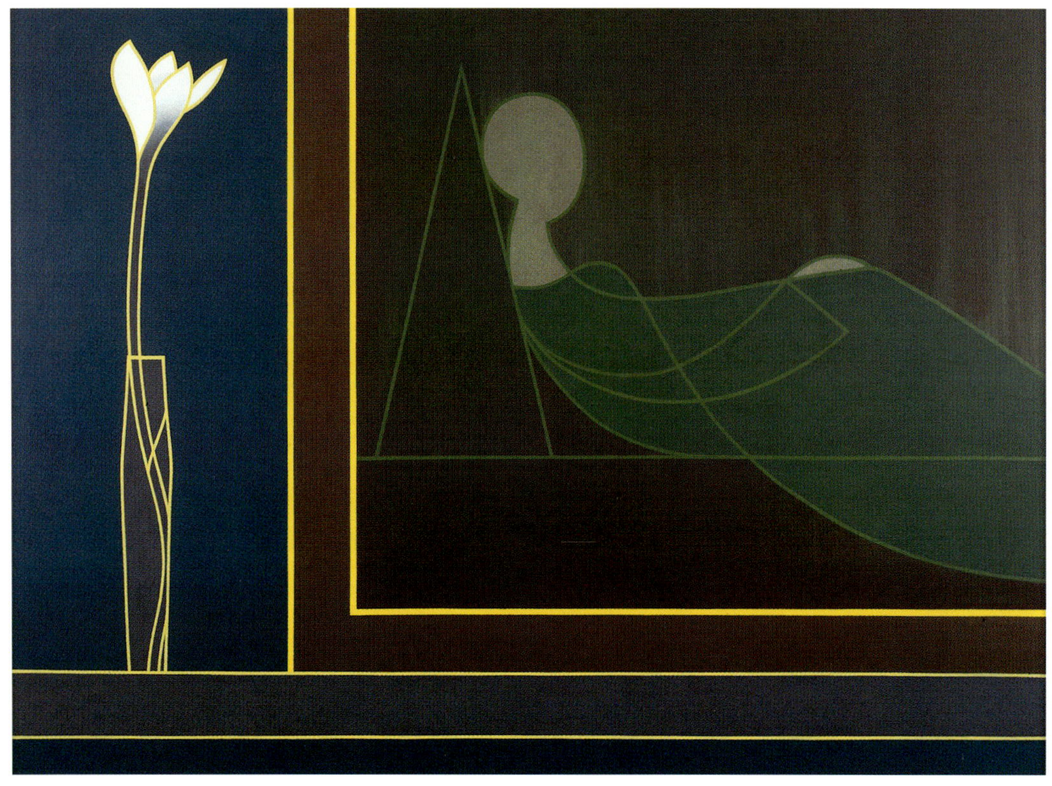

119 *Recamier (Still Life with Picture)*,
2002
Oil on canvas
121 × 169cm (47.6 × 66.5in)
Private Collection, London

Good News for Archaeologists (1966), *Greece – The Museum of Eggs* (1981) and *Odalisque Disturbed* (1983) exemplify this continual entwining of the thoughtful and the playful, illustrating a witty response to imagery which characterises much of Greaves's work even if it has a darker edge. This good humour is especially evident in Greaves's response to the past and, above all, to classical civilisation. A perfectly preserved jar is indeed good news for archaeologists, a museum of eggs pokes fun at the cult of preservation and the proliferation of museums, and the disturbed odalisque subverts the stability of any number of reclining nudes from classical times, through David and Ingres to Picasso and Matisse, suggesting the naughtier pleasures of a fun-fair side show. Meanwhile, Greaves's appreciation of this classical lineage has also resulted in the striking composure of *Sally Butler in a Sarong* (plate 118) and the equally regal *Recamier (Still Life with Picture)* (plate 119).

In continuing to push his own language, one of Greaves's most powerful recent achievements is his use of a horizontal bar that crosses several large-scale paintings. This shelf-like structure runs through *Laocöon* (plate 120), *Border* (plate 121), *Two Trees (Spring)* (plate 122) and *Sunset* (plate 123), allowing Greaves to situate still-life objects without having to present a table-top or locate subjects without the need for an horizon line. The result objectifies each element, even giving substance to the insubstantial, whether it is a flower, a sculpture, a tree or even the sun:

> *I like formal structures that can do more than one job in a painting. I like the viewer to be led beyond the painting only to come back to it. So the single bar passing through the picture is like a continuous shelf in the mind. I also like the way the bar acts chromatically. It allows one to pitch the line to a different key from the objects on the line.*[9]

These paintings provide a compendium of multifarious sources. In *Border*, Greaves presents a row of African spearheads, which previously he had drawn at the Museum of Mankind, London. In *Laocöon*, the snakes of the famous Hellenistic sculpture dance with delight. In *Two Trees (Spring)*, each tree is distinct yet their equivalent weights give an overall harmony to a composition with two competing centres of attention, and in the climactic *Sunset* the red ribbons of the sun are set against the deepest blue and are accentuated by the horizontal bar of purple-grey with yellow edges. Within the sun, an arrow points downwards affirming that this is indeed a sunset, not a sunrise.

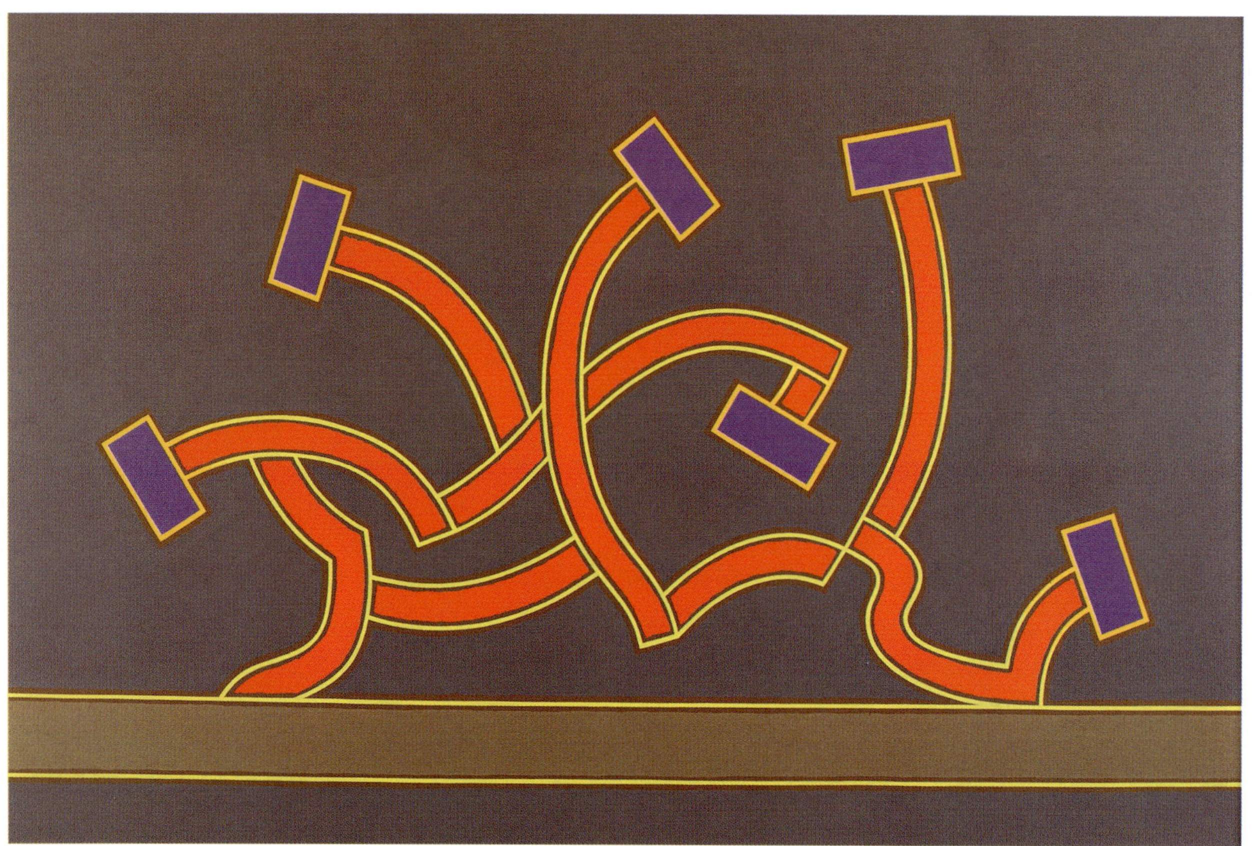

120 *Laocöon*, 2001
Oil on canvas
108.5 × 167.5cm (42.7 × 65.9in)
Private Collection, London

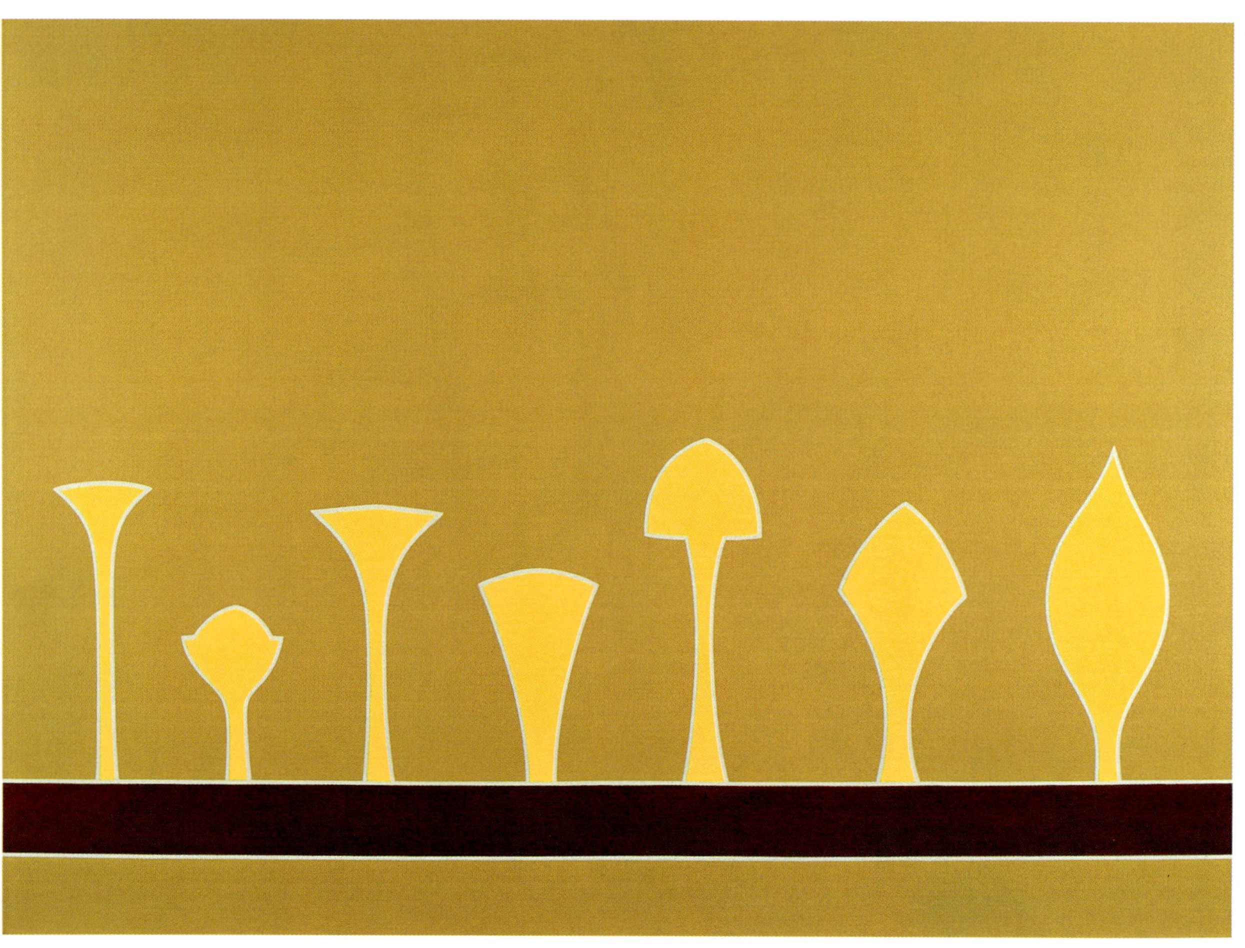

121 *Border*, 1997
Oil on canvas
120 × 166cm (47.2 × 66.5in)

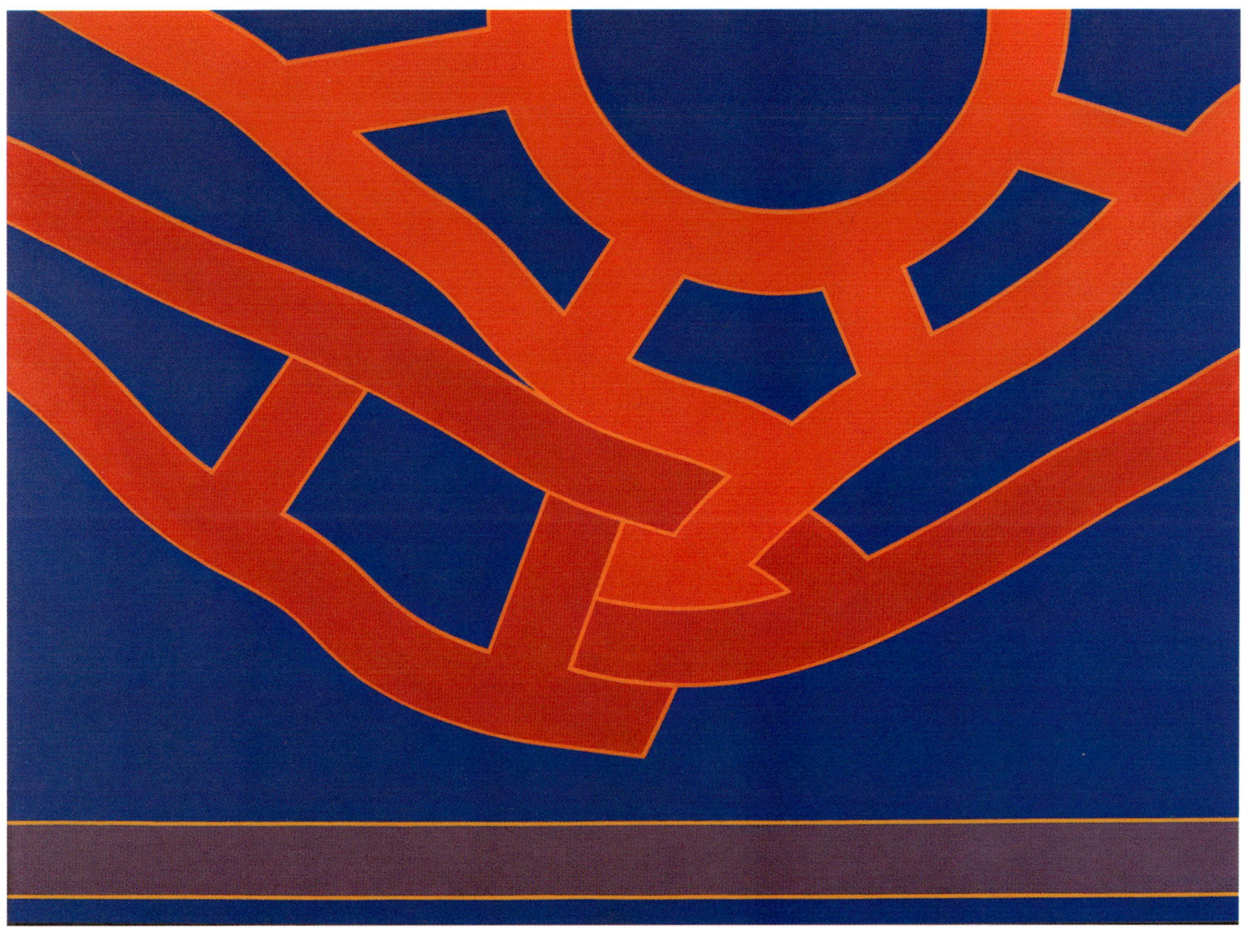

122 *Two Trees (Spring)*, 1999
Oil on canvas
108 × 167cm (42.5 × 65.7in)

123 *Sunset*, 1997
Oil on canvas
120 × 166cm (47.2 × 65.4in)
Claire and James Hyman, London

Greaves's recent paintings also bestow an iconographic boldness on more mundane objects, that translates them into heraldic forms that are both solid and dignified, playful and witty. Greaves does not discourage a semiological approach to his work, although he does distinguish between the 'exotic insights' of a writer such as E.H. Gombrich and the 'rough and tumble of the studio'.[10] It would not be an exaggeration to assert that at the centre of Greaves's work is drawing and at the heart of his drawing is line. In *Rope Tricks* (2004), all is movement: a line twists and turns, dancing with an inner life, the possibilities apparently limitless. The effect is lyrical, a 'Mozartian lightness', yet to use line so precisely and so sparingly is hard-won, and the artist himself comments that 'I've not aimed for elegance or simplicity. I've aimed for clarity.'

Greaves also often speaks of his practice as 'drawing a line around my thoughts', like in a cartoon. He has explained that line not only delineates forms and carries colour, but also relates dynamically to the picture ground.[11] These grounds are painted as impassively as possible but Greaves builds them up in thin layers to retain their vibrancy:

I realise there is an audience that likes the bravura, the attack, the spirit of the painter: from John Singer Sargent to Vincent van Gogh – they love the brushstrokes. People feel after my fifties work, the brushstrokes are missing. I feel however that this showiness gets in the way. I don't want traces of the hand or finicky touches. I don't want to make a great show of me on the canvas. I'm the opposite of an expressionist painter trying to grab the spectator. I want to paint myself out of a picture so that the feeling of a painting is everything. I want people to bring themselves to the picture.[12]

Colour is no less important. Indeed it is the artist's boldness as a colourist that is one of the most dramatic impressions and one that is carried through from his earliest works. Colour is frequently unmodulated and flat and what is depicted is a shadowless world. In fact, shadows had been abolished by Greaves since the beginning of the 1960s when objects stopped having a light side and a dark side, and they were modelled as though a light shone on them from outside the picture. The shadows were found by him to be unnecessary, thus the modelling of the objects and the shadows disappeared simultaneously, giving the chance of a newer, more freshly found rebirth of forms. Later on in his development, these forms could be completely restructured, as has been mentioned, and this refiguring of the forms continues to this day. One colour is often given even greater resonance by its proximity to another. Sometimes complementary, sometimes clashing, the effect of placing one colour against another at times echoes this central aspect of Bridget Riley's exploration of colour. The result in Greaves's work is especially vibrant in paintings in which he introduces closely painted dots of colour which dance across the canvas, as in *The Meeting (Max Ernst and Brancusi)* (2001), *Pandora* (2001) and *Landscape with Conifers* (plate 124). More subtly, it also accounts for the shimmering effect that Greaves achieves in paintings such as *Rain* (2002), where the lines of falling water are depicted using one colour set against another:

> *I have to fight for the colour, it has to be right. My colour is very personal, I follow my instincts, but it is also very measured. I want clarity in all the parts of the painting. This is why you can count the colours. You can see three different yellows, two reds, a blue. The lines, the ground each is countable, like in a Léger. But the final painting is a total feeling that comes from all these countables.*[13]

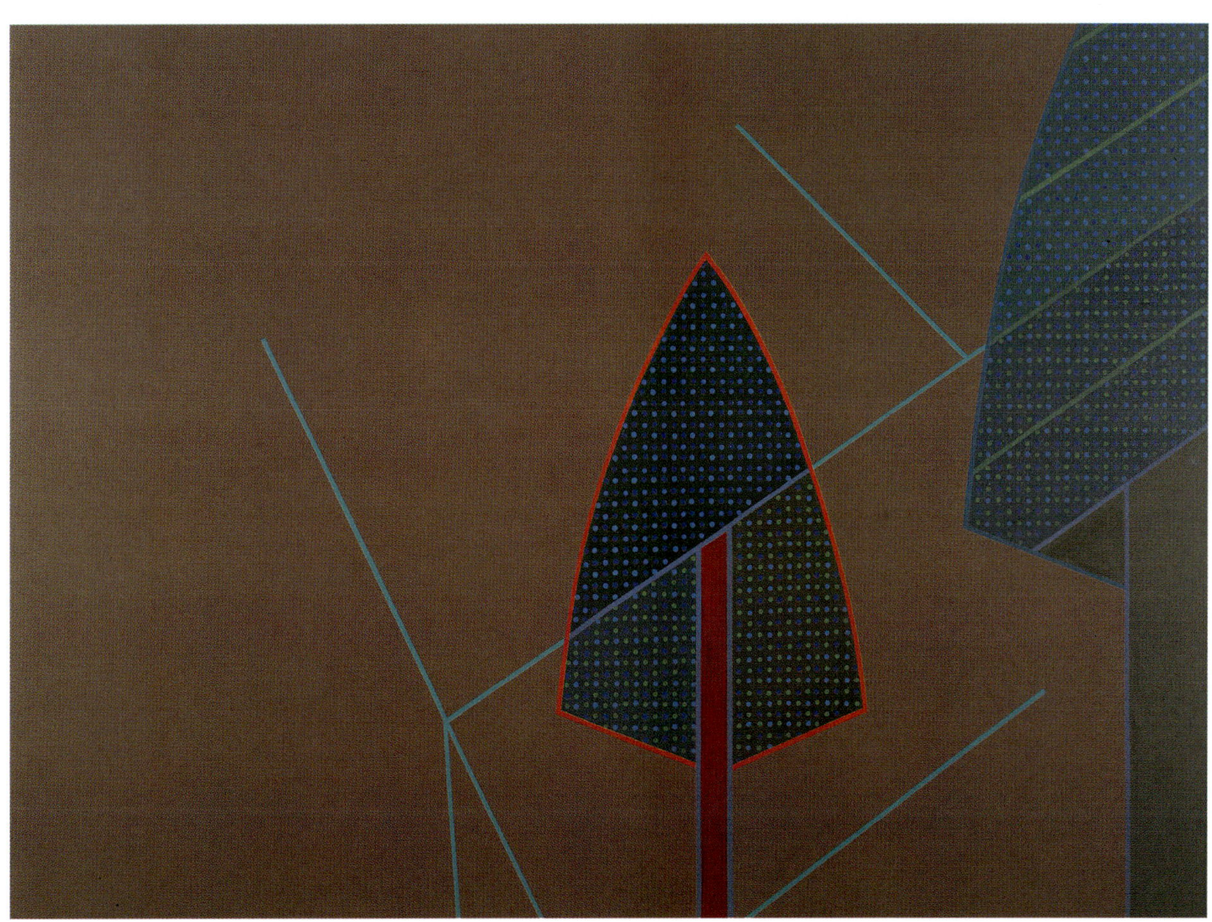

124 *Landscape with Conifers*, 2000–01
Oil on canvas
117 × 162.5cm (46.1 × 64in)

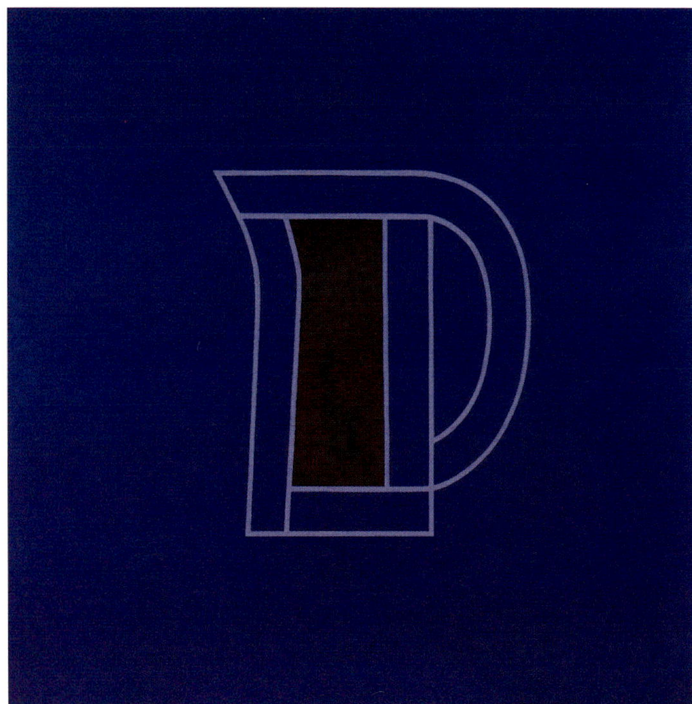

Coffee (plate 125) is characteristic, occupying a distinct space between the late paintings of William Scott and Peter Kinley, to which there are superficial affinities. However, whilst Scott sought to convey the substance and volume of his pared down forms and to set his table-top, still-life motifs against a field of colour, Greaves's objects have a 'lightness of being' and there is no such separation of form and ground. Kinley meanwhile used his delicate touches of thinned paint to unify the picture and soften his contours to allow forms to melt into the surrounding space. Greaves, however, hides his touch to allow the colour to dominate and uses lines that are firm, but do not necessarily relate to the subject's outline.

The emblematic, even heraldic, quality recalls Greaves's days as a sign writer, illustrating Marmite pots and Raleigh bicycles. *Coffee,* for example, began as a depiction of a coffee pot on a shelf, partly in remembrance of a café in Belsize Park in London; he even included a decorative cross pattern derived from the café's tiled walls (as in the watercolour *Coffee II*, 2001). Eventually, as he deconstructed the coffee pot, Greaves felt able to leave out the situating shelf and the decorative tiles, reconstructing the jug, as though from a model, to create a new schematic form: 'the structure was pushed through the sieve of the mind and remade as a painting, as something which could not be made in reality'. Such boldness was a breakthrough, leading to recent works that similarly reinvent form.

The spare, unadorned beauty of the resulting work is nowhere more evident than in the refined *Cascade* (plate 126) which parallels the qualities that Greaves admires in such diverse achievements as Matisse's *papier collés*, the paintings of Piet Mondrian and Elsworth Kelly, Jean Muir's clothes and Lucie Rie's ceramics. In other works, there is a greater syntactical complexity. Frequently, in these later works Greaves aims for the coexistence of different visual languages. Collage drawings of the 1980s and recent large-scale paintings are linked by their marriage of clear line to a use of transparency that allows forms to interlock and coexist, whilst retaining their distinctiveness.

The approach is elliptical, a way of lateral thinking that Greaves himself admires in Hans Keller's approach to music, Jacob Bronowski's *The Ascent of Man* and Kenneth Clark's approach to eroticism through the medium of art. Indeed, the analogies Greaves makes are frequently with music. A series of paintings, *Bird Song,* begun in 1997, even took the layering of bird song in his garden as a

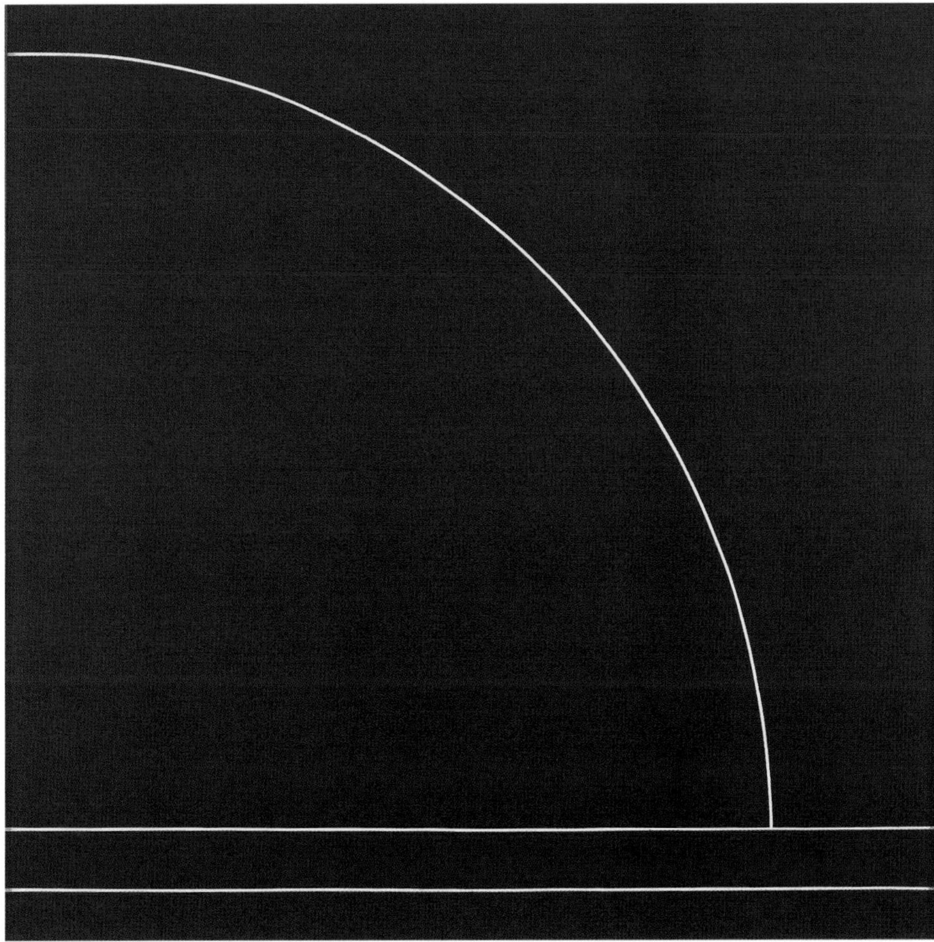

126 *Cascade*, 2000
Oil on canvas
152.5 × 152.5cm (60 × 60in)

metaphor for the way that forms can overlap in a painting and the high notes led him to heighten the chroma of his palette.

Greaves may consider Mozart's G minor Symphony No. 40 to be one of his favourite pieces and may identify with Ravel, admiring the combination of eroticism and humour in *Scheherazade*, but it is frequently to more avant-garde composers that he is drawn, including Olivier Messiaen and Charles Ives. Just as the musicians in an ensemble may play in different keys simultaneously, so Greaves, in his paintings, seeks to fit together different keynotes like jigsaw pieces. The results may be as bizarre as a brass band in an orchestra piece by Ives, but frequently cacophony gives way to harmony.

Greaves has consistently sought to translate this sort of bizarre structure into his painting. Certainly in his collage drawings there is a rupture between form and ground, and in recent paintings one often finds that each disparate element is rendered in a different style. At times the effect recalls the way that the late transparencies of Francis Picabia might combine a monster or pinup with a landscape, each painted in a different manner. Admiring these paintings, Greaves equates their impact to atonalism in music, in which there is a fruitful coexistence of different, precisely considered forms and the application of a linear construction. This is what Greaves particularly admires in the award-winning animation, *Flat World* (1998), by his son Daniel Greaves.[14] This half-hour animation presents a world of two-dimensional cut-outs into which intrudes a three-dimensional world: the main character cuts through a road cable and picks up the two ends. Pulses spark from each end and out leaps a variety of characters from cartoons to realist films, set against different coloured grounds.

In *Acropolis* (plate 127), Greaves combines a small sketchbook drawing of the Acropolis with a separate, totally unrelated drawing of a geometric form. Jamming these two pictorial structures together, he encapsulates an evening in which a cacophony of voices discussed their thoughts on Athens. The hillside and Acropolis are a single-coloured structure that is left without infilling, while the geometric form is polychrome. Superficially, such a painting may resemble the combining of languages to be found in the paintings of Patrick Caulfield, yet the use of line and conception of space is fundamentally different. In Greaves's work, the line may or may not relate to the form and the visibility of an all-over ground may be used to suggest transparency, whereas in Caulfield's work line often indicates the contour of an object, which is then filled in like a *cloisonné* or enamel inlay. For Greaves, the repercussions are not merely formal; this is not

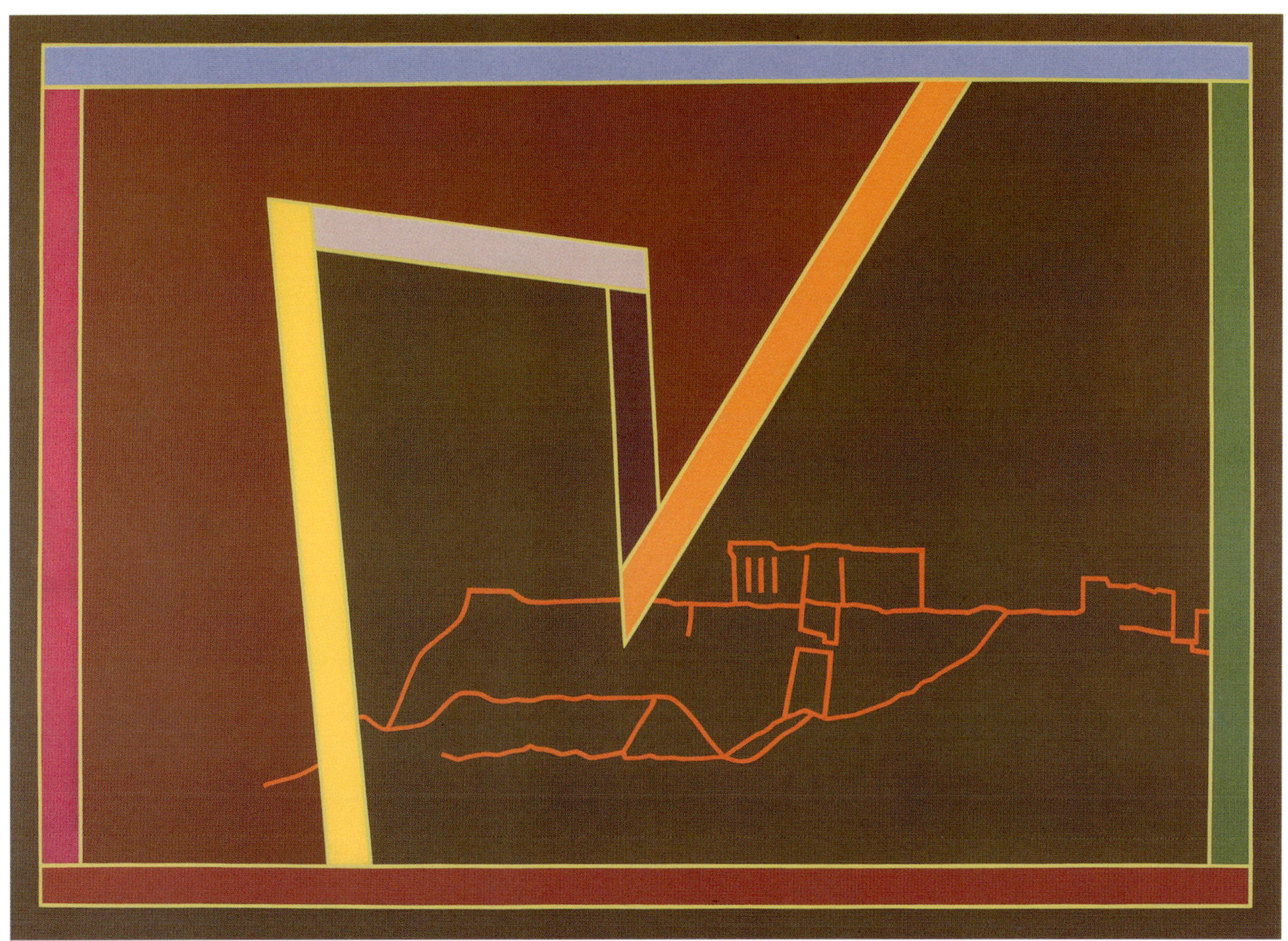

127 *Acropolis*, 1999
Oil on canvas
120.5 × 166.5cm (47.4 × 65.6in)
Claire and James Hyman, London

simply a formal device or a means of complicating the picture space. It also has a psychological dimension and an existential resonance that reflects his admiration for such Modernist classics as T.S. Eliot's *The Wasteland* and James Joyce's *Ulysses* with their inventive syntax, multiple voices and interpenetrating realities.

Acropolis is multilayered, like the conversations that inspired it, and in seeking such an equivalence in painting Greaves 'began to feel existentialist about the way things look different today than they did for Gustave Courbet'.[15] In contrast to Lucian Freud's alchemical desire for paint to be flesh, for Greaves 'paint is not flesh and cannot be; the painter's job is to invent a new language of painting and to speak with a contemporary voice. One cannot redo Courbet.'[16] The enemy is the prevalent preoccupation with volumes created through chiaroscuro and the conventional rendering of a heavy positive form in a negative space. Greaves deplores the conventional separation of figure and ground, and in discussing his own work talks instead of transparency, interpenetration and all-over equality: 'we have become more transparent than this; our corporeal presence is not as solid as it once was'.[17] This transparency may suggest insubstantiality but is none-theless concrete and allows Greaves remarkable freedom in his latest paintings to combine images from the external world with those from dreams, rendering them starkly, with ambiguity perhaps, but not with haziness. The challenge, then, has been to portray the subject in a new way that reflects new circumstances and a new worldview. In this sense, the artist has never stopped being a realist.

Other paintings are more elliptical. In contrast to Edward Middleditch, for whom the landscape was a more purely visual phenomenon, or David Bomberg and his followers, who dramatised the skin of the land, the bulk of the landscape and the drama of a slope or a hillock, for Greaves a rural motif may be specific in form but not place. *Green* (2001) suggests a mass of tree and trunk or the shelter of a bivouac, whilst *At the Farm* (2000–01) appears to show a pile of chopped wood and a hatchet or pan.

This impression of a subject sensed but not seen, of a thing encapsulated but not described, of a glimpsed view rather than a sustained gaze, is a leitmotif of Greaves's approach to landscape. But if Greaves is, above all, a rural artist then he is a particularly unusual example. His painting is the antithesis of English land-scape painting with its romanticism and love of metamorphic transformation, and it is distanced, too, from the anthropomorphism of a range of artists from Graham Sutherland to Peter Lanyon.[18] As in the poems of Seamus Heaney, which he admires, Greaves does not romanticise the farmer on the land. These are modern images rooted in today and the nature of Greaves's response is far removed from the extremes represented, on the one hand, by the gestural imprecision of Ivon Hitchens and, on the other, by the topographic fidelity of Michael Andrews. Nor does he concern himself with *genius loci* like Paul Nash.

Landscape of a new kind entered Greaves's work in the run up to the second Iraq War. Greaves felt moved to respond and once more this found focus in still-life motifs as well as nature. But perhaps in acknowledgement of the limitations of painting as direct political invention, what Greaves was painting was an escape. Just as Matisse spent the World Wars painting luxuriant studio interiors and lush landscapes, so Greaves produced an epic series of idylls under the title *Shangri-La*, among the boldest of which are *Shangri-La (Two Trees)* and *Shangri-La (Tree and Sea)* (plate 130): 'My depiction of exotic birds, plants and trees and through the tree glimpses of calm lagoons or seas appears extreme, escapist fantasy, but with their colour pitched to a new heightened level of expression the "escapist fantasy" was pushed to extremely un-pretty levels. Meanwhile the political world and the situations of Iraq and Afghanistan became darker than ever.'

In the two small, elegant paintings *Shangri-La (Exotic Bird)* (plate 128) and

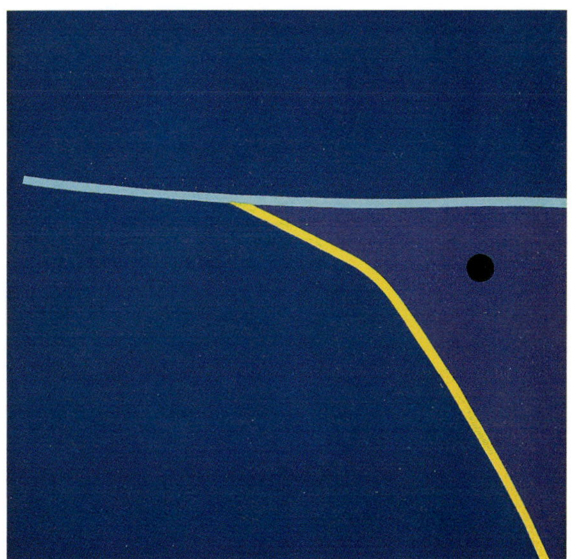

128 *Shangri-La
(Exotic Bird)*, 2003
Oil on canvas
40.5 × 40.5cm (15.9 × 15.9in)

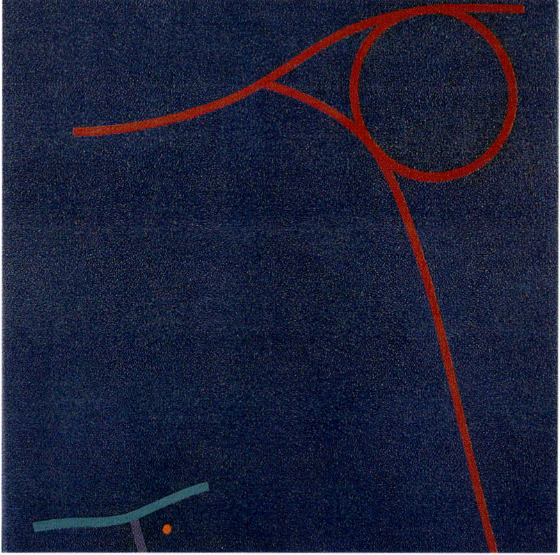

129 *Shangri-La
(Two Exotic Birds)*, 2002
Oil on canvas
40.5 × 40.5cm (15.9 × 15.9in)

Shangri-La (Two Exotic Birds) (plate 129), there is an enjoyment in the flow of line as well as precision. In *Shangri-La (Exotic Bird)*, an extended line from top to bottom helps create a space in which the artist places a circle; at once representational and abstract, the lines trace the beak, neck and eye of a bird as well as being quite simply two lines and a circle.

Many of the recent pictures start from dream images, although none are as literal as merely illustrating a dream.[21] Greaves passes through the studio to the bedroom and is very often snagged on the way by the painting of the day. Conversely, in the morning he passes through the studio to go to the kitchen, and uses a pad of yellow 'Post-it' notes to draw the fag ends of dreams. He sticks them on the studio wall to inspire a drawing or painting. The starting point may be personal and even trivial but, as with the work of his friend, the late Prunella Clough, the result is at once bold and subtle. Greaves has commented of Clough: 'In her own words, she "paints a small thing edgily". She does it freshly and unexpectedly. Her touch is beautiful – the way she uses the surface – and in her later work she takes risks she couldn't early on.'[22] A key to understanding both artists is to appreciate that however grand the resulting painting, its starting point might have been the most casual of doodles, in Greaves's case on the Post -it notes. When Greaves commented on this to Clough, she laughed that he had at last discovered the secret of her own way of working. External and internal worlds combine as Greaves has finally, 'after all these years been able to get an easy carpet slipper relationship with my unconscious'.[23]

Greaves likens this shift in sensibility and the combination of impressions that feed each new work to shifts in music: 'it's like atonalism in music: Tchaikovsky fits rural Russia at a particular time, but Ligeti's strung out style, absorption of world music and polyphonic voices is more relevant to our own times. It's part of our environmental and cultural matching set.'[24]

These multifarious sources also include Greaves's own earlier works and several recent paintings possess an overtly self-referential element. *Shooting the Crows* (plate 132) adds a crueller element to the earlier *Shadow of a Bird on a Road* (plate 73), while *Diptych – One Step Forward* (plate 136) and *Ten Thorns* (plate 131) echo Greaves's paintings of the late 1960s. Meanwhile, *Man into Bird* (plate 133) recalls Greaves's many pictures on the theme of Icarus but replaces their pathos with something jauntier. *Wall Drawings* (plate 135) is more explicit. A large painting, it references more recent works, specifically Greaves's Post-it note doodles. In *Wall Drawings*, Greaves achieves his ambition of allowing forms

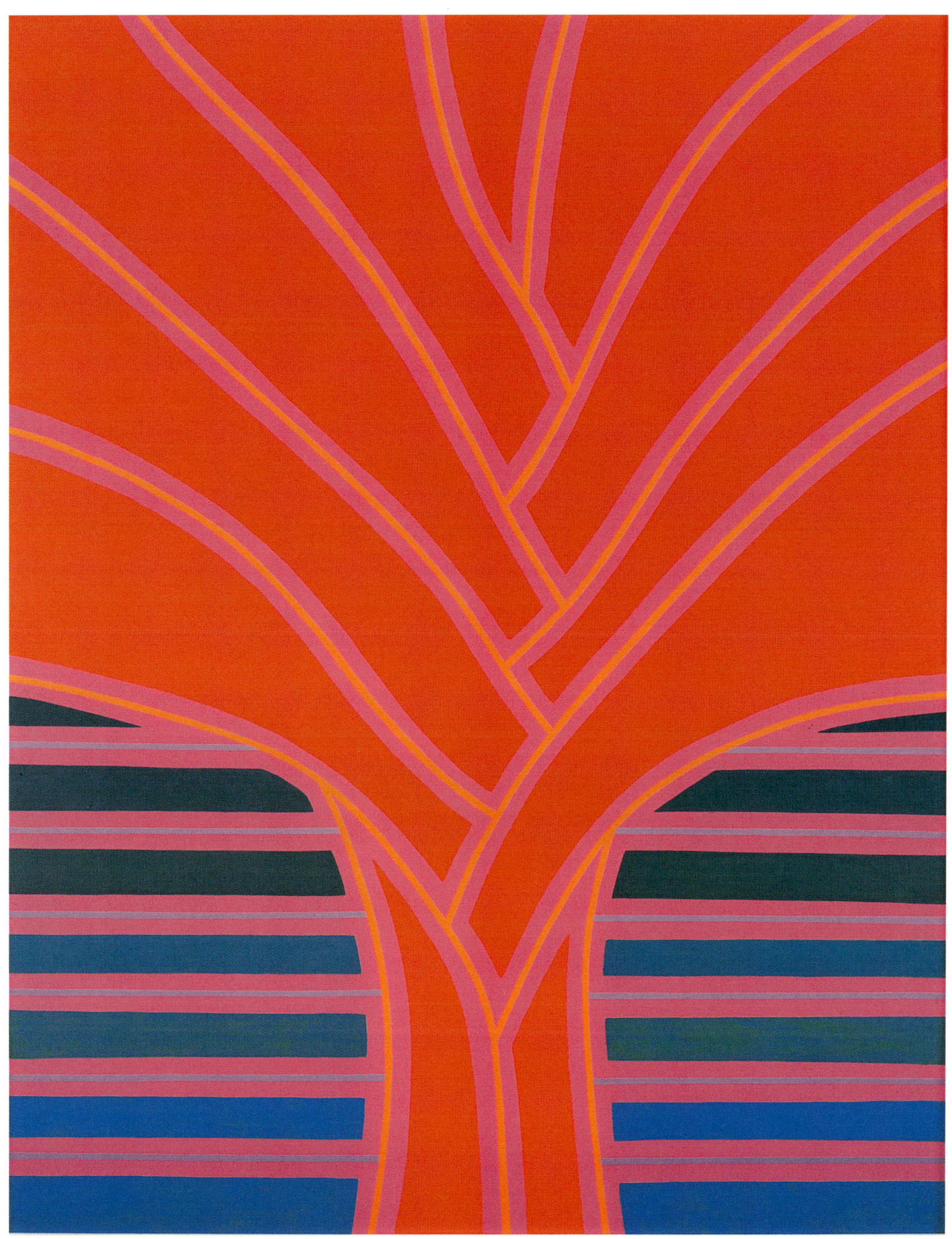

130 *Shangri-La (Tree and Sea)*, 2005
Oil on canvas
152.5 × 122cm (60 × 48in)

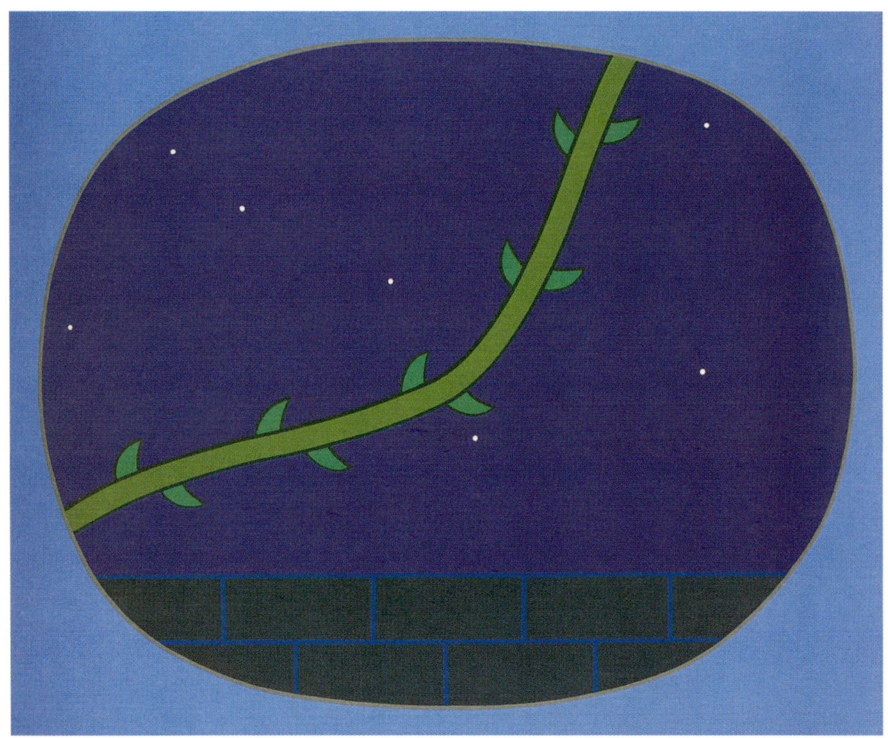

131 *Ten Thorns*, 2005–06
Oil on canvas
122 × 152.5cm (48 × 60in)

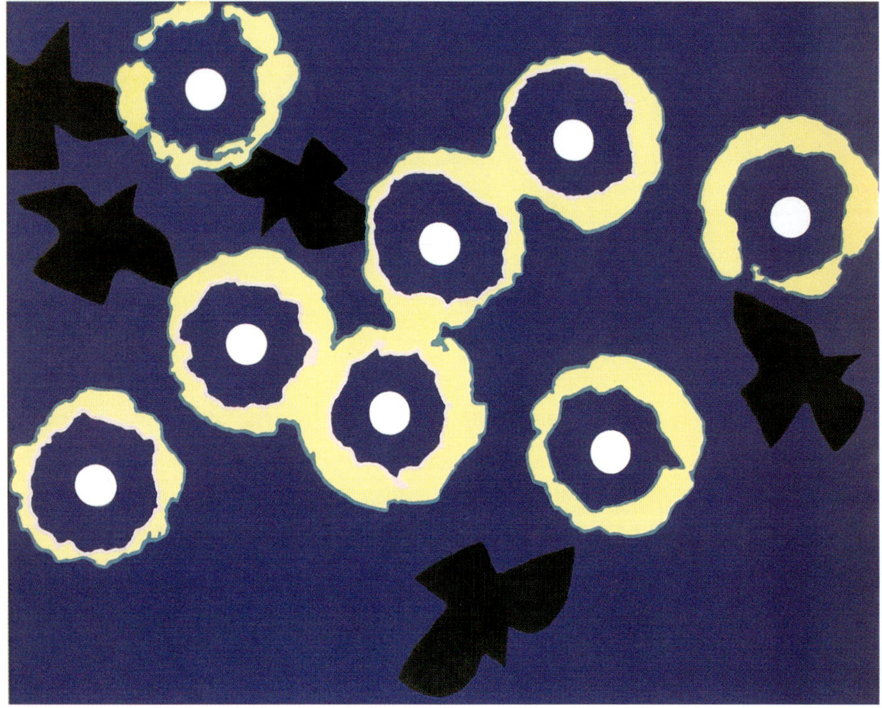

132 *Shooting the Crows*, 2003–04
Oil on canvas
101.5 × 127cm (40 × 50in)

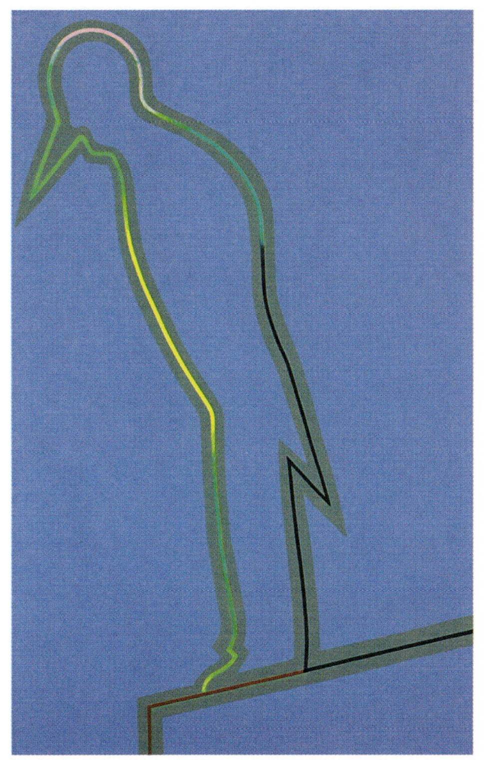

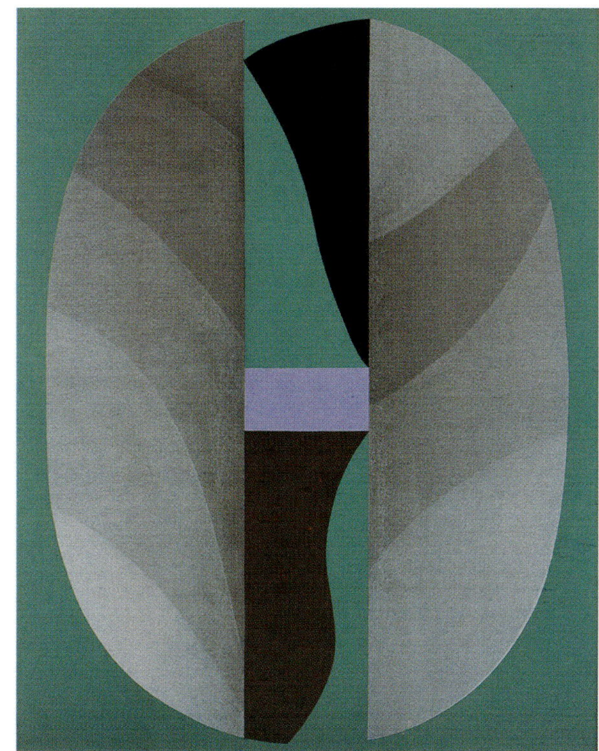

133 *Man into Bird*, 2003–04
Oil on canvas
137 × 91.5cm (53.9 × 36in)

134 *Et in Arcadia Ego*, 2005
Acrylic on canvas
152.5 × 122cm (60 × 48in)

to interpenetrate. Transparency is a key as images flit in and out of focus. Possessing the soft translucence of a reverie, the painting retains the intimacy of Post-it notes. In so doing, it combines the escapism of his *Shangri-La* paintings of exotic birds, which it samples, with the more immediate concerns of creating a synthetic landscape.

Elsewhere, however, the mood is bleaker, with fighting in the Middle East provoking engagement, rather than escape to an earthly paradise. Greaves's largest painting of recent years, *War Triptych* (plate 137) is a powerful return to the mural format of his earliest paintings and a reprise of the triptych format of the late 1960s and early 1970s. Drawing from existing imagery, including an earlier screenprint of a bound figure, Greaves provides a brooding image of a menacing war machine, imprisonment and torture. The bold iconography and emblematic imagery speak for and of our times in a strong and distinct voice, a voice that is both individual and universal, classical and contemporary.

Such paintings are the legacy of Greaves's earlier paintings and deserve to become his iconic images. Indeed, they stand proudly alongside the youthful paintings with which the artist first established his reputation half a century

ago. But this is to look backwards. The journey still continues, as Greaves recently
explained:

> *I work everyday in the quiet atmosphere of the studio which, year upon year, has*
> *suited me well. I like it, and the hours of prolonged contemplation it brings.*
> *Interestingly there's no sense of repetition for, over the months and years, work*
> *changes under the hand, becoming porous, absorbing the most unexpected clues,*
> *transforming its own form. Paintings become palimpsests and drawings spawn*
> *dozens more formal variations. They all seem to do themselves, by themselves,*
> *more and more, to determine their own form and future and the way they finally*
> *look. And just as importantly, look back at you. For, as Klee says, 'don't think*
> *you are just looking at pictures – they are also looking at you'.*[25]

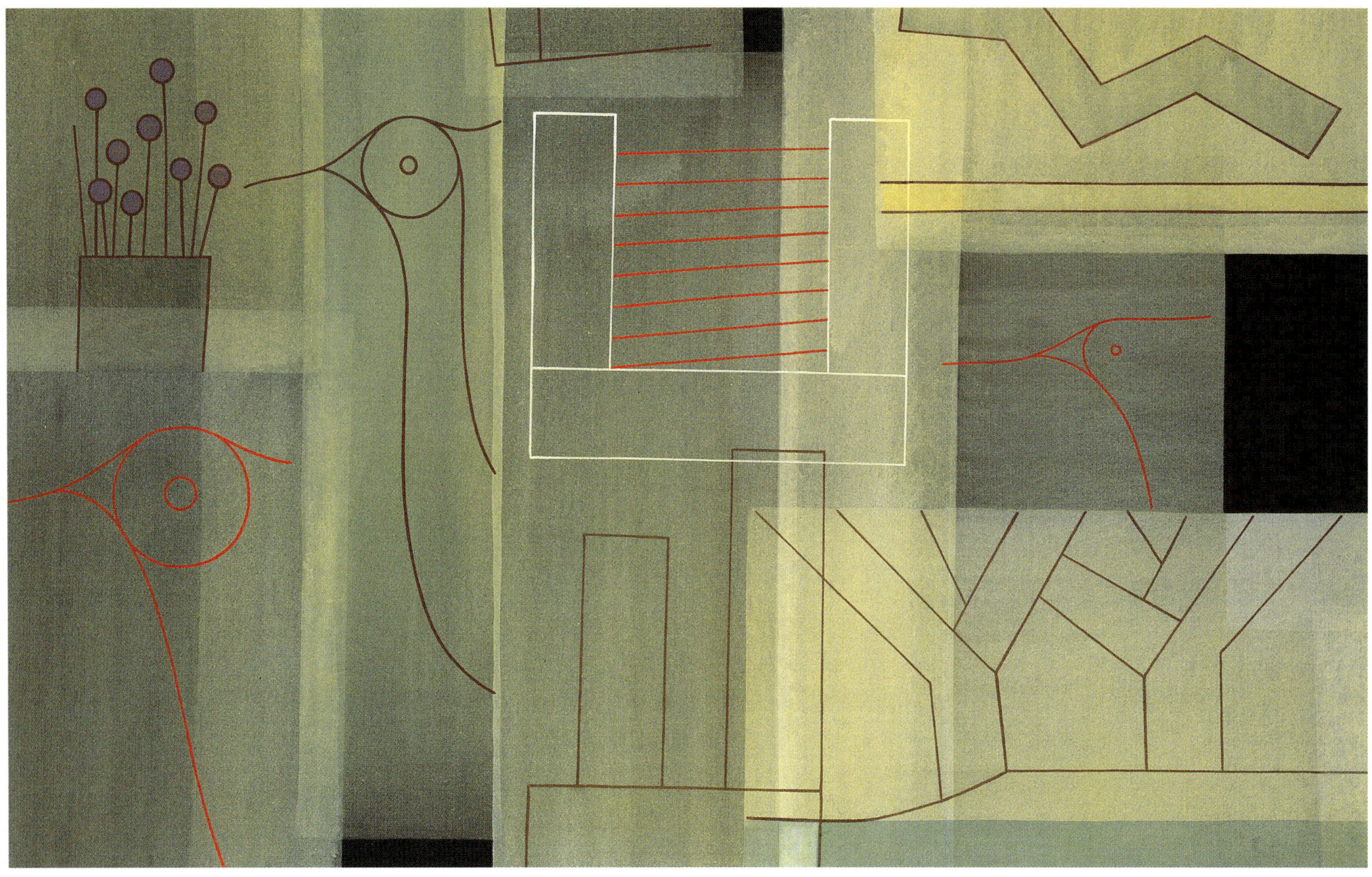

135 *Wall Drawings*, 2004–06
Acrylic on canvas
94.5 × 152.5cm (37.2 × 60in)
Private Collection, London

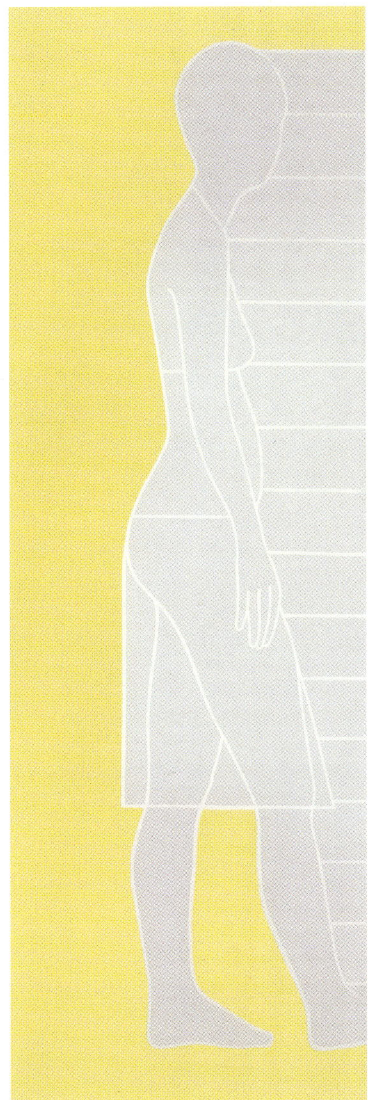

136 *Diptych – One Step Forward*, 2004–06
Oil on canvas
163 × 56cm (64.2 × 22in)

Notes

1. Derrick Greaves, interview with James Hyman, 20 November 2004.
2. Tim Hilton, 'Hanging the Edwardians', *Guardian*, 1990, p.33. Artist's Archive. Hilton has been a consistent champion, writing in 1990: 'Greaves's retrospective two years ago was not enough noticed. He has links with Pop Art, though he is not one of them. Was there a link between Kitchen-Sink and RCA Pop? I think so.' Tim Hilton, 'Stages on the exhibition road', *Guardian*, 16 March 1988, p.21. Then, in 1991, Hilton added: 'Three years ago Greaves, to my mind a seriously underrated artist, had a touring exhibition that really should have come to London.' Tim Hilton, 'The Perfectly awful John Bratby', *Guardian*, 27 March 1991, p.37.

3. Robert Medley, letter to Derrick Greaves, referring to *Forty from Ten*, 21 April 1987.
4. This exhibition presented Greaves's 24 silkscreen prints inspired by Pierre Louys's *Les Chansons de Bilitis*, printed by Mel Clark during 1978–9, Middleditch's landscape and nature studies, and Medley's illustrations for Milton's *Samson Agonistes*. The catalogue included short essays on each artist, respectively by Victor Musgrave, Bryan Robertson and Mel Gooding.
5. Derrick Greaves, interview with James Hyman. November 2002.
6. Op. cit.
7. Op. cit.
8. Courtney, tape 3, side 1.
9. Derrick Greaves, interview with James Hyman. 23 December 2002.

10. Greaves has a great admiration for the BBC Third programme, now BBC Radio Three, both for its music coverage and the talks it broadcasts. He recalls making notes of a broadcast by Professor Gombrich on signs and symbols.
11. Courtney, tape 10, side 2.
12. Courtney, tape 4, side 2.
13. Courtney, tape 10, side 2.
14. Daniel Greaves, *Flat World*, BBC, 1998.
15. Derrick Greaves, interview with James Hyman, 23 December 2002.
16. Derrick Greaves, interview with James Hyman, 23 December 2002.
17. Derrick Greaves, conversation with James Hyman, June 2005.
18. Greaves recalls that whilst at the British School in Rome, Peter Lanyon came to visit. They walked in the

Abruzzi mountains, arguing about how to respond to their environment. While Lanyon was interested in metamorphosis and poetry, Greaves's approach to landscape was at that time direct and matter-of-fact.
19. Derrick Greaves, unpublished journal entry, undated.
20. Derrick Greaves, unpublished journal entry, undated.
21. Courtney, tape 5, side 1.
22. Derrick Greaves, interview with James Hyman, March 2003.
23. Courtney, tape 3, side 2.
24. Courtney, tape 3, side 2. The Hungarian composer György Ligeti (1923–2006) came to prominence with *Atmosphères* (1961).
25. Derrick Greaves, unpublished journal entry, undated.

137 *War Triptych*, 2003–06
Acrylic and oil on canvas
147.3 × 91.4cm (58 × 36in),
147.3 × 187.3cm (58 × 73.8in),
147.3 × 91.4cm (58 × 36in)

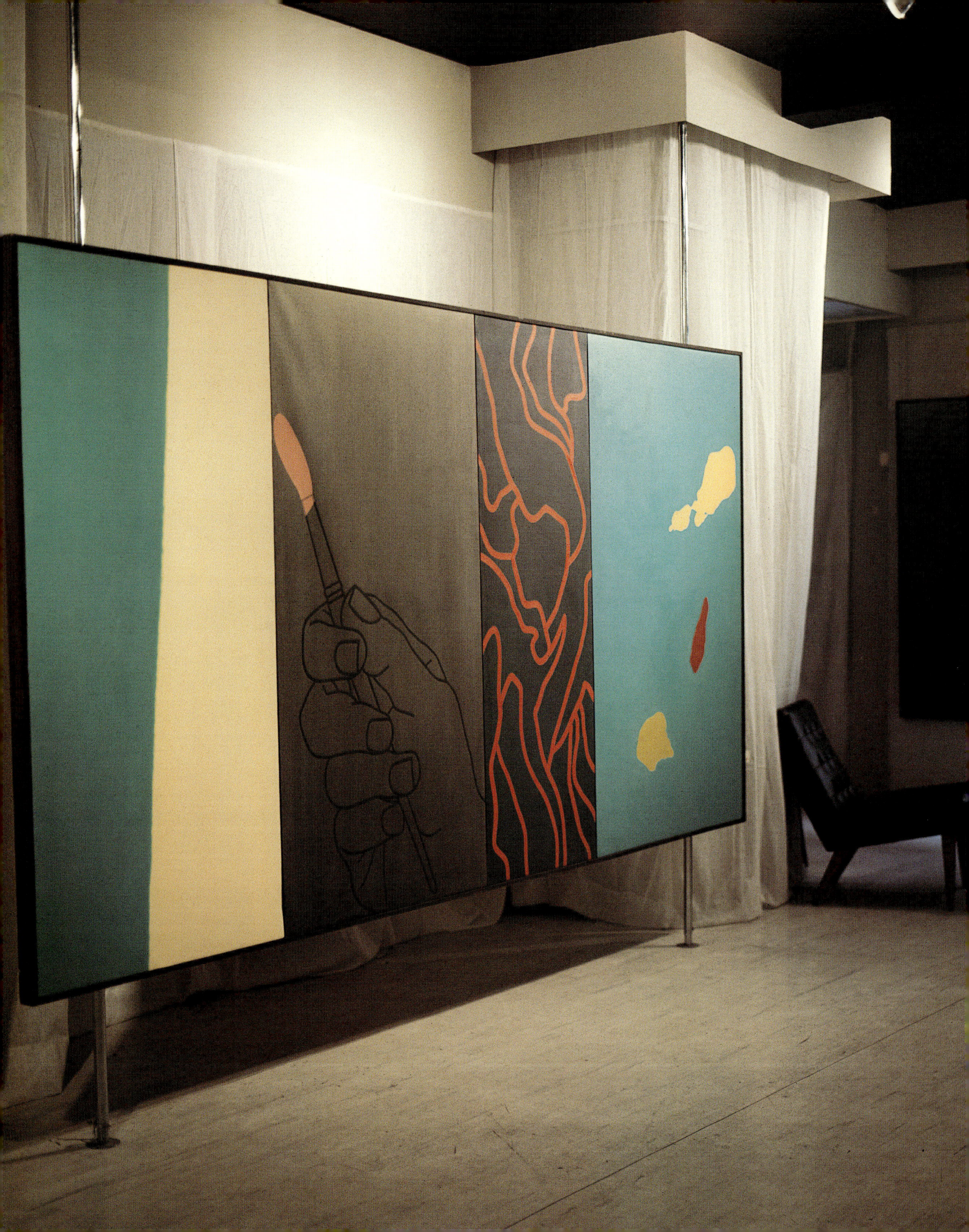

Key Dates, Exhibitions, Public Collections, Selected Reading

Key Dates

1927 Born 5 June, Sheffield

1943–8 Apprenticed as a sign writer

1948–52 Won a scholarship to study at the Royal College of Art, London

1950 Married Margaret Johnson

1952–4 Abbey Major Scholarships to study in Italy

1954–63 Taught part-time at St Martin's School of Art, London

1956 Represented Britain at Venice Biennale (with John Bratby, Edward Middleditch and Jack Smith)

1957 Visited USSR. Awarded Gold Medal for painting at Moscow Youth Festival. Awarded prize at John Moore's Exhibition, Liverpool

1962 Awarded purchase prize in Belfast Open Painting Exhibition

mid 1960s Taught part-time at Maidstone College of Art and Royal Academy schools

1979 Visited Israel with nine other British artists to produce work for 'Israel Observed' project

1983–91 Head of Printmaking at Norwich School of Art

1994 Married Sally Butler

Solo Exhibitions

1953 *Derrick Greaves*, Beaux Arts Gallery, London

1955 *Derrick Greaves*, Beaux Arts Gallery, London

1958 *Derrick Greaves; Paintings and Monotypes*, Zwemmer Gallery, London

1960 *Derrick Greaves; Paintings 1959–60*, Zwemmer Gallery, London

1962 *Derrick Greaves; New Paintings, Drawings and Aquatints*, Zwemmer Gallery, London

1963 *Derrick Greaves; Paintings and Wash Drawings*, Zwemmer Gallery, London

1968 *The Sower as Self-Portrait: Homage to Van Gogh*, Curwen Gallery, London

1969 *Derrick Greaves*, Institute of Contemporary Art, London
Derrick Greaves, Ewan Phillips, London

1970 *Derrick Greaves*, Bear Lane Gallery, Oxford
Derrick Greaves, Galleria La Citta, Padua and Verona, Italy
Derrick Greaves: Paintings, Drawings, Graphics, McCleaf Gallery, Philadelphia, USA

1971 *Derrick Greaves*, Institute of Contemporary Art, London

Derrick Greaves; Recent Paintings, Basil Jacobs Fine Art, London

1972 *Derrick Greaves*, Arts Council Gallery, Belfast, Northern Ireland
Derrick Greaves, David Hendriks Gallery, Dublin, Ireland
Derrick Greaves, Bruton Gallery, Bruton

1973 *Derrick Greaves*, Bear Lane Gallery, Oxford
Derrick Greaves, Whitechapel Gallery, London
Derrick Greaves, Monika Kinley, London

1974 *Derrick Greaves*, David Hendriks Gallery, Dublin, Ireland
Derrick Greaves, Monika Kinley, London

1975 *Derrick Greaves*, Monika Kinley, London
Derrick Greaves, City Gallery, Milton Keynes

1976 *Derrick Greaves*, Monika Kinley, London
Derrick Greaves, City Gallery, Milton Keynes

1977 *Derrick Greaves*, Monika Kinley, London
Derrick Greaves, City Gallery, Milton Keynes

Facing page:
138 Installation, Ewan Phillips, London, 1969

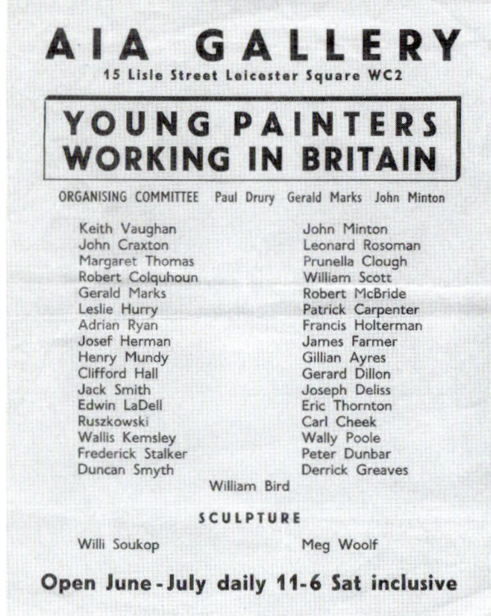

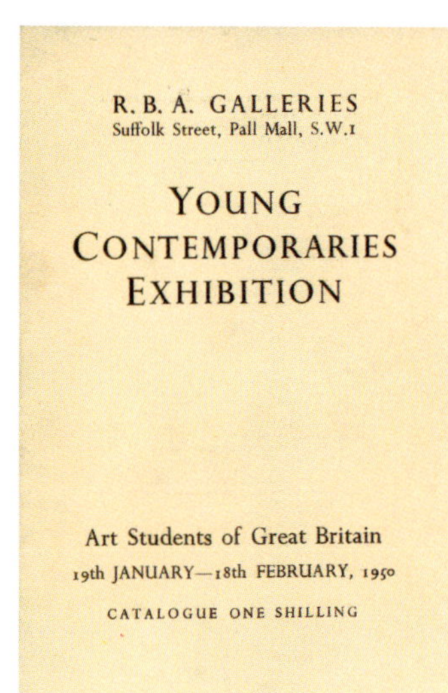

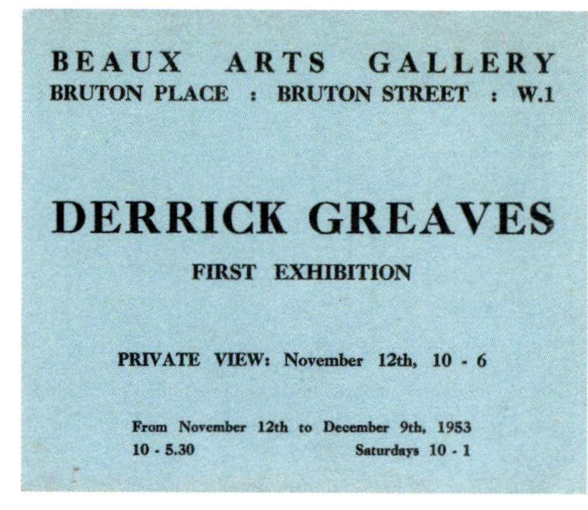

1978 *Derrick Greaves*, Monika Kinley, London
Derrick Greaves, City Gallery, Milton Keynes
Derrick Greaves, Cranfield Institute of Technology, Cranfield

1980 *Derrick Greaves: Retrospective Exhibition of Paintings 1953–1980*, Graves Art Gallery, Sheffield
Derrick Greaves: Retrospective Exhibition of Prints 1969–1980, Leicester Museum and Art Gallery, Leicester
Derrick Greaves: Collage Drawings, Fischer Fine Art, London

1986 *Derrick Greaves – Forty from Ten*, Loughborough College of Art and Design, Loughborough

1992 *Derrick Greaves: Masks, Torsos, Flowers*, King of Hearts Gallery, Norwich

1996 *Derrick Greaves*, Gallerie Daniel Wahrenberger, Zurich, Switzerland

1997 *Derrick Greaves*, Hart Gallery, London
Derrick Greaves, King of Hearts Gallery, Norwich

1999 *Derrick Greaves: Drawing for Paintings 1953–1997*, School House Gallery, Wighton

2001 *Collage Drawings*, Chappel Galleries, Chappel

2002 *Six Decades of Painting*, Wingfield Arts Centre, Wingfield

2003 *Derrick Greaves: Paintings and Drawings 1952–2002*, James Hyman Fine Art, London

2005 *Derrick Greaves: The Pleasures of Drawing*, James Hyman Fine Art, London

2006 *Pop Classical: Derrick Greaves, Paintings from the 1970s*, James Hyman Fine Art, London

2007 *Derrick Greaves: An Eightieth Birthday Tribute*, James Hyman Fine Art, London

Selected Group Exhibitions

1949 *Young Painters*, Lisle Street Gallery, A.I.A., London

1950 *Paintings by Contemporary Artists*, A.I.A., London
Young Contemporaries, R.B.A. Galleries, London

1952 *Artists for Peace*, Adams Gallery, London
Looking Forward, Whitechapel Art Gallery, London (curated by John Berger and including Peter de Francia, L.S. Lowry, Edward Middleditch, John Minton, Rodrigo Moynihan, Ruskin Spear and Carel Weight)

1953 *Looking Forward*, Whitechapel Art Gallery, London, touring exhibition (curated by John Berger)

1955 Heffer Gallery, Cambridge (with John Bratby, Edward Middleditch and Jack Smith)
The Artist's View of an Industry: Recent Drawings and Paintings of the Oil Industry, Arts Council of Great Britain (including Michael Andrews, Peter Coker and Edward Middleditch)

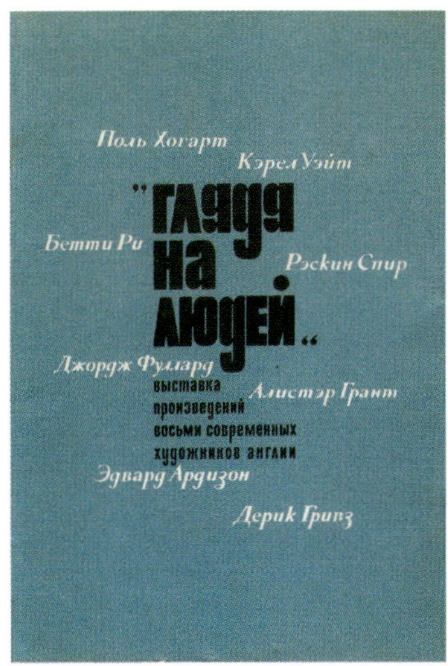 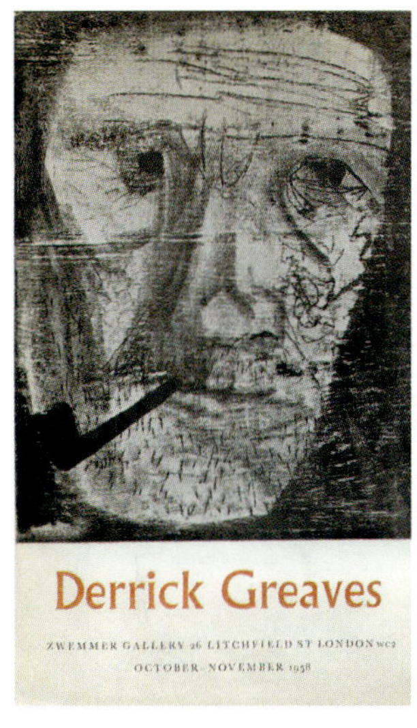 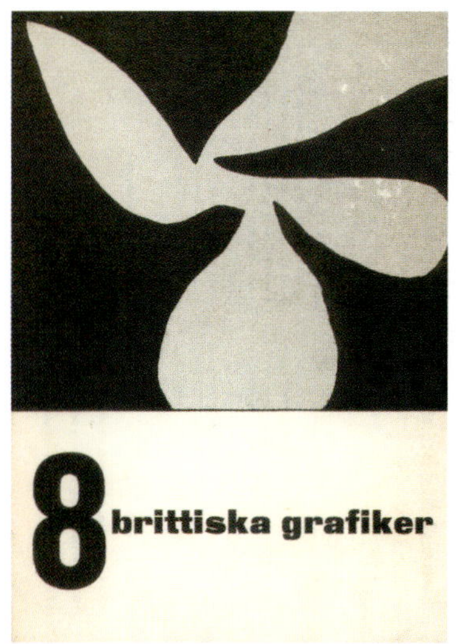

1956 Contemporary Arts Society, London
Quatro Giovani Pittori Inglesi, British
Pavilion, Venice Biennale, Venice, Italy
(with John Bratby, Edward Middleditch
and Jack Smith)
Landscape Painting, I.C.A., London
Three British Painters, Adams Gallery,
London (with Edward Middleditch and
Peter de Francia) and Piccadilly Gallery,
London (with Edward Middleditch and
Alistair Grant)

1957 *Six Young Painters*, Arts Council
of Great Britain (including Michael
Andrews, John Bratby, Harold Cohen,
Martin Froy and Philip Sutton)
Looking at People, Pushkin Museum,
Moscow, Russia
Yorkshire Artists' Exhibition, City Art
Gallery, Leeds
John Moore's Exhibition, Liverpool
Looking Forward, South London Art
Gallery, London

1959 *16 Paintings by 16 Painters: Aspects
of Realism*, A.I.A. Gallery, London
John Moore's Exhibition, Liverpool

1960 Guggenheim Selection, Pittsburgh,
USA and London

Das Junge England, Neue Galerie der
Stadt Linz, Linz, Austria

1961 John Moore's Exhibition, Liverpool

1962 *Towards Art; The Contribution of the
RCA to the Fine Arts 1952–62*, Royal
College of Art, London

1963 John Moore's Exhibition, Liverpool
British Painting in the 60s, Whitechapel
Gallery, London
Brittiska Grafiker, Stockholm, Sweden

1964 *The Pittsburgh International*,
Carnegie Institute, Pittsburgh, USA
Prints 64, A.I.A. Gallery, London

1966 *Print Workshop*, Curwen Gallery,
London
Six Sheffield Artists, Mappin Art Gallery,
Sheffield

1969 John Moore's Exhibition, Liverpool

1974 *British Painting '74*, Haymarket
Gallery, London

1975 *The Wavendon Season 1975*, City
Gallery, Milton Keynes (with Edward
Middleditch and Jason Monet)

1976 *The Gordon Lambert Collection of
Contemporary Art*, Ulster Museum,
Belfast, Northern Ireland

1977 *British Painting 1952–1977*, Royal
Academy, London

1978 *Exposicion International de la
Plastica*, Museo de San Francisco,
San Francisco, Chile

1979 *The British Art Show*, toured
Sheffield, Newcastle and Bristol
(recent paintings and sculpture,
selected by William Packer)
Five Artists, City Gallery, Milton Keynes
(with Stephen Gregory, Sonia Lawson,
Paolo Serra and John Watson)
*Contemporary Art for 17 Charterhouse
Street*, Mall Galleries, London

1981 *Israel Observed*, Israel Museum,
Jerusalem, Israel; Mall Galleries,
London; Royal Northern College
of Music, Manchester
*Books and Folios – Screenprints by
Derrick Greaves, Robert Medley and
Edward Middleditch*, Arts Council of
Great Britain, touring exhibition
*Artists for Nuclear Disarmament at the
Acme Gallery*, Acme Gallery, London

1982 *A Taste of British Art Today*, C.A.S.
Exhibition, Brussels, Belgium

1983 *Twelve by Twelve*, Leicester Museum
and Art Gallery, Leicester
New Work from Norwich School of Art,
University of East Anglia, Norwich

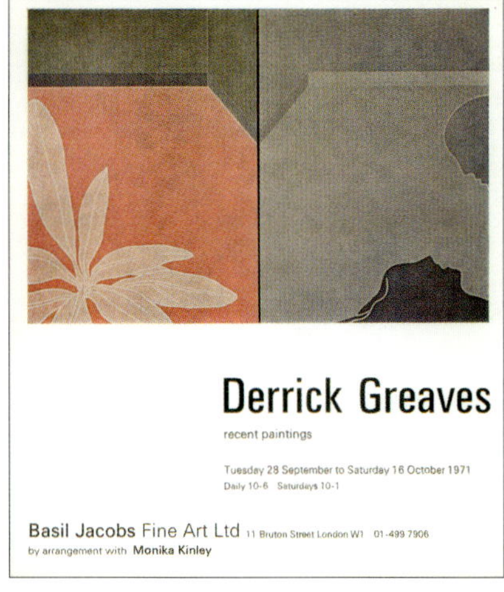

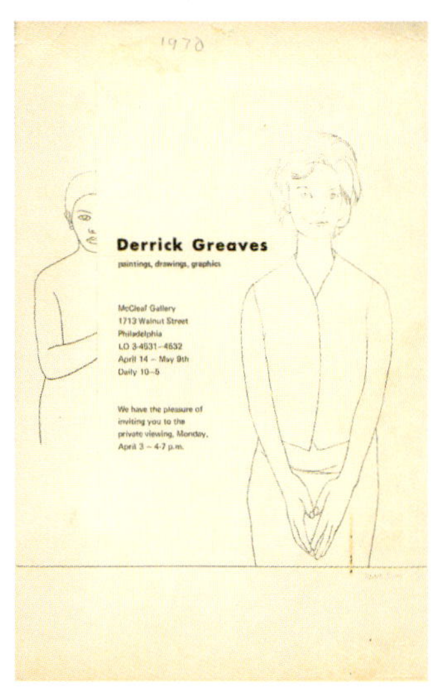

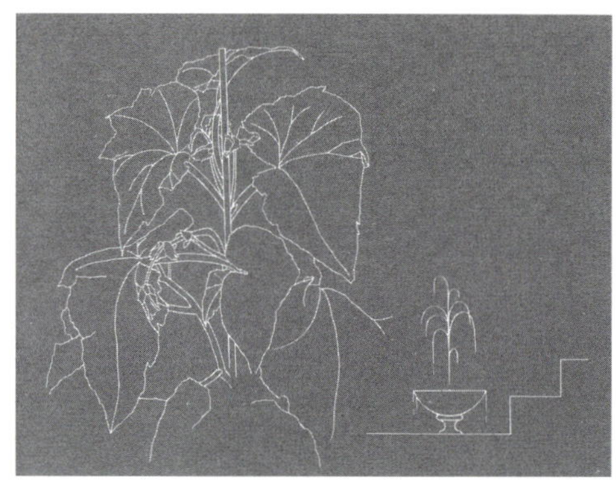

1984 *The Forgotten Fifties*, Sheffield City Art Galleries, touring exhibition to Graves Art Gallery, Sheffield, Castle Museum, Norwich, Herbert Art Gallery and Museum, Coventry and Camden Arts Centre, London (among those included were David Bomberg, Peter de Francia, Leon Kossoff, Edward Middleditch, Claude Rogers, Jack Smith and Carel Weight)
British Artists' Books 1970–1983, Atlantis Gallery, London

1986 *Generations Apart*, Mappin Art Gallery, Sheffield

1987 *150th Anniversary Exhibition of Printmaking from the Royal College of Art*, Barbican Art Gallery, London
Exhibition Road: Painters at the Royal College of Art, Royal College of Art, London (among those included were Frank Auerbach, Edward Burra, Patrick Caulfield, Donald Hamilton Fraser, David Hockney, R.B.Kitaj, Leon Kossoff, Rodrigo Moynihan, John Piper and Jack Smith)

1988 *Summer Exhibition*, Royal Academy, London
New Prints from Norwich, University of London, London and Wingfield College, Wingfield

1989 *Summer Exhibition*, Royal Academy, London
Portrait of the Artist, Tate Gallery, London
Within these Shores: A Selection of Works from the Chantrey Bequest 1883–1985, Tate Gallery, London in association with Sheffield City Art Galleries

1990 *Summer Exhibition*, Royal Academy, London

1991 *The Kitchen Sink Painters*, Mayor Gallery, London
Norfolk Portfolio, Castle Museum, Norwich (with Roger Ackling and Anthony Benjamin)
Summer Exhibition, Royal Academy, London
The Discerning Eye, Mall Galleries, London

1991–2 *New Year Exhibition*, Chappel Galleries, Chappel

1992 *Summer Exhibition*, Royal Academy, London

1993 *Summer Exhibition*, Royal Academy, London
New Norfolk Drawings: Derrick Greaves, Roger Ackling, Anthony Benjamin, King's Lynn Arts Centre, King's Lynn
Open Exhibition, King's Lynn Arts Centre, King's Lynn
Christmas Exhibition, King of Hearts Gallery, Norwich

1994 *Kitchen Sink and Other Drawings of the Fifties*, Julian Hartnoll and Mayor Gallery, London
The Kitchen Sink and the Beaux Arts Gallery, Mayor Gallery, London

1995 *The Kitchen Sink Painters*, Michael Haas Gallery, Berlin-Charlottenburg, Germany

1996 *Private Views*, Contact Gallery, Norwich
Flowers in May, King of Hearts Gallery, Norwich

1997 *Revolutions: 1950-1960-1970*, Nicosia Municipal Arts Centre, Nicosia, Cyprus

1998 *Summer Exhibition*, Royal Academy, London

2002 *Transition: The London Art Scene in the Fifties*, Barbican Art Gallery, London (inc. Francis Bacon, Peter Blake, Lucian Freud, Allen Jones, William Turnbull)
The Naked Truth, Fermoy Gallery, King's Lynn

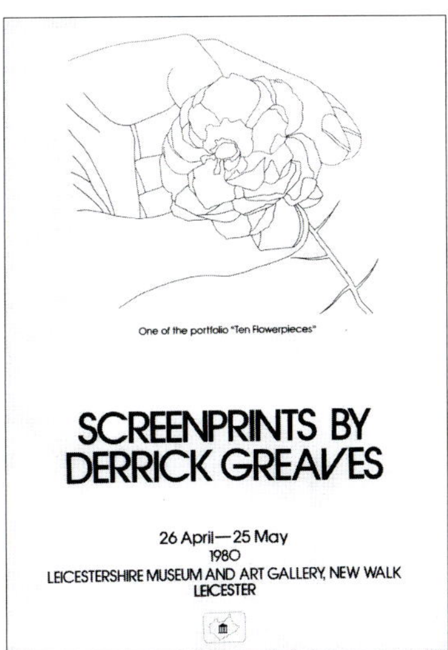

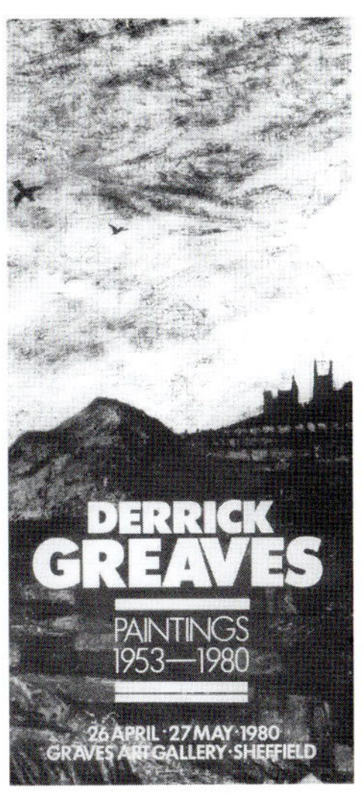

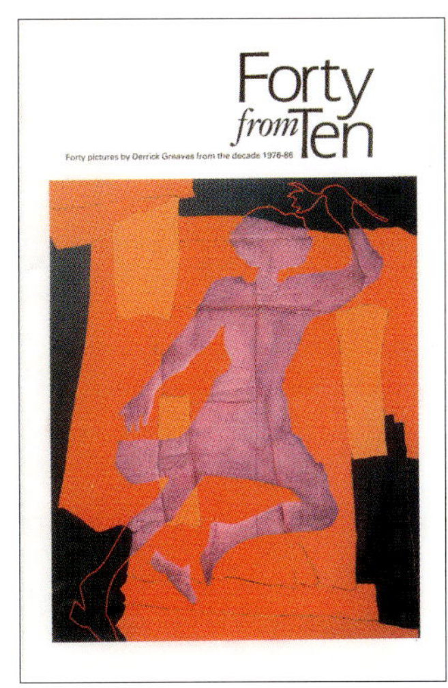

2005 *Fifty Years of British Landscape Painting*, James Hyman Fine Art, London (with Michael Andrews, Frank Auerbach, Lewis Chamberlain, Sheila Fell, Terry Frost, Roger Hilton, Ivon Hitchens, Leon Kossoff, Robert Medley, Henry Moore, Graham Sutherland, Arnold van Praag)

2006 *New Directions*, James Hyman Fine Art, London (with Michael Andrews, Peter de Francia and Robert Medley)
Drawing Inspiration, Abbot Hall Art Gallery, Kendal (among those included were Frank Auerbach, Peter de Francia, Lucian Freud, Damien Hirst, David Hockney, Leon Kossoff and Paula Rego)
Travellers' Tales, Graves Art Gallery, Sheffield
Home and Away: Andrews, de Francia, Greaves, Medley, Middleditch, Townsend, van Praag, James Hyman Fine Art, London

Public Collections

Arts Council of England
Bank of Ireland, Dublin, Ireland
Berardo Collection, Sintra, Portugal
British Council
British Museum, London
Cambridgeshire County Council, Cambridge
Castle Museum, Norwich
Chantrey Bequest
City of Milton Keynes Collection, Milton Keynes
Contemporary Art Society
Cranfield College of Technology, Cranfield
Department of the Environment
Government Art Collection
Graves Art Gallery, Sheffield
IBM, New York, USA
Johannesburg Public Gallery, South Africa
Leeds Art Gallery, Leeds
Leicestershire County Collection
Municipal Gallery of Modern Art, Dublin, Ireland
National Museum of Wales, Cardiff
National Portrait Gallery, London
New York Public Library, New York, USA
Norfolk Contemporary Arts Association, Norfolk
North Wales Association of Arts
Northwestern University, Chicago, USA
Pallant House Gallery, Chichester
Pembroke College, Oxford University, Oxford
Philadelphia Museum of Art, Philadelphia, USA
Public Gallery, Adelaide, Australia
Reading Art Gallery, Reading
Southampton Art Gallery, Southampton
Tate Gallery, London
University of Wales, Aberystwyth
Walker Art Gallery, Liverpool
Wesleyan University, Illinois, USA

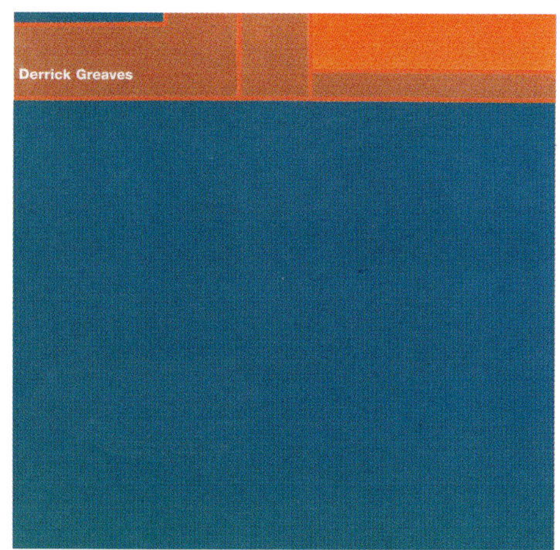

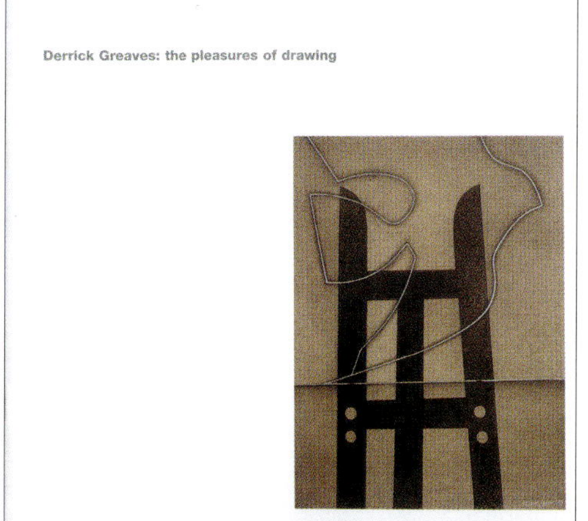

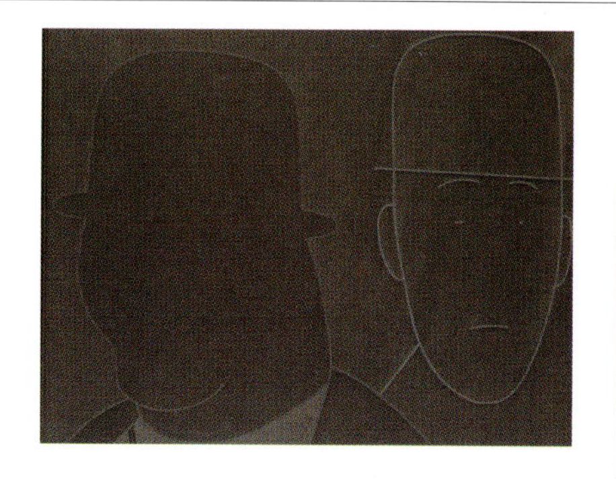

Selected Reading

Books:

Exhibition Road – Painters at the Royal College of Art, Phaidon-Christies Ltd, Oxford, 1988

Portrait of the Artist, Tate Gallery Publications, London, 1989

Hyman, James, *The Battle for Realism: Figurative Art in Britain during the Cold War 1945–1960*, Yale University Press, New Haven and London, 2001

Catalogues:

The British Art Show, Recent Paintings and Sculpture by 112 Artists Selected by William Packer, toured Sheffield, Newcastle and Bristol, catalogue, 1980

Books and Folios – Screenprints by Derrick Greaves, Robert Medley and Edward Middleditch, Arts Council Touring Exhibition, catalogue, 1981

British Artists' Books 1970–83, Atlantis

Israel Observed; An Exhibition by 10 British Artists, catalogue, 1981

Morris, Lynda and Radford, Robert, *The Story of the Artists International Association*, Oxford, 1983

Spalding, Julian (ed.), *The Forgotten Fifties*, Sheffield City Art Galleries, catalogue, 1984

Wheeler, Peter, essay in *Derrick Greaves – Forty from Ten*, Loughborough College of Art and Design and tour, 1986

150th Anniversary Exhibition of Printmaking from the Royal College, catalogue, 1987

Within these Shores – A Selection of Works from the Chantrey Bequest 1883–1985, Tate Gallery Publications, catalogue, 1989

The Kitchen Sink Painters, Mayor Gallery, London, catalogue, 1993

Texts by the artist:

Greaves, Derrick, 'Painter's Purpose', *Studio*, March 1959

'The Kitchen Sink School', *Arts Review*, 1994

Greaves, Derrick, 'Except the Kitchen Sink', *Art Review*, June 1994

Greaves, Derrick, 'Studios I Have Known', *Art Review*, 1995

Greaves, Derrick, 'The Artist's Eye', *Art Review*, March 1997

'Artist's Profiles – Derrick Greaves', *Printmaking Today*, 1997

Artists' Books and Folios:

Also, seven screenprints with text by Roy Fisher, published by Tetrad Press, London, 1972

The Songs of Bilitis, suite of 25 screenprints, published by the artist, 1977

The Sower as Self-Portrait, Homage to Van Gogh, a portfolio of screenprints and etchings, published by the artist, 1986

Sanskrit Love Poems, nine screenprints with text, published by Tetrad Press, London, 1987